# The Care and Education of Young Bilinguals

## An Introduction for Professionals

### Colin Baker

in association
with Anne Sienkewicz

**MULTILINGUAL MATTERS LTD**
Clevedon • Buffalo • Toronto • Sydney

**Library of Congress Cataloging in Publication Data**
Baker, Colin
The Care and Education of Young Bilinguals: An Introduction for Professionals
Colin Baker
Includes bibliographical references and index.
1. Bilingualism in children. I. Title.
P115.2.B348 2000
404'.2'083 21–cd21          99-045551

**British Library Cataloguing in Publication Data**
A CIP catalogue record for this book is available from the British Library.

ISBN 1-85359-466-0 (hbk)
ISBN 1-85359-465-2 (pbk)

**Multilingual Matters Ltd**
*UK*: Frankfurt Lodge, Clevedon Hall, Victoria Road, Clevedon BS21 7HH.
*USA*: UTP, 2250 Military Road, Tonawanda, NY 14150, USA.
*Canada*: UTP, 5201 Dufferin Street, North York, Ontario M3H 5T8, Canada.
*Australia*: P.O. Box 586, Artarmon, NSW, Australia.

Printed and bound in Great Britain by Cambrian Printers Ltd.

# Contents

Acknowledgements. . . . . . . . . . . . . . . . . . . . . . . . . . . . . . vi

Introduction . . . . . . . . . . . . . . . . . . . . . . . . . . . . . . . vii

**Chapter 1: Getting to Know Bilingual Children**

Introduction . . . . . . . . . . . . . . . . . . . . . . . . . . . . . . 1

Theme 1:  Who Is Bilingual? Essential Definitions And Distinctions For
Professionals. . . . . . . . . . . . . . . . . . . . . . . . . . 1

Theme 2:  Double Meanings? The Child's Mother Tongue. . . . . . . . . . . 3

Theme 3:  Two Equal Languages? Balanced Bilinguals. . . . . . . . . . . . 5

Theme 4:  Two Underdeveloped Languages? Double 'Semilingualism' . . . . . 6

Theme 5:  Crème de la Crème? Prestigious Bilinguals . . . . . . . . . . . 8

Theme 6:  Triple Tongues? Multilingual Children. . . . . . . . . . . . . . 8

**Chapter 2: The Advantages of the Bilingual Child**

Introduction . . . . . . . . . . . . . . . . . . . . . . . . . . . . . . 11

Theme 1:  Do Bilingual Children Have Advantages? The Modern View . . . . 11

Theme 2:  Two Views of Bilinguals: Fractional or Holistic?. . . . . . . . 15

Theme 3:  Bilingual Characters: The Personality and Social Development
of Bilinguals . . . . . . . . . . . . . . . . . . . . . . . . . 17

Theme 4:  Insiders or Outsiders? Bilingualism and Immigration. . . . . . 20

Theme 5:  Bilingual Belonging? Identity Issues and Solutions . . . . . . 21

**Chapter 3: The Everyday Use of Language by Bilingual Children**

Introduction . . . . . . . . . . . . . . . . . . . . . . . . . . . . . . 26

Theme 1:  Choice Language: The Language Use of Bilingual Children . . . . 26

Theme 2:  Sensitive Listeners? Bilingualism and Sensitivity in
Communication . . . . . . . . . . . . . . . . . . . . . . . . . 28

Theme 3:  To Rephrase – Children as Interpreters . . . . . . . . . . . . 30

Theme 4:  Moving Between Languages – Codeswitching. . . . . . . . . . . . 31

Theme 5:  In Other Words – The Functions and Results of Codeswitching . . . 34

## Chapter 4: Bilingual Children and Families

Introduction . . . . . . . . . . . . . . . . . . . . . . . . . . . . . . 37
Theme 1: Types of Bilingual Families. . . . . . . . . . . . . . . . . . . 37
Theme 2: The Development of Bilingualism in Children . . . . . . . . . . . 41
Theme 3: Childhood Trilingualism . . . . . . . . . . . . . . . . . . . . 47
Theme 4: Bilingualism and Marriage . . . . . . . . . . . . . . . . . . . 48

## Chapter 5: Bilingual Children in Communities

Introduction . . . . . . . . . . . . . . . . . . . . . . . . . . . . . . 51
Theme 1: Language Communities. . . . . . . . . . . . . . . . . . . . . . 51
Theme 2: Language Minorities . . . . . . . . . . . . . . . . . . . . . . 53
Theme 3: A Categorization of Language Minorities. . . . . . . . . . . . . 54
Theme 4: Immigration, Emigration and Language . . . . . . . . . . . . . . 55
Theme 5: Ethnic Identity . . . . . . . . . . . . . . . . . . . . . . . . 57
Theme 6: Diglossia . . . . . . . . . . . . . . . . . . . . . . . . . . . 61
Theme 7: Language Boundaries: The Territorial and Personality
Principles . . . . . . . . . . . . . . . . . . . . . . . . . . . . . . . 62
Theme 8: Dialects and Bilingualism. . . . . . . . . . . . . . . . . . . . 63

## Chapter 6: Bilingual Children and Thinking

Introduction . . . . . . . . . . . . . . . . . . . . . . . . . . . . . . 66
Theme 1: Bilingualism and Intelligence. . . . . . . . . . . . . . . . . . 66
Theme 2: Bilingualism and Creative Thinking. . . . . . . . . . . . . . . . 69
Theme 3: Bilingualism and Metalinguistic Awareness . . . . . . . . . . . . 70
Theme 4: Common Underlying Proficiency and Separate Underlying
Proficiency . . . . . . . . . . . . . . . . . . . . . . . . . . . . . . . 72
Theme 5: Thresholds Theory. . . . . . . . . . . . . . . . . . . . . . . . 75

## Chapter 7: The Education of Bilingual Children

Introduction . . . . . . . . . . . . . . . . . . . . . . . . . . . . . . 82
Theme 1: Home and School Relationships . . . . . . . . . . . . . . . . . 82
Theme 2: Community Language Education . . . . . . . . . . . . . . . . . . 85
Theme 3: The Empowerment of Bilingual Children. . . . . . . . . . . . . . 86
Theme 4: The Nature and Aims of Bilingual Education . . . . . . . . . . . 90
Theme 5: Different Styles of Bilingual Education . . . . . . . . . . . . . 92

## Chapter 8: The Bilingual Classroom

Introduction . . . . . . . . . . . . . . . . . . . . . . . . . . . . . . 95
Theme 1: Language Allocation in Bilingual Classrooms . . . . . . . . . . . 95
Theme 2: Recent Approaches to Bilingual Teaching and Learning . . . . . . 103

**Chapter 9: Developing Biliterate Children**

Introduction . . . . . . . . . . . . . . . . . . . . . . . . . . . . . . . . . . 107

Theme 1: Literacy Among Bilingual Students . . . . . . . . . . . . . . . . 107

Theme 2: The Development of Biliteracy . . . . . . . . . . . . . . . . . . 117

**Chapter 10: Bilingual Children with Special Needs**

Introduction . . . . . . . . . . . . . . . . . . . . . . . . . . . . . . . . . . 120

Theme 1: Explanations of Under-Achievement in Bilinguals. . . . . . . . 120

Theme 2: Bilingualism and Learning Difficulties. . . . . . . . . . . . . . 124

Theme 3: Language Delay and Language Disorder . . . . . . . . . . . . 126

Theme 4: Language and Speech Therapy in a Bilingual Context. . . . . . 128

**Chapter 11: The Assessment and Education of Bilingual Children
with Special Needs**

Introduction . . . . . . . . . . . . . . . . . . . . . . . . . . . . . . . . . . 130

Theme 1: Assessment of Bilingual Children . . . . . . . . . . . . . . . . 130

Theme 2: Bilingual Special Education . . . . . . . . . . . . . . . . . . . . 136

**Chapter 12: Multiculturalism, Racism and Bilingual Children**

Introduction . . . . . . . . . . . . . . . . . . . . . . . . . . . . . . . . . . 141

Theme 1: Multicultural Education for All. . . . . . . . . . . . . . . . . . . 141

Theme 2: Anti-Racism and Prejudice Reduction in School . . . . . . . . . 147

Theme 3: Immigrants and Refugee Children . . . . . . . . . . . . . . . . 150

Theme 4: Curriculum Adaptation with Immigrants and Refugee Students. . 152

**Chapter 13: The Politics Surrounding Bilingual Children**

Introduction . . . . . . . . . . . . . . . . . . . . . . . . . . . . . . . . . . 153

Theme 1: Language as a Problem, a Right and a Resource . . . . . . . . . 153

Theme 2: The Assimilation of Language Minorities . . . . . . . . . . . . . 160

Theme 3: Integration and Language Minorities . . . . . . . . . . . . . . . 162

Theme 4: Cultural Pluralism . . . . . . . . . . . . . . . . . . . . . . . . . . 163

Glossary . . . . . . . . . . . . . . . . . . . . . . . . . . . . . . . . . . 166

Bibliography . . . . . . . . . . . . . . . . . . . . . . . . . . . . . . . . . . 189

Index . . . . . . . . . . . . . . . . . . . . . . . . . . . . . . . . . . 197

# Acknowledgements

Much appreciation is due to the following who have, in many and varied ways, helped shape the ideas, style and the contents of the book. They will recognize their major contributions to the topics in the book, and I thank them for their help, encouragement and support over the last 20 years: Jim Cummins, John Edwards, Viv Edwards, Joshua Fishman, Ofelia García, François Grosjean, Charlotte Hoffmann, Nancy Hornberger, Meirion and Sylvia Prys Jones, Suzanne Romaine, Tove Skutnabb-Kangas, Terry Wiley, Cen Williams and Colin Williams.

My wife, Anwen deserves much praise for all her love and support over many years. Sara, Rhodri and Arwel, our children, have taught me so much about bilingualism that is not found just by researching the literature.

The idea for the book came from Mike Grover of Multilingual Matters, my fellow Essex man. His enthusiasm for the book has been long-standing, and his facilitation of the book has been crucial to its completion.

Anne Sienkewicz was appointed by Multilingual Matters to edit the original text. She was not just a wise choice, she was a brilliant one. My academic text has been turned around to become more active in voice, efficient and focused. Without changing the essential ideas, she expertly created a much more readable text for busy professionals.

A thousand thanks.

# Introduction

This book is the outcome of an initiative by Multilingual Matters to produce a text for a wide spectrum of professionals. It was felt that existing texts on bilingualism were either focused on a specific market (e.g. parents, graduates) or were too detailed or complex as a first general introduction for professionals.

Thus the book aims to provide a first but comprehensive introduction for busy professionals working with bilingual children. It assumes no previous training in this area but aims to provide the kind of information needed by those who deal with bilingual children. For speech therapists, doctors, psychologists, counselors, teachers, special needs personnel and many other professionals, the contents will sensitize and inform on the following: the nature of the bilingual child; bilingual children in families, bilingual children and their communities, the psychology of bilingual children, home–school relationships, bilingual schooling, bilingual children with special needs, racism and bilinguals, and the future for bilingual children.

Bilinguals can only be understood through a cross-disciplinary and inter-disciplinary perspective. Hence, this book contains psychological, sociolinguistic, educational, linguistic and cultural aspects. Each chapter assumes no previous knowledge and is presented in a simple, clear, concise and comprehensible style.

Bilingualism has become an important topic. It reflects a surge of interest in bilinguals as people with different characteristics from monolinguals. It also reflects the increased interest in minority languages and cultures. The last decades of the twentieth century have brought swift changes in international travel, international communications, the global economy, ease of travel between countries, greater internationalism and the need for ethnic harmony. This has led to debates about the place of the languages of the world, including the need to preserve linguistic and cultural diversity. There are many indigenous and immigrant languages that are endangered. Just as there have been movements to save endangered species of animals and plants, so endangered languages need protection. The colorful diversity of human existence as expressed in its many languages and cultures is threatened, and therefore bilingualism becomes a central issue. Bilingual children are at the heart of this.

In the last decade, the advantages of bilingualism and multilingualism have become clearer. The cultural, communication, cognitive and curriculum advantages of being a bilingual are increasingly agreed. Yet bilinguals often live in circumstances where there is relatively little power, little political influence, sometimes being marginalized and the targets of racial or ethnic attack. Therefore, this book aims to help reduce the prejudice and stereotyping that surrounds bilingual children and to inform about the beauty of bilingualism.

# Chapter 1

# Getting to Know Bilingual Children

## INTRODUCTION

Bilingual children are varied and diverse in their language profiles, advantages and problems. The first professional necessity in dealing with them is a refined view of their nature and variety. Only with that knowledge can secure and sensitive advice be given and decisions made. This chapter provides the essential foundations to discuss bilinguals with sensitivity and sympathy. Who is bilingual? What is included or excluded in this term? What is the likelihood of a child having two equal languages rather than two underdeveloped ones? What about multilingual children? The issue of 'mother tongue' shows that individuals connect rapidly with bilingual communities and their politics. This discussion will be addressed under six theme headings:

- Who is a Bilingual? Essential Definitions and Distinctions for Professionals
- Double Meanings? The Child's Mother Tongue
- Two Equal Languages? Balanced Bilinguals
- Two Underdeveloped Languages? Double 'Semilingualism'
- Crème de la Crème? Prestigious Bilinguals
- Triple Tongues? Multilingual Children

## THEME 1: WHO IS BILINGUAL? ESSENTIAL DEFINITIONS AND DISTINCTIONS FOR PROFESSIONALS

Who is bilingual? The answer seems simple. A person who speaks two languages is bilingual. Unfortunately, the question is more complex. The following selection of issues will lead to different definitions.

### Language competence

If someone is considerably less fluent in one language than the other, should that person be called bilingual? Few people are equally skilled in both languages, even

1

though this is often expected. One language tends to be stronger and better developed than the other. This 'dominant' language is not always the first or native language of the bilingual.

### Use or ability

Is ability in two languages the only criterion for assessing bilingualism, or should the use of two languages also be considered? Maybe one person tends to speak only one language in practice. Perhaps another regularly speaks two languages, but with halting fluency in one of them. Ability or proficiency in languages may be separate from their use. This distinction is sometimes referred to as the difference between **degree** (proficiency, ability or competence in a language) and **function** (actual use of two languages).

### Specific language skills

What about a person who can understand a second language perfectly, but cannot speak it? What about people who can speak a second language but are not literate in it? An individual's proficiency may vary across the four skills of speaking, listening, reading and writing. One person may use one language fluently for conversation, but switch to a second tongue to read and write. Another person may understand the spoken and written forms of a second language very well but be unable to speak or write it at the same level. Such a person can be said to have a passive, or receptive competence in a second language.

### Self-categorization or categorization by others

Is 'bilingual' a label people give themselves? Should self-perception and self-categorization be pre-eminent? Often people lack the confidence to describe themselves as bilingual when they do not speak a second language very fluently or are not literate in it. An assessment through testing by professionals such as psychologists or speech therapists may be the means of categorization, instead.

### Change in language use and choice

Bilingualism is a state which changes over time and according to circumstances. A monolingual person becomes bilingual by acquiring a second language. A bilingual person can also become monolingual by forgetting a second tongue. Competence in a language may vary, as the situation changes. A child may learn a minority language at home, then later acquire a majority language in the community or at school. Over time, the acquired language may become stronger or dominant. If that individual moves away from the area where the first language is spoken, or loses contact with those who speak it, fluency in the minority language may be lost.

It is thus impossible to create any concise, all-inclusive definition of a bilingual. Professionals need a refined understanding which takes into account the number of dimensions, distinctions and variations involved in the umbrella term 'bilingualism'.

## Bilingualism in Society

Bilingualism exists as a possession of an individual. However, it is also possible to talk about it as a characteristic of a group or community. Bilinguals and multilinguals are most often located in groups, communities or a particular region, such as Latinos in California, Texas, Arizona, New York, Florida and elsewhere. Some live in smaller clusters, as do some Chinese scattered in many communities across the United States.

There is no language without a language community (see Chapter 5). However, co-existing languages can change rapidly, in harmony or in conflict. One language may rapidly advance at the expense of the other. Where many language minorities exist, there is often language shift.

Thus an important distinction exists between **individual** and **societal bilingualism**. Some professionals, such as teachers, speech therapists and psychologists, are particularly interested in bilingualism within an individual. However, geographers, political scientists, social psychologists, policy makers and sociolinguists are interested in bilingualism within societies. While the distinction is important, there are many interconnections between the two. Individual attitudes about a minority language, for example, may affect the maintenance, restoration or demise of that language within a speech community.

The term 'bilingualism' is usually reserved to describe two languages within an individual. When the focus is on two languages in society, the term **diglossia** is often used (see p. 61).

### Further Reading

Hoffmann, C. (1991) *An Introduction to Bilingualism*. London: Longman.
Romaine, S. (1995) *Bilingualism* (2nd edn). Oxford: Blackwell.

## THEME 2: DOUBLE MEANINGS? THE CHILD'S MOTHER TONGUE

The term **mother tongue** is often used conversationally to refer to an individual's original language and also to discuss the heritage, or native, language of a group of people, especially a language minority within a language majority region. However, the term 'mother tongue' is ambiguous. For example, is it the language used first? The best known? The most used? The most closely identified with an individual? The term also has negative connotations and can be politically loaded.

On the surface, 'mother tongue' refers to the language a mother speaks to her child. It implies that such a language is embedded within the child. However, not all children are raised by their biological mothers. Some children are raised by fathers or other relatives. Some live with adoptive or foster parents. Others spend most of their time in day care from birth on. What is the 'mother tongue' of such children?

Again, the term 'mother tongue' reflects the positive qualities of a mother, nurturing, protecting, and caring for her child. As part of this loving role, the mother is portrayed as developing the child's language. While in many (but not all) countries and families, the mother is indeed the regular and major language model for the child, does the term 'mother tongue' understate the language role of the father? The importance of a father in language development is a recent theme in the psychology of child development. Fathers are increasingly primary caregivers, thus the regular and enduring models for language growth. There are many cases of two parents speaking different languages to their child. Such children learn one 'mother tongue' from the father.

One interpretation of 'mother tongue' is the first language learned. Many bilinguals learn two languages simultaneously. If the 'mother tongue' is the first, what is the implication if a child soon becomes dominant in a second language? If the family emigrates and starts to switch to the majority language in a new region, which is the mother tongue, the first language or the language which becomes dominant in the family, particularly outside the home?

Competence in a language can change easily over time, as circumstances change. The balance between two languages varies with family situations, with school and peer group norms, and with socioeconomic and geographic mobility created by employment and marriage. Identification of a language and its use may change with context and time. If competence is the criterion for the 'mother tongue', then that too may change.

Skutnabb-Kangas (1981) and Skutnabb-Kangas & Phillipson (1989) have argued that the term 'mother tongue', when applied to different ethnic groups, often reveals bias and prejudice. When Mexicans in the United States, Maori peoples in New Zealand, Finns in Sweden, Kurds from Turkey in Denmark, or Asians in Canada and England are referred to in terms of their 'mother tongue', the expression may refer to oppressed minorities. Thus the term has assumed evaluative meaning, qualifying guest and migrant workers, oppressed, indigenous peoples, and language minorities. 'Mother tongue' tends to identify minorities, not majorities, and therefore can infer separation of the two groups, or of individuals with less power and status from those with more.

## The Role of the Father in Childhood Bilingualism

There is a danger that using the term 'mother tongue' may place responsibility for bilingual development on mothers. Fathers play their part too. Research shows the language(s) of the father sometimes dominate in decision making, even to the point of creating monolingualism. When fathers are initially monolingual they may develop some fluency in a second language, as children grow up in it. When the mother is monolingual, the father may still use another language with the child, giving the mother some opportunity to learn it. For both partners, language classes may encourage bilingualism.

Recent research shows that the chances of children becoming bilingual depend heavily on home language constellations and patterns. In a study of Welsh–English homes, Jean Lyon (1996) found particular trends in the use of two languages in a family:

- Welsh-speaking mothers were more likely than Welsh-speaking fathers to speak Welsh to their children in mixed language families.
- English-speaking mothers were more likely than English-speaking fathers to try to learn and speak Welsh in the home and neighborhood.
- A husband and wife do not have an equal influence on home languages. The

preferred language of the husband tends to dominate. Women are more likely to change to suit their partner.

- More Welsh-speaking mothers than fathers wanted their children to be fully bilingual, that is, encouraged the use of Welsh as well as English. Mothers influence the language of their children more than the language of their husbands and home.
- More Welsh-speaking mothers than fathers read to their children in the minority language.

### Further Reading

Lyon, J. (1996) *Becoming Bilingual: Language Acquisition in a Bilingual Community.* Clevedon: Multilingual Matters.
Skutnabb-Kangas, T. and Phillipson, R. (1989) Mother tongue: The theoretical and sociopolitical construction of a concept. In U. Ammon (ed.) *Status and Function of Languages and Language Variety.* New York: W. de Gruyter.

## THEME 3: TWO EQUAL LANGUAGES? BALANCED BILINGUALS

One of the myths of bilingualism is that of two equally developed languages. In reality, individuals rarely have a balance between their two languages. Terms such as **balanced bilingual, equilingual** or **ambilingual** define idealized concepts unrelated to the great majority of bilinguals. Rarely will anyone be equally competent in speaking, reading and writing both languages across all different situations and domains, nor does language stay constant over time.

The literal interpretation of '**balanced bilinguals**' may include those who are less than proficient in both languages. However, most related literature identifies a 'balanced bilingual' as a person with age-appropriate competence in both languages. In other words, that person would equal the competence of a native speaker of the same age in both languages. One example is a student who understands the school curriculum in either language.

Research on bilingualism and intelligence, as well as on bilingualism and thinking, tends to show that 'balanced bilingual' children may have some cognitive advantages over monolinguals. For example, they appear to be more flexible in their thinking and more able to 'look inside' their language. This illustrates that this idealized concept has nevertheless been found of value in research. Several core issues are involved in this concept:

- Most bilinguals use their two languages for **distinct purposes and functions**. A young Muslim Panjabi might speak Panjabi in the family. With adults in the community, the same person learns Urdu for literacy purposes and Arabic to recite prayers and follow the Qur'an, then acquires English for school socialization and employment purposes. Thus dominance in languages varies according to the contexts where they are used.
- With the majority of bilinguals, one language dominates. However, this **dominance** sometimes changes with age, education, work, area of residence, friends and motivation. For a child in a Spanish speaking family, Spanish is

dominant in the early years. However, if the school and neighborhood are predominantly English speaking, dominance may shift to English. Later in life, when working in a Spanish speaking country, the individual may revert to Spanish dominance. If ever an approximate balance does exist, it is usually temporary.

- If individuals are not particularly proficient in either language, are they still 'balanced bilinguals'? Should the term be reserved for those who are relatively skilled in both languages? In the technical sense employed by many researchers in the field, the latter case is the one included.

- While the term 'balanced bilingual' has research value, it is still unclear who belongs to this group. Must individuals be biliterate, or are only speaking and listening skills of account in this category? What skill levels are required in listening, speaking, reading and writing to constitute a 'balanced bilingual'? What constitutes 'age appropriate' proficiency or fluency in both languages?

- The danger is that we classify too rigidly and make the term 'balanced bilingual' too elitist. The term tends to refer to a privileged group with the choice and opportunity to use two languages, and the educational chances for both languages to blossom.

### Further Reading

Grosjean, F. (1994) Individual bilingualism. In R.E. Asher and J.M. Simpson (eds) *The Encyclopedia of Language and Linguistics* (three volumes). Oxford: Pergamon.
Romaine, S. (1995) *Bilingualism* (2nd edn). Oxford: Blackwell.

## THEME 4: TWO UNDERDEVELOPED LANGUAGES? DOUBLE 'SEMILINGUALISM'

One category has been proposed as distinct from 'balanced' and 'dominant' bilinguals. Sometimes termed pejoratively as **semilinguals** or **double semilinguals**, these individuals are regarded as having 'insufficient' competence in either language.

Hansegård (1975) described '**semilingualism**' in terms of deficits in six language competencies:

- Size of vocabulary
- Correctness of language
- Subconscious processing of language (automatism)
- Language creation (neologization)
- Mastery of the functions of language (e.g. emotive, cognitive)
- Meanings and imagery

Thus a semilingual is seen as having deficiencies in both languages when compared with monolinguals. Such a person is considered to possess a small vocabulary and incorrect grammar, to consciously think about language production, to be stilted and uncreative in both languages, and to find it difficult to think and express emotions in either.

There are six major problems with the notion of semilingualism, or double semilingualism, which has received much criticism, for example, from Cummins (2000).

- Semilingualism may be used as a negative label, which invokes failure and underachievement, particularly in Scandinavia and with immigrant groups in the United States.
- The term may be a political rather than a linguistic concept. If languages are relatively undeveloped, the reasons may not lie in bilingualism but in economic, political and social conditions. The danger of the term is that it locates the origins of underdevelopment in the individual, rather than in external factors, which coexist with bilingualism.
- Language may be specific to a context. Many people use their two languages for different purposes and events. Thus, a person may be competent in one language in only certain situations.
- A person may 'fail' on quantitative educational tests most often used to measure language proficiencies, and still be a competent speaker in the street and home, since such testing may be insensitive to the unquantifiable aspects of communication and the great range of language competencies. Tests may measure a small, unrepresentative sample of total language behavior.
- The frequency of double semilingualism is disputed, for example among Finnish–Swedish speakers (see Skutnabb-Kangas, 1981). There is a lack of sound empirical evidence, and attempts to establish a cut off point for who is defined as semilingual, without evidence will be arbitrary and value-laden.
- An apparent deficiency may be due to unfair comparisons with monolinguals. It is important to distinguish if bilinguals are 'naturally' qualitatively and quantitatively different from monolinguals in their use of their two languages.

These criticisms raise considerable doubts about the value of the term 'semilingualism'. However, people do indeed differ on many language abilities, with some remaining at the earliest stages of development. Moreover, bilinguals themselves may worry about their language abilities. In the presence of higher status monolinguals, there may be concern over competence in the majority language. Minority language speakers, immigrants, and workers who frequently change countries with their employment are often anxious that their difficulties in the local prestige language makes them appear inferior. Even when they communicate with ease, there is still residual worry over weakness in comparison with monolinguals.

Being at an early stage in language development may not be caused by bilingualism. Economic or social factors, or educational opportunity may also cause delay. Rather than highlight the apparent 'deficit', it is more positive to emphasize that, when suitable conditions prevail, languages easily evolve beyond the 'semi' state.

**Further Reading**

Edelsky, C. *et al.* (1983) Semilingualism and language deficit. *Applied Linguistics* 4 (1), 1–22.
Martin-Jones, M. and Romaine, S. (1986) Semilingualism: A half-baked theory of communicative competence. *Applied Linguistics* 7 (1), 26–38.

## THEME 5: CRÈME DE LA CRÈME? PRESTIGIOUS BILINGUALS

Prestigious bilinguals are those who typically (but not exclusively) own two high status languages. They can also be those who are of high status in their own society and are bilingual. Often the social elite speak two or more high status tongues. Children who speak French and English or Japanese and German fluently will tend to be prestigious bilinguals. Such individuals often come from middle and upper class families. Thus linguistic prestige is often paralleled by social, cultural and economic prestige. Such families often regard bilingualism as a way of preserving family status and educational and employment advantage. High status bilingualism tends to exist at an individual or family level but is not organized at a group or society level.

People who regularly travel abroad, such as diplomats or bureaucrats in international bodies and their children, will be among the number of prestigious bilinguals. With an increase in study abroad programs, prestigious bilingualism is sometimes reproduced by university and graduate education.

'Elite' bilinguals may be produced by a nanny or governess who speaks a different language to the children. Swiss Finishing schools also enable the daughters of more affluent families to polish their cultural and behavioral repertoire and become fluent in one or more prestigious European languages, especially French. Bilingualism in this sense is often planned and purposeful.

Among prestigious bilinguals, there has been no historical debate about the disadvantages and problems of bilinguals. During the 20th century, the economic, social and educational advantages of such bilingualism have been recognized. Prestigious bilinguals have continually accepted that use of two languages causes no problems in thinking, academic achievement or cultural acceptance.

### Further Reading

Baker, C.R. and Jones, S.P. (1998) *Encyclopedia of Bilingualism and Bilingual Education.* Clevedon: Multilingual Matters.

Tosi, A. (1991) High-status and low-status bilingualism in Europe. *Journal of Education* 173 (2), 21–37.

## THEME 6: TRIPLE TONGUES? MULTILINGUAL CHILDREN

The word 'bilingual', used about an individual, primarily describes the possession of two languages. However, it also serves as an umbrella term for the many people who have varying degrees of proficiency in three or more languages.

In many parts of Africa and Asia, several **languages co-exist**, and large sections of the population speak two or more languages. In such countries, individual multilingualism is the result of a process of industrial development, political unification, modernization, urbanization and greater contact between different local communities. Many individuals speak one or more local or ethnic languages, as well as another indigenous language, which has become the medium of communication between different ethnic groups or speech communities. Such individuals may also speak a colonial language such as English, French or Spanish. This latter language is often the vehicle of education, bureaucracy and privilege.

In many Western countries, individual monolingualism, rather than multilingualism, is the norm. This is often the result of a drive toward political and national unification, which required the establishment of an official language or languages to be used in education, work and public life. However, some immigrant minorities may be multilingual. In Asian communities of Britain and Canada, many individuals are trilingual, in their native language or dialect, in another Asian language often associated with literacy (such as Urdu or Hindi) and in English. In addition, a Muslim child will learn Arabic, the language of the Qur'an and the mosque.

**Multilingualism** also occurs with individuals who do not live within a multilingual community. Families can be trilingual when the husband and wife each speak a different language as well as the majority language of the country of residence. A person can learn multiple languages at school or university, at work, or in leisure hours. The motives for such language learning include personal enrichment, travel, educational betterment and economic advantage.

Like 'prestigious bilingualism' (see p. 8) this type of individual multilingualism is usually voluntary and planned. It brings economic, educational and social advantages. It is more widespread in countries where the native tongue is not an international, high prestige language. In such countries, the inhabitants see the economic, employment and travel value of multilingualism.

Many mainland European children learn two languages in school, such as English, German, or French, as well as being fluent in their home language, for example, Finnish, Swedish Danish, Luxembourgish, or Dutch. In Scandinavia, people seem particularly experienced and successful in producing trilingual offspring, and language learning has relatively high status there. The economic, employment and travel value of speaking several languages is one partial explanation of Scandinavian multilingual accomplishment.

## The Reality of Multilingualism

As these examples from around the world indicate, individual multilingualism is possible, non-problematic, and potentially valuable. Human beings have the brain capacity to learn and retain several languages. In many countries, not only the advantaged 'elite', but also the majority of the population, in all social classes, is multilingual. For example, in Calcutta, a *rickshaw-wallah* may speak a native language with family and close friends, Hindi to some customers, Bengali to others, and also have a working knowledge of English.

However, it is important to realize that different languages serve **different purposes** for most multilingual people. The individual typically does not possess the same level or type of proficiency in each language. In Morocco, a native Berber speaker may also be fluent in colloquial Moroccan Arabic, but not be literate in either of them. This Berber speaker will be educated in modern standard Arabic and use it for writing and formal purposes. Classical Arabic is the language of the mosque, used for prayers and to read the Qur'an. Many Moroccans also have some knowledge of French, the former colonial language.

In addition, languages within an individual may **grow and decay** over time. One or two of them may become stronger, another may weaken. This is even truer of multilinguals than of bilinguals. As opportunities for practice vary and motivations change, so may language dominance. Few individuals live in a situation that allows regular use of their three or more languages over a lifetime. The topic of child trilingualism is considered later (see p. 47).

As friends, work and residence change, so will the balance of languages within an individual. The co-existence of multiple languages will shift within an individual or family, according to religious, cultural, social, economic, political and community pressures. A person's languages may be surrounded by 'market forces', external manipulation, internal motivations, honest advice and active hostility. Where multilingualism is seen as unnatural, unnecessary, a deficiency rather than a proficiency, in need of compensatory or remedial action, then reward structures in society, such as employment or preferment, may favor a monolingual or bilingual norm.

### Further Reading

Cook, V.J. (1992) Evidence for multicompetence. *Language Learning* 42 (4), 557–591.
Edwards, J.R. (1994) *Multilingualism*. New York: Routledge.

# Chapter 2
# The Advantages of the Bilingual Child

## INTRODUCTION

The aim of this chapter is to provide a modern view of the bilingual child. Historically the bilingual individual has been seen as having thinking, personality and identity problems (see Chapter 6). Recent research has shown how such views reflect prejudices derived from nationalism, xenophobia and early studies grounded in a negative or 'subtractive' view of bilinguals.

This chapter will provide a 'state of the art' perspective of the nature of the bilingual child. It will examine the many advantages of bilingualism, as well as the occasionally-cited problems of social development and identity, self-esteem and acculturation.

This chapter's themes are:

- Do Bilingual Children Have Advantages? The Modern View
- Two Views of Bilinguals: Fractional or Holistic?
- Bilingual Characters: Personality and Social Development
- Insiders or Outsiders? Bilingualism and Immigration
- Bilingual Belonging? Identity Issues and Solutions

## THEME 1: DO BILINGUAL CHILDREN HAVE ADVANTAGES? THE MODERN VIEW

Why is bilingualism important for children? The reason is that it will affect the rest of their lives and those of their parents. Being bilingual, multilingual or monolingual is likely to affect a child's identity, networks of friends and acquaintances, schooling, employment, marriage, preferred area of residence, travel and thinking. Does bilingualism increase or decrease opportunities and choices? The answer is that there are indeed **many advantages** and very few disadvantages in becoming

---

### The Advantages of Being Bilingual

Some of the potential advantages of bilingualism and bilingual education are:

**Communication Advantages**

- Wider communication (extended family, community, international links, employment).
- Literacy in two languages.

**Cultural Advantages**

- Broader enculturation, deeper multiculturalism, two 'language worlds' of experience.
- Greater tolerance and less racism.

**Cognitive Advantages**

- Thinking benefits (e.g. creativity, sensitivity to communication)

**Character Advantages**

- Raised self-esteem.
- Security in identity.

**Curriculum Advantages**

- Increased curriculum achievement.
- Ease in learning a third language.

**Cash and Career Advantages**

- Economic and employment benefits.

---

bilingual. These are summarized below. Some of these advantages are discussed immediately, but others require detailed explanation and are considered later.

These advantages will be considered throughout the book. For the moment, some of the major advantages need mentioning.

Where parents have different first languages, bilingual children are able to **communicate** in each parent's preferred language. This allows a subtle, finer texture of relationship. Alternatively, children will be able to communicate with parents in one language and friends in the community in another.

For many parents, it is important to be able to speak to the child in their own first language. Many can only communicate with full intimacy, naturally and expressively in their first (or preferred, dominant) language. A child who speaks to each parent in that language enables a maximally close relationship with the parents. At the same time, both parents are passing part of their past, their heritage, to that child.

Bilingualism also allows communication between generations. When the extended family in another region speaks a different language from the child, the monolingual child may be unable to communicate within the family. The bilingual child has the chance of bridging that gap, building relationships, and feeling a sense of belonging and roots within the extended family.

A bilingual has the chance of communicating with a wider variety of people. When traveling, bilingual children have the distinct advantage that their languages provide bridges to new relationships. While a monolingual can communicate with a variety of people in one language, monolingualism sometimes raises barriers to relationships within other nationalities and ethnic groups. Bilingualism enables the individual to move between cultures.

Adapted, with permission, from *Negotiating Identities: Education for Empowerment in a Diverse Society*, by Jim Cummins (CABE, 1996)

When bilinguals are **biliterate** (literate in two languages), they have another communication advantage; they can access two literatures, open up different traditions, ideas, ways of thinking and acting. Biliteracy doubles the pleasures of reading novels or magazines, of writing to friends, it enhances educational writing and reading, and satisfies doubly the literacy requirements of employment.

The bilingual individual has two or more **worlds of experience**. Each language implies different systems of behavior, folk sayings, stories, histories, traditions, greetings, rituals, even conversation. Compare Italians, Arabs and English people when they are speaking! Literature, music, entertainment, religious traditions, ways of understanding and interpreting the world, all are distinct. With two languages go a wider cultural experience, greater tolerance of cultural difference, less racism.

The monolingual also experiences a **variety of cultures**, from neighbors and communities which use the same language but have different ways of life. The monolingual also can travel to other countries and other cultures. But penetrating a different society requires the language of that culture. Participation and involvement in the cultural core requires knowing its language. The bilingual has an improved chance of actively penetrating both language cultures.

Within any language, there is a kaleidoscope of cultures. Monolinguals experience the periphery of the kaleidoscope of another culture. The full experience of the inner colors and excitement of that kaleidoscope requires knowledge of its language.

Apart from social, cultural, economic, personal relationship and communication advantages, research has shown that bilinguals may have particular advantages in **thinking** (and in curriculum achievements and hence higher self esteem). Bilingual children have two or more words for each object and idea: 'kitchen' in English, 'cuisine' in French, for example. Consequently, the link between a word and its concept is usually looser. Sometimes corresponding words in different languages carry different connotations. 'Kitchen' in English traditionally implies hard work, as in the phrase 'tied to the kitchen sink'. The French 'cuisine' is a place for creativity, where the family congregates to socialize as well as to eat.

When each word carries slightly different associations, bilinguals may be able to think more fluently, flexibly and creatively. Mobility between languages may lead to greater language awareness and sensitivity in communication. When meeting weaker speakers of their language, bilinguals may be more patient listeners than monolinguals. (Details in Chapter 3)

Potential **economic advantages** in bilingualism are increasing. A bilingual may have a wider choice of jobs in the future. As economic trade barriers fall, international relationships become closer, as international trade unions and partnerships grow more widespread, ever more jobs will require bilingual or multilingual workers. These workers are in increasing demand in the international retail sector, tourism, international transport, public relations, banking and accountancy, information technology, secretarial work, marketing and sales, the law, teaching and overseas aid work.

**Careers** in multinational companies, sales and export jobs, and an increasingly global economy make the future of employment more flexible for bilinguals than monolinguals. In particular areas of Wales and Catalonia, for example, knowledge of the minority language is required for teaching and administrative posts, and is of prime value in business and commerce. Bilingualism guarantees nothing, but as the global village rises, and trade barriers fall, it may provide a relatively strong position in the race for employment.

Language is sometimes seen as a barrier to communication and friendship across social groups and countries. Bilinguals in the home, community and society, can lower such barriers. They can be **bridges** within the family, community, and across societies. Those who speak two different languages personify this bridging of gaps between peoples of different color, creed, culture and language.

### Further Reading

Baker, C.R. and Jones, S.P. (1998) *Encyclopedia of Bilingualism and Bilingual Education.* Clevedon, Multilingual Matters.
Edwards, J.R. (1994) *Multilingualism.* New York: Routledge.

## THEME 2: TWO VIEWS OF BILINGUALS: FRACTIONAL OR HOLISTIC?

Many people do not see the definite advantages in bilingualism. Two contrasting views are posed by François Grosjean, one defines bilinguals as two halves, the other as one whole. The **fractional view** of bilinguals sees the individual as 'two monolinguals in one person.' The **holistic view** asserts that the bilingual has a unique linguistic profile, rather than embodying two monolinguals. The contrast between these views is important.

### Monolingual, or fractional, Bilingualism

Many professionals see the bilingual as two monolinguals in one body. For example, if English is the second language, scores on English tests will normally be compared against monolingual averages and norms. A bilingual's English language competence is measured against a native monolingual Anglophone. Is this fair? Should a bilingual be expected to show the fluency and proficiency of a monolingual?

One consequence is to limit the definition of bilingualism to those who are equally fluent in both languages, with proficiency comparable to a monolingual. If that competence or proficiency does not exist in both languages, especially the majority language, the bilinguals may be denigrated and classed as inferior. In the United States, for example, children of language minority families have sometimes been classified as LEP (Limited English Proficient). Bilinguals who exhibit an apparent lack of proficiency in both languages are described as semilingual. When tests compare bilinguals' proficiency in either of their languages with monolinguals, they don't take into account that bilinguals will often use the two languages in different situations with different people.

While bilingualism is the norm in Africa, India and Asia, in countries such as the

United States and England, the dominant view of the world is monolingual. In these two countries in particular, the monolingual is seen as normal, and the bilingual as an exception or oddity, although one half to two-thirds of the world's population is bilingual to some degree. This monolingual view often predicts negative consequences in cognitive processing, because of the potential confusion between two languages perceived as underdeveloped.

Many bilinguals themselves feel insufficiently competent in one or both of their languages compared with monolinguals, accepting and reinforcing the monolingual view of bilinguals. A bilingual may apologize to monolinguals for not speaking their language as well as they do. Bilinguals may feel shy and embarrassed when using one of their languages in public among monolinguals of that language. Some bilinguals strive to reach monolingual standards in the majority language, even to the point of avoiding use of their minority language.

## The Holistic View of Bilingualism

François Grosjean presents a more positive alternative. Monolinguals should not be the point of reference. Comparing bilinguals and monolinguals does not compare like to like. In athletics, we could fairly judge a sprinter or high jumper against a hurdler? The sprinter and high jumper concentrate on excellence in one event. The hurdler develops two different skills, trying to combine a high standard in both. The hurdler will be unable to sprint as fast as the sprinter or jump as high as the high jumper. This is not to say that the hurdler is a worse athlete than the other two. Any such comparison makes little sense. Comparing the language proficiency of a monolingual with a bilingual's dual or multiple language proficiency is similarly unjust.

However, should bilinguals be measured and compared only by reference to other bilinguals? When someone learns English as a second language, should that competence in English be measured only against other bilinguals? Obviously, this is not practical. In countries like the United States, where first language Spanish-speaking children will have to compete against monolingual English speakers in an English language job market, a common view is that they should face the same English assessments in school.

However, Grosjean stresses that any assessment of a bilingual's language proficiency should avoid the traditional language tests with their emphasis on form and correctness and evaluate the bilingual's general communicative competence. This appraisal would be based on a totality of the bilingual's language usage, whether this involves the choice of one language in a particular domain, or mixing the two languages.

Sometimes political realities prevent a holistic view of the bilingual. In Australasia, most of Canada, the United States and Great Britain, dominant English-speaking politicians and administrators will not accept a different approach or standard of assessment (one for monolinguals, another for bilinguals). If there is a double approach, will less be expected of bilinguals in their school achievement? Will they be expected to under-perform? (see p. 90).

Yet the bilingual is a **complete linguistic entity**, an integrated whole. Bilinguals use their two languages with different people in particular contexts and for distinct purposes. Levels of language proficiency may depend on the contexts and frequency of use. Communicative competence may be stronger in some domains than in others. This is natural and to be expected. Any test of a bilingual's competence in two languages must be sensitive to such differences of when, where, and with whom bilinguals use either of their languages.

### Further Reading

Grosjean, F. (1985) The bilingual as a competent but specific speaker–hearer. *Journal of Multilingual and Multicultural Development* 6, 467–477.

Grosjean, F. (1994) Individual bilingualism. In R.E. Asher and J.M. Simpson (eds) *The Encyclopedia of Language and Linguistics (Volume 3)*. Oxford: Pergamon.

## THEME 3: BILINGUAL CHARACTERS: THE PERSONALITY AND SOCIAL DEVELOPMENT OF BILINGUALS

### Introduction

Until recently, negative views about the personality and social development of bilingual children have been frequently expressed. Bilingualism was long associated with, and even said to cause, schizophrenia, mental confusion, identity and emotional problems, social attachment deficits, loyalty conflicts, and poor self-esteem and self-concept. Problems as diverse as stuttering and poor moral development were regarded as likely consequences of bilingualism.

There will always be some individuals who think of their bilingualism as a problem. But as Grosjean found (1982), the majority of bilinguals and trilinguals find no inconvenience in speaking multiple languages. If we trawl for advantages, they will be found in bilinguals. The question is not 'Are there bilinguals who show personality, identity or social problems?' Among bilinguals, as among monolinguals, there will always be individuals with such problems. The issue is whether bilingualism causes them. For example:

- The question is not 'Do bilinguals stutter?' Some bilinguals stutter. So do many monolinguals. The important concern is whether bilingualism *per se* causes stuttering. Research suggests that bilinguals are neither more nor less likely to stutter than other groups. Bilingualism does not seem to produce stuttering.
- One frequent concern is that mixing two languages is cognitively and socially undesirable. Here, bilingualism would appear more causally linked to potential problems. However, in some societies, such as particular Puerto Rican groups in New York, switching between languages is normal and accepted. Codeswitching can have advantages, as in further explanations of ideas (see Codeswitching, p. 31).

## Negative Viewpoints

One particular author presents a negative, prejudiced view about bilingual personalities. Adler (1977) describes bilingual children as having split minds, being
'neither here nor there,' marginal people. Using early research, he wrote of the bilingual child: 'His standards are split, he becomes more inarticulate than one would
expect of one who can express himself in two languages, his emotions are more
instinctive, in short, bilingualism can lead to a split personality and, at worst, to
schizophrenia' (p. 40).

Much of what has been written about this topic is anecdotal, irrational and
unscholarly. There is only a small amount of research in this area. For example,
there are currently believed to be five main personality dimensions: extroversion–introversion; agreeableness; conscientiousness; neuroticism–stability;
openness. Despite the considerable research on personality traits, bilinguals have
yet to figure as a line of inquiry. Tests such as the Myers-Briggs Type Indicator,
Cattell's Sixteen Personality Factor Scale or Eysenck's Personality Tests have rarely
been used in research on bilinguals.

When such formal personality tests have been included, it is rare to find any
personality trait difference between bilinguals and monolinguals. Ekstrand (1989)
found evidence of little or no difference. One reason for such minimal connection is
that the expression of personality in everyday behavior is filtered and changed by
the particular context and situation. For example, an undertaker has little scope for
extroversion, even if so disposed. The individual's personality and environment are
inextricably linked and interdependent.

Another reason why personality traits may have little causal connection to bilingualism is expressed in *Troilus and Cressida*: 'No man is the Lord of anything ... Til
he communicates his parts to others. Nor does he of himself know them for aught.
Til he behold them formed in th'applause' (spoken by Ulysses in Act 3, Scene 3).
Shakespeare was centuries ahead of the social-constructivist argument of modern
psychologists. We require our friends and others to help define and endorse the
personality qualities we seek to communicate. How we see ourselves is based on us
(the actor or actress), the audience, ourselves observing the interaction, other cast
members, the scenery and props, the story line, and the drama enacted. We express
personality through the reactions (social meanings) assigned by others to behavior
as well as through our behavior itself. What we believe about our personalities
reflects a negotiation and construction of meaning derived from our behavior. Seen
in this light, bilinguals and monolinguals may have many similarities in most
personality areas. A consideration of self-esteem and self-identity will show how
consideration of personality connects with bilingualism.

## Bilingualism and Self-esteem

Bilingual children are popularly believed to have lower self-esteem. Children of
guest workers, recent or long term immigrants and language minority children are
sometimes thought to share this problem. One argument against Submersion or
Transitional Bilingual education (see p. 92) is that it may cause a lowering of a

child's self-esteem. However, one major justification for the inclusion of an ethnic heritage language and culture in the curriculum is the positive effects on the self-esteem of language minority children. Educating a child in the minority language is often believed to have the same effect.

There is little research in this area. Generally, research finds no difference between the self-concept or self-esteem of bilingual children compared with monolinguals. Self concepts are difficult to measure validly. Tests tend to measure self-report instead, what students are willing or what they prefer to say about themselves, rather than their true, inner self-image. Also, specific language minority situations affect the relationship between personality and bilingualism. Bilinguals in impoverished, low-status conditions can be expected to differ from elite bilinguals such as diplomats. That is, bilingualism and sociopolitical conditions must be distinguished in their effect on self-esteem.

Those who believe that self-esteem is lower among some language minority bilinguals disagree in their remedies. Some argue that education in the minority language is essential. Only then will children appreciate their home language and culture, gain security in their ethnic identity and raise self-esteem. Others maintain that low self-esteem among bilinguals exists because of isolation from the majority society, thus, learning the majority language will improve self-esteem.

Alexander and Baker (1992) even suggest that bilingualism or a bilingual education will result in negative labels for bilingual children which, in turn, will result in lower self-esteem. They argue that a bilingual education program means separation from the majority. The message is that segregation makes a child deviant or disadvantaged, with consequent damage to self-esteem. Alexander and Baker show a preference for assimilation of minority language groups, eradicating language and cultural variations, producing a monolingual, mainstream society in the United States.

## Cause and Effect

When bilingual or bicultural individuals suffer a detrimental effect on personality, bilingualism is not likely to be the cause. It is not language *per se* that causes personality or social problems. Rather, the **social, economic and political conditions** surrounding the development of bilingualism generate the problems. Where the bicultural community is stigmatized, seen as socially or economically inferior, and where there is symbolic or physical violence toward the minority community, personality problems within children may arise. Where language communities are oppressed and downtrodden, prejudice, discrimination and hate by other communities, not the ownership of bilingualism, may affect character and personality.

If there are problems of self-esteem, social and personal identity among bilinguals, they may be caused by antagonistic pressure from the dominant monolingual society. If a bicultural community is stigmatized as socially inferior, the bilingual may suffer in terms of self-esteem and identity. Thus, the environmental circumstances in which individuals are located, not bilingualism, is the cause.

Particular examples, such as migrant workers and immigrants into a dominant monolingual society, show that race and religion may be part of that discrimination.

Therefore, the key variable may be whether an individual is in a subtractive or additive bilingual and bicultural environment. Where bilingualism and biculturalism are additive, the chances of negative effects on personal adjustment may be minimal. Instead, there may be positive effects. In a society where they are subtractive, where the first language is depreciated and replaced, potential harmful effects on personality and adjustment may be increased (see **additive** and **subtractive bilingualism**, p. 52).

Where bilinguals are encouraged toward monolingualism in the majority tongue, personality problems may arise. Such integration and assimilation may be demanded but difficult to achieve. The majority community may resist newcomers. Where race and skin color are factors, bilinguals may not be admitted. There may be a bar on access to better jobs, educational opportunities and affluence.

Learning English as a second language in England and the United States is often demanded, but it may increase discrimination and racist attitudes, rather than dispelling them. The more a teenager moves into English cultural and English-speaking groups, the more problems of acceptance, identity and integrity of character may occur. In such subtractive situations, individuals may strive to identify with mainstream, monolingual cultural and social values or come to reject everything about the majority language culture, thus embracing the heritage language and culture more warmly.

### Further Reading

Baetens Beardsmore, H. (1986) *Bilingualism: Basic Principles*. Clevedon: Multilingual Matters.
Hoffmann, C. (1991) *An Introduction to Bilingualism*. London: Longman.

## THEME 4: INSIDERS OR OUTSIDERS? BILINGUALISM AND IMMIGRATION

Another popular worry is whether bilinguals are caught between two languages and cultures. Will an individual belong to neither language group, feel neither North American nor Latino, English nor Irish, Japanese nor English? In learning another language and culture, will a bilingual experience social alienation, a conflict of personal and ethnic identity, disorientation, isolation and anxiety?

A potentially poignant example is immigrants. Some immigrants may feel bewilderment and frustration when expected to adapt to a new culture and language. A conflict of loyalties may arise. For example, in the United States, such immigrants may wonder whether they are still Mexicans (or Puerto Ricans) or North Americans, whether they are a mix of the host and the native cultures, or without identity.

Some immigrants to the United States quickly switch to the North American culture and lifestyle. Others, often for social and cultural reasons, strive to retain their native culture and language, or are influenced to do so. Still others manage to bridge the two. A few may feel a sense of rootlessness. Some have the choice of a new identity, others have no choice, and are unable to escape economic, social and political oppression.

At the worst, shame and guilt, lawlessness or powerless resignation may set in among immigrants. Others attempt to lose their language identity and show a preference for majority cultural values and language. Alienation from the family unit may result. Some resign themselves to apathetic withdrawal, others strive to retail their heritage language and culture. Some reject the past and assume a new identity. Between rejection and acceptance are temporary or permanent confusion of ethnic and self-identity. Some assimilate more or less successfully. Some integrate while retaining the family's traditional culture and language.

**Children of immigrants**, in particular, may be between two language communities. The home culture supports the heritage language. The host culture requires a different set of values and behaviors. When a teenager is trying to find a core self-concept and integrated self-image, perhaps during an adolescent identity crisis, there is an extra layer of ambivalence. The teenager may have to move between two sets of values, solitudes, cultures. Some switch cultures and identities as easily as languages. Others are disoriented. Conflicts of loyalty arise, as learning a language often involves acquiring the values, attitudes and behaviors of the target language community.

Nevertheless, acceptance is possible when bridging two languages and cultures. It is possible to hold different yet **integrated identities**. A Yiddish-speaking Jew, an English-speaking Jew, a Yiddish-speaking North American and English-speaking North American can coexist as an individual and as a combination of multiple identities. Cuban-Americans, Gaelic-Canadians, Chinese-Malays and German-Australians experience relatively few problems of identity. A hyphenated variety is possible in an individual cognitive and affective psyche.

The choice of withdrawal or rejection is replaced by acceptance of the possibility of living in two language groups. Given appropriate motivation and environmental support, identity confusion is replaced by a unique integration of values and beliefs, allowing people to bridge language groups and mingle. Unfortunately, not all bilinguals have the drive or favorable circumstances to enable biculturalism and bilingualism to live peacefully and creatively within the psyche.

### Further Reading

Dicker, S.J. (1996) *Languages in America: A Pluralist View*. Clevedon: Multilingual Matters.

## THEME 5: BILINGUAL BELONGING? IDENTITY ISSUES AND SOLUTIONS

Professionals often face identity questions with individual children, parents, community groups and background politics. Is the child American, Mexican or Mexican-American? Does a bilingual child have a contorted, mixed up mish-mash identity or is s/he adjusted to a hyphenated variety, secure in a valued inheritance, delighting in moving between cultures? When politicians clamor for loyal citizens, what pressures are placed in the identities of bilinguals, especially immigrants?

At the end of one 'identity adjustment' dimension are children who learn to switch between two cultures as easily as they switch between languages. They are Hebrew-speaking Jews in Israel and Yiddish-speaking Jews in the New York home,

English speaking Americans in school. For some there are few problems of cultural mixing or identity. Theirs is **biculturalism** fully flowered, easily exhibited and admired by all.

Close to this are those whose identity is securely rooted within their minority language culture. Welsh speakers, for example, primarily belong to their language minority and also to a larger group (British or European), sometimes with reluctance, sometimes marginally. Welsh speakers often regard themselves as Welsh first and foremost, British possibly, European reluctantly but increasingly, English definitely not. For them there is little identity crisis, as there are strong roots in a minority language culture.

One Canadian study investigated the effect on teenagers of **mixed language marriages** (Aellen & Lambert, 1969), testing them on ethnic identification, identification with (or rejection of) one of their ethnic groups, self-esteem and stability, perception of parents, peer relationships, attitudes and values. Analysis of the data in comparison with children from monolingual homes, showed that bilingual teenagers had no problem in identifying with both their parents, nor suffered at all in self-esteem or identity. They showed a positive attitude toward both their parents' cultural groups. Children from monolingual homes tended to favor their own group.

Aellen and Lambert (1969) concluded that teenagers of mixed language background marriages were characteristically socially and emotionally healthy in each measured dimension. They showed no signs of personality disturbances, social disorientation or anxiety. Their self-concepts were positive and they saw their parents as giving them relatively more attention. Their values reflected the influence of both ethnic backgrounds. Rather than developing a divided allegiance or rejecting one of their dual language backgrounds, they had developed a dual allegiance. Mixed language background marriages did not produce division, only multiplication and integration of languages and cultures. For the children of such marriages, a double inheritance is more likely than division of loyalties.

This result concerns children from middle class Canadian backgrounds, where both languages and cultures have status and prestige. In immigrant situations in England and the United States, a slightly less rosy picture might be obtained.

Indeed, at the other end of the 'identity adjustment' dimension, there are those who experience rootlessness or dislocation between two cultures. For example, with older immigrants, there is sometimes a passive reaction, isolation, numbness and loss of rooted identity. In younger immigrants, there can be an aggressive reaction with the loss of home and heritage and the difficulty of penetrating thick walls to enter the new host culture. For some immigrants, there may be a sense of rootlessness, identity confusion, feeling neither ethnic identity. This can lead to despair, cultural ambiguity, or wandering in a cultural wilderness.

**Reactions among immigrants** include (sometimes in approximately this order):

- a honeymoon period of optimism, pleasure in new surroundings and hope for the future;

- a period of frustration, when hopes are dashed and barriers to integration seem overwhelming;
- a period of anger, when wrong decisions seem to have been made (internalized anger) or when others prevent access to jobs, integration, friendships and success (externalized anger);
- a period of isolation when pessimism and gloom dominate. The immigrant may become marginalized. Or
- rejection of the 'old' language and culture and desire for total assimilation and identification with the new. A person may suppress the home country, concentrating on being a true citizen of the new land. Or
- integration, retaining the best from the past and adding good things from the new way of life. Or
- conformity without conviction to an allegiance to the new language and culture.

**Adjustment** among immigrants thus takes many different forms, happy integration, uncomfortable assimilation, isolation, rejection or anomie. Bilingualism is greatly affected by the outcome of adjustment.

Among immigrants, ethnic identity begins around three to five years of age. By the age of seven or eight, it is well established, while continuing to develop. During adolescence, ethnic differences may become increasingly conscious and considered. Overt and covert discrimination, racial abuse and harassment, color, religion, dress and dietary differences surface, increasingly focusing ethnic awareness, identity, inequity and the need for social justice.

**Identities** are never static or permanent, they are becoming rather than being, never singular and rarely unified. It is natural for an individual to have different identities in contexts, which change through time. 'Who we are' or 'where we come from' are not so important as 'how we are represented' and 'what we may or cannot become.' Cultural, ethnic or language identity is often less about a return to roots than making sense out of our past, present and future routes.

We are all on stage. As the script changes, the cast changes, props, scenery and audience change, so do the roles we play. Parents have to assume different identities in changing situations with new people. Varied and different personalities are displayed at home, at work, in worship, in cafes or bars, in private or public roles.

As we move in and out of **different roles**, we naturally have different identities. Children assume different identities and role-playing behavior in school with teachers, on the playground with friends, on the street during evenings and weekends. They are different at worship, as Granny's little one, as the sophisticated socialite at parties or dazzling disco dancer. With different people and in different situations, the individual learns to play varied roles, wear 'costumes' and harmonize with changing casts. It is important that such roles and resultant sub-identities integrate into a satisfactory, harmonized whole. We all need coherence and wholeness around those sub-identities. From this consideration, something important can be said about bilingualism and self-identity.

First, a bilingual child needs experience of and exposure to successful play in different roles. Acting on stage with varying people and unusual props is difficult. The more exposure and experience to changing scenery, cast, and scripts, the more harmonized with a role we become. Therefore, a child needs plenty of exposure and experience of the cultures of the two languages.

Second, if the minority language culture is to be retained within the child, continuous participation through that language is desirable. Otherwise, there may be a break away from that language and culture, during adolescence especially. Exposure to the majority language culture is automatic, it almost takes care of itself. Movies and television, newspapers and magazines, sports and shops, the World Wide Web and pop music all contain powerful, pervasive influences that ensure experience in majority language and culture.

For the recent immigrant, there is the dual task. **Retention** of continuity of cultural experience within the heritage language culture is necessary. For the family, recently settled in the host country, harsh dislocation from the home and heritage culture may mean an identity crisis for the child. Throwing off all vestiges of the drama one has enacted in the home language is like denying the past and the value of the home language, killing a part of the Self.

At the same time, a **transition** into the host culture is necessary. To open economic prospects, employment and equality of opportunity the family often needs to learn the lines of a new play, to become comfortable with a new script, people, props and scenery. This is rarely easy. Sometimes the host cast does not want to accept newcomers in their drama. To preserve economic and social advantages, establish clear racial and ethnic boundaries, difficulties may be raised for immigrants in penetrating established relationships. As much as the immigrants may want to assimilate and integrate, they will often be barred from privileged circles. Of all the different bilingual situations, this is the most frustrating and resistant to harmonization.

In such a situation, identity conflicts may well arise. Wearing different dress, speaking foreign tongues, having different color, ethnic identity and religion may make the establishment of a new identity a difficult drama. There are no rehearsals, only a stage facing a skeptical audience. There is a danger that children will not know who they are, their origins nor their destinations.

To help, parents may wish to look for opportunities for children to integrate into the host culture, while retaining the home culture. If there are particular playgroups, evening activities, churches and mosques where harmonization can occur without sacrificing heritage language and culture, a child may be encouraged to adopt new identities. The school plays an important role in resolving this paradox: retaining heritage languages, identities and cultures while allowing entry into the host language and culture. The school must ensure there be addition, not subtraction, that is, loss of the heritage language and culture. The school is responsible for developing a harmonic multiplication of identities within the child, not a division of identities that makes a child feel lost or despairing.

Professionals must face the issue of whether experiencing two cultures means watering one down while the other gains. At the optimum, the Latino-American, Anglo-French, Swedish-Finn, Chinese-Canadian bilingual child will be a fresh species in a colorful language garden. This hyphenated variety is neither French nor English, Finnish nor Swedish, Chinese nor Canadian. The bilingual, bicultural child needs a dual repertoire of custom and culture that allows high self-esteem, a positive self-concept, optimism for the future, and a potential for choosing for oneself which cultures to accent in the future.

The **demands** of a language community are important in identity formation. If bilinguals are criticized for their accents, dual cultural norms or split loyalties, a dual identity may be more difficult. Speaking English and Arabic, being Western and Islamic, for example, may cause conflicts of identity and loyalty, within the individual and also the language community. Cultural inappropriateness may be admonished. The relative status of languages and cultures affects the accommodation of dual identity.

Bilingual identity is a particularly Western problem. In many African and Asian language communities, bilingualism (or multilingualism) is the accepted norm. The monolingual and monocultural person, who cannot switch between cultures and language communities, is the oddity. In many countries, linguistic diversity within society as well as in individuals, is accepted as natural, normal and desirable.

While bilingualism and biculturalism may superficially appear to have a detrimental effect on identity, language does not cause identity problems. Rather, it is often the **social, economic, and political environment** surrounding bilinguals that generates problems. Where the bicultural community is stigmatized, socially inferior, economically underprivileged, and where there is symbolic or physical violence toward the minority language community, personality problems within children may arise. It is not bilingualism, but the condition in which that language community lives that may be the cause of the problem. Where language communities are oppressed and downtrodden. It is prejudice and discrimination, not bilingualism, that affect identity.

## Further Reading

Aellen, C. and Lambert, W.E. (1969) Ethnic identification and personality adjustments of Canadian adolescents of mixed English–French parentage. *Canadian Journal of Behavioural Science* 1 (2), 69–82.

Harris, P.R. and Moran, R.T. (1991) *Managing Cultural Differences: High Performance Strategies for a New World of Business*. Houston: Gulf Publishing Company.

# Chapter 3
# The Everyday Use of Language by Bilingual Children

## INTRODUCTION

**Children are born ready to become bilinguals**. Too many are restricted to one language, one language culture. Bilingual children typically switch effortlessly between languages, using them for different reasons with different people. This chapter studies how bilingual children use their languages, why and when they move between them, their sensitivity advantages in communication and skills in interpretation. Finally, the chapter concludes with the important topic of codeswitching – a major topic in linguistics.

The themes of the chapter are:

- Choice Language: The Language Use of Bilingual Children
- Sensitive Listeners? Bilingualism and Sensitivity in Communication
- To Rephrase – Children as Interpreters
- Moving between Languages – Codeswitching
- In other Words: The Functions and Results of Codeswitching

## THEME 1: CHOICE LANGUAGE: THE LANGUAGE USE OF BILINGUAL CHILDREN

### Introduction

Monolinguals can change the **register** or type of language they use, depending on their context or interlocutor. An English-speaking teenager in the United States may speak formally to a teacher, less formally to parents, and in an informal, slangy style with classmates and friends. Italians or Germans may use the standard form of their language with people from other regions, but switch to dialect with locals. Bilinguals can also change their register in either language. They also can move between their two languages, an ability which is the focus of this topic.

Not all bilinguals can use both languages regularly. In a largely monolingual community, there may be little choice about day-to-day language use. A resident of Pennsylvania may be bilingual in English and German, yet rarely use the latter. However, in communities where multiple languages are spoken, bilinguals may use both languages on a frequent basis. Some individuals do not have mastery of both languages, yet communicate successfully in both in varying circumstances.

When bilinguals use both their languages on a day-to-day basis, language use is neither haphazard nor arbitrary. Rather, bilinguals use their languages in different contexts or domains, with different people. Many bilinguals use both their languages in conversation with similar bilinguals.

## Functions and Uses of Language

Many factors are necessary to describe bilingual language use. To study how a person employs two languages, these questions are helpful:

- Who is speaking?
- Who is the addressee? Who is listener or co-participant?
- What is the situation or context? Is it the temple, mosque or church, factory, office, home, classroom?
- What is the topic of conversation? Is it the weather, food, sport, work, leisure, family, health?
- What is the purpose of the conversation? What is its expected outcome, hidden agenda or intended effect?

These questions illustrate how language choice varies along five dimensions: speaker, addressee, context/situation, topic and purpose.

## Language Choice

Many subtle and overlapping factors affect a bilingual's language choice, particularly in a new, unrehearsed situation. It may not always be simple. Two major factors will now be considered, as indications of the complex way in which a bilingual monitors language choice.

### The other person in the conversation

If the interlocutor is already known, a relationship has usually been established through one language. If both are bilingual, they may change to their second language, perhaps to include other people.

If the other speaker is a stranger, the bilingual may quickly pick up clues about the language to use, responding to suggestions from dress, appearance, age, accent and command of a language. In parts of Africa, a well-dressed African may automatically be addressed in English. In bilingual areas of Canada and Wales, employees dealing with the general public may use personal names to indicate which language to speak. Pierre Rougeau or Bryn Jones might be addressed first in French or Welsh, rather than English.

Children as young as two or three soon learn which language to speak to which person and tend to do so consistently. However, even young children learn to base their language choice on appearance, accent or age of the conversation partner.

### Individual preference

An individual's **attitudes** and preferences influence language choice. In a minority/majority language situation, older people may prefer the minority language. Younger folk, such as second-generation immigrants, may reject it in favor of the higher status and fashionable image of the majority tongue. Where the native language is perceived as threatened, some bilinguals assert and reinforce the status of the first language by avoiding the dominant language. Francophone Quebecois sometimes refuse to speak English in shops and offices, to underline the status of French.

Some minority languages are often confined to a private, domestic role, when such languages have historically been disparaged and deprived of status. In western Brittany, many people speak Breton only with family and close friends. They are often offended if addressed in Breton by a stranger, believing that such a stranger implies they are uneducated and unable to speak French.

An individual may also change languages, whether deliberately or unconsciously, to accommodate the perceived preference of the conversation partner. The perception of relative prestige or convenience of language may depend on the nature of the listener. To gain acceptance or status, someone may deliberately and consciously use the majority tongue. Alternatively, the minority language may serve as a form of affiliation or group identity.

At other times, bilinguals may mix and **switch languages**. They may deliberately explain an idea in one language, then switch to another to reinforce or further explain. Another example arises in narration, where relating a conversation may authentically mirror dual language use. The conversation which occurred in English is related in English; commentary is added in the minority language (see Codeswitching, p. 31).

## Further Reading

Appel, R. and Muysken, P. (1987) *Language Contact and Bilingualism*. London: Edward Arnold.

Grosjean, F. (1982) *Life with Two Languages*. Cambridge, MA; Harvard University Press.

Romaine, S. (1995) *Bilingualism*. Oxford: Basil Blackwell.

## THEME 2: SENSITIVE LISTENERS? BILINGUALISM AND SENSITIVITY IN COMMUNICATION

Because individuals living in a bilingual environment often switch languages, they subconsciously develop sensitivity to the communication needs of particular situations. They constantly but latently monitor the language in which they respond or into which they must switch. A telephone conversation starts in English, but the bilingual picks up, from an accent or speech style, that Spanish may be the interlocutor's preferred language. The bilingual then switches to Spanish to encourage a more intimate and friendly conversation. In an unfamiliar shop, a bilingual monitors, subconsciously, the conversational language preferred by the shopkeeper, or the bilingual merchant tries to pick up clues about which language to speak to each customer.

Bilinguals typically monitor and restrict mixing languages when speaking to monolinguals or writing. They also tend to be continuously alert for signals about when to switch languages. Bilinguals may thus have increased sensitivity to language use. They may also be more **aware of their listeners' needs**. They constantly subconsciously monitor different situations and people to establish the need to move between languages. Bilinguals may be more latently aware of different language functions and purposes, and of the importance of using the appropriate language. Very young children, such as two- or three-year-olds, have been found quite sensitive to the language preferences of the listener and the communicative context (de Houwer, 1995). Such children also usually avoid mixing languages when speaking to monolinguals.

Research by Ben-Zeev (1977b) found bilinguals more responsive to hints and clues in a social situation. In an experimental situation, they seemed more sensitive to the required form of language and to instruction. They corrected their errors faster than monolinguals. This is an early research indication that bilinguals may have increased sensitivity in interpersonal communication.

Genesee, Tucker and Lambert (1975) studied sensitivity in communication. They compared children in bilingual and monolingual education on performance in a game. Students aged between five and eight were asked to explain a board and dice game to two classmates. One listener was blindfolded, the other not. They were not allowed to ask any questions after the explanation. The listeners then attempted to play the game with a person giving the explanation. Children in a total immersion bilingual program proved **more sensitive** to the needs of listeners than children in the monolingual control group. They also gave more information to the blindfolded children than to the sighted ones. The authors concluded that such bilingual children, 'may have been better able than the control children to take the role of others experiencing communicational difficulties, to perceive their needs, and consequently to respond appropriately to these needs' (p. 1013)

Thus, bilingual children may be more sensitive than monolinguals in a social situation requiring careful communication. A bilingual child may be more aware of the needs of the listener, more sensitive and empathic. Possibly the listener's understanding is enhanced by the extra communicative sensitivity of the bilingual.

There are currently more hypotheses and hunches than clear evidence here. Much more research is needed to define precisely how bilingualism affects sensitivity in communication in interpersonal relationships. Such research is important to connect bilingualism with interpersonal relationships. It moves from questions about skills of the bilingual mind to social skills. While research showing a bilingual tendency toward advantages in thinking skills is relatively plentiful, there are only small pieces of evidence, needing replication and extension, suggesting particular **bilingual social skills** compared with monolinguals.

## Further Reading

Ben-Zeev, S. (1977) The effect of bilingualism in children from Spanish–English low economic neighbourhoods on cognitive development and cognitive strategy. *Working Papers on Bilingualism* 14, 830122.

Bialystok, E. (ed.) (1991) *Language Processing in Bilingual Children*. Cambridge: Cambridge University Press.

De Houwer, A. (1995) Bilingual language acquisition. In P. Fletcher and B. Macwhinney (ed.) *The Handbook of Child Language*. Oxford: Blackwell.

Genesee, F., Tucker, G.R. and Lambert, W.E. (1975) Communication skills in bilingual children. *Child Development* 46, 1010–1014.

## THEME 3: TO REPHRASE – CHILDREN AS INTERPRETERS

In language minority families, children often interpret for their parents. In first and second generation immigrant families, parents may have little or no competence in the majority language, and their children must step in. There are a variety of possible contexts. When there are visitors, such as sellers or traders, religious prose-lytizers and local officials, a parent may call a child to help translate the conversation. The child interprets for both parties, parent and caller. Similarly in the hospital, in the doctor's, dentist's, optician's offices, or at school, the child may be taken to help interpret. Interpretation is needed in more informal places, in the street, with television or radio, reading a newspaper or working on the computer.

Kaur and Mills (1993) found that children accustomed to interpreting sometimes took the initiative. Such children may answer a question rather than relaying it to the parent. This puts the children in a position of power, even of language censor-ship. The teacher's comments, written or oral, may be transformed from something negative to something positive.

Linguistic, emotional, social, attitudinal pressure is placed on **child interpreters**. Children may find exact translation difficult, as their language is still developing. They may be hearing information which is the preserve of adults, perhaps medical or financial troubles, arguments. They may be expected to be adult-like when inter-preting, and child-like at all other times, to mix with adults as interpreters and 'be seen and not heard' on other occasions. Also, seeing their parents in an inferior posi-tion, when the language of power, prestige and purse is the majority language, may lead to children despising their minority language.

However, interpreting can also bring parental praise, reward, and family status. The child learns adult information quickly and acts with authority and trust. Early maturity has its own rewards in the teenage peer group.

When parents become dependent on children for interpretation, it may make the family closer and more integrated. Such interpretation is a lifeline for those who must yield much power to their children. Yet it may make parents aware of their own language inadequacies, frustration and resentment, particularly in cultures where children are expected to remain subordinate for a long time.

The **cognitive outcomes** for child interpreters may be valuable. Children who regularly translate for their parents may quickly realize the problems and possibili-ties in translating words, figures of speech and ideas. Such children learn early that one language never fully parallels another. Sometimes, it is hard to translate exactly the inner meaning of words and metaphors. Such children may thus become more introspective about their languages. This **metalinguistic awareness** is considered on p. 70.

Another possible advantage for the child interpreter is gaining **empathy**. The children negotiate between two different social and cultural worlds, trying to understand both, bridging between them. This negotiation may increase maturity, astuteness, independence and self-esteem. Being expected to carry an adult role early in life may produce a positive self-concept, an adult feeling of responsibility, and a privileged family position. Through language skills, a child may feel more responsible, more grownup, and more valuable in the family and community.

### Further Reading

Kaur, S. and Mills, R. (1993) Children as interpreters. In R.W. Mills and J. Mills (ed.) *Bilingualism in the Primary School: A Handbook for Teachers*. London: Routledge.

## THEME 4: MOVING BETWEEN LANGUAGES – CODESWITCHING

**Codeswitching** is a change of language within a conversation, most often when bilinguals are with other bilinguals. When they converse, bilinguals consciously or subconsciously select the conversational language. The factors governing this initial choice have been discussed in the previous topic. This selected language may be called the **base**, **recipient**, or **matrix language**. Codeswitching occurs when items from another language are introduced into the base language. The second language may be called the **donor** or **embedded language**. Codeswitching may occur in large blocks of speech, between or within sentences, even involving single words or phrases. It may occur between a base language and more than one donor language. While bilinguals do consciously codeswitch, usually the event is subconscious.

Monolinguals who hear bilinguals codeswitch may view it negatively, believing it shows a deficit in mastery of both languages. Bilinguals themselves may be defensive or apologetic and attribute codeswitching to laziness or sloppy language habits. However, studies have shown that it is a valuable linguistic strategy. It does not happen at random. There is usually considerable purpose and logic in changing languages.

### The Monolingual and Bilingual Modes

The term 'codeswitching' embraces a complex variety of phenomena. Very few bilinguals keep their two languages completely separate. The ways in which they mix them are complex and varied. Grosjean (1992) distinguishes between the 'monolingual mode,' when bilinguals use one language with monolingual speakers of that language, and the 'bilingual mode,' when bilinguals are together and have the option of codeswitching. Even in the 'monolingual mode,' bilinguals occasionally mix languages. Few speak both languages with native speaker fluency. One language may influence the other. Often the dominant language influences the less dominant. Such influence is sometimes called **interference**, although the term **transfer** avoids the negative connotations of 'interference'.

Grosjean (1992a) distinguishes between **static** and **dynamic interference**. Static interference describes relatively permanent influence from one of the bilingual's languages in the other. Accent, intonation and the pronunciation of individual sounds are common areas where static interference may be present. A native German speaker speaks English with a German accent and intonation, and pronounces various sounds in a 'German' way, such as hardening soft consonants at the end of words ('haf' for 'have, 'goot' instead of 'good'). Because few bilinguals who have acquired a second language after early childhood attain complete native speaker pronunciation, these features tend to be permanent.

Dynamic interference recognizes when features from one language are transferred temporarily into the other. Interference can occur at any level of language (syntax, phonology, vocabulary) and in either written or spoken language. An English speaker with some competence in French demonstrates dynamic interference by using the word *librairie* to mean 'library', whereas it means 'bookshop'.

Because interference (transfer) usually occurs from the dominant language into the less dominant, it is often a feature of second language acquisition (see Interlanguage, p. 175). 'Language interference' is often used when young children studying two languages mix them. When a child has temporary difficulty in separating two languages, interference has often been the ascribed term. Many bilinguals find this negative and pejorative, revealing a monolingual perspective. For the child, switching between languages may serve to convey thoughts and ideas in the most personally efficient manner. The child may also realize that the listener understands such switching. When interference is temporary in bilingual development, the more neutral term 'transfer' is preferable. As children grow older, there is less transfer between languages and more separation (see p. 42).

According to Grosjean (1992a), when bilinguals interact among themselves, they are in the bilingual language mode, where both languages are activated and the resources of both are available. Codeswitching tends to occur in the bilingual language mode.

## Terminology

Various terms describe switches between languages in bilingual conversation. **Codemixing** is sometimes used to describe changes at the word level, when one or two words in a sentence change. A mixed language sentence, such as '*Leo un magazine*' ('I read a magazine'), is an example. In contrast, '*Come to the table, Bwyd yn barod*' ('food is ready'), might be called codeswitching. The first phrase is in English, the second in Welsh. However, 'codeswitching' is now generally used for any switch within the course of a single conversation, whether at the level of word, sentence, or blocks of speech.

**Language borrowing** indicates foreign loan words or phrases that have become an integral and permanent part of the recipient language. '*Le weekend*' in French, '*der Computer*' in German are examples. All languages borrow words or phrases from others with which they come in contact. Codeswitching may often be the first step in this process. Individuals codeswitch, using words or phrases from the donor language for a variety of purposes. As these elements are widely used, they become accepted and perceived as part of the recipient language. Some linguists have tried to distinguish between 'nonce borrowings' (one time borrowings, as in codeswitching) and established borrowings. Myers-Scotton (1992) argues against distinctions between codeswitches and loans, as they form a continuum, rather than two distinct and separate entities.

## How and Why do People Codeswitch?

Codeswitching is complex and subtle, capable of linguistic description, but also understandable in social and psychological terms. The presence of linguistic restraints universally applicable to any pair of languages, has not yet been established. However, research has shown both the existence of such linguistic constraints and that codeswitching reflects linguistic skill, not incompetence. Social and psychological factors, rather than linguistic ones, trigger many instances of codeswitching. Some of the most common functions of codeswitching are listed below.

## Codeswitching as the Norm

Swigart (1992) distinguishes between **marked** and **unmarked codeswitching**. 'Marked' and 'unmarked' are commonly used in linguistics. 'Unmarked' generally means conventional, neutral, unremarkable. 'Marked' tends to mean different, unconventional, out of the ordinary, remarkable. Most research concentrates on marked codeswitching, used strategically or purposefully to achieve an aim.

However, in many bilingual situations throughout the world, codeswitching between two languages has become the norm. Among Wolof–French bilinguals in Dakar, the capital of Senegal (the subject of Swigart's paper), there is continuous, acceptable mixing of the two languages. A similar pattern is found in India, where there is a relatively stable use of codeswitching between Hindi and English. In such cases, Swigart (1992) argues, codeswitching is unmarked and lacks the stylistic or sociological significance of marked codeswitching. Rather, it is a general marker of belonging to a mixed group with a multiple identity. From a linguistic and grammatical point of view, such stable codeswitching should not be analyzed in terms of donor or recipient language, but on its own terms as a third code or language.

## The Absence of Codeswitching

Hinglish (Hindi–English), Spanglish (Spanish–English), Tex-Mex (Texan–Mexican) and Wenglish (Welsh–English) are often used derogatorily to describe standardized and accepted language borrowing within a particular community. However, in other bilingual communities, strict separation of languages is the acceptable norm, for political, cultural or social reasons. In cases of power conflict between ethnic groups, language may be a prime marker of separate identity; codeswitching is then unacceptable. Traffers-Daller (1992) illustrates how

French–Flemish codeswitching in the Belgian capital, Brussels, was acceptable to the older bilingual generation, who identified with both the French and Flemish groups. It has become less acceptable, however, among younger Belgians, because of the gradual polarization of the Walloon and Flemish ethnic groups.

Similarly, French–English codeswitching is unacceptable among some Canadian francophone groups, because of the power and ethnic identity struggle with anglophones. The African country of Tanzania illustrates the reverse situation. English, the colonial language, was marginalized for many years after independence in 1964, while Swahili was promoted as the national language. Although older Tanzanians still associate English with colonialization and do not favor codeswitching, it has become more widespread among young Tanzanians, as English has become the fashionable medium of Anglo-American culture.

### Further Reading

Myers-Scotton, C. (1992) *Duelling Languages: Grammatical Structure in Codeswitching*. Oxford: Oxford University Press.
Myers-Scotton, C. (1996) Code-switching. In F. Coulmas (ed.) *The Handbook of Sociolinguistics*. Oxford: Blackwell.

## THEME 5: IN OTHER WORDS – THE FUNCTIONS AND RESULTS OF CODESWITCHING

Codeswitches have a variety of purposes and aims and change according to who is talking, the topic, and the context of the conversation. The languages may be negotiated between speakers and may change with the topic.

Codeswitches may be used for **emphasis**, to stress a particular word or its central function in a sentence.

When a speaker does not know a word or phrase in one language, another language may be **substituted**. This often happens because bilinguals use different languages in different domains of their lives. A young person may switch from the home language to the school language to discuss mathematics or computers. Myers-Scotton (1972) describes how a Kikuyu University student in Nairobi, Kenya, switched constantly from Kikuyu to English to discuss geometry with his younger brother. 'A *tiriri* angle *Iniati* has *ina* degree eighty; *nayo* this one *inamirongo itatu*.' Similarly, an adult may codeswitch to discuss work, because the technical terms associated with work are only known in that language.

Bilinguals may switch languages to express a concept **without an equivalent** in the culture of the other language. A French–English bilingual living in Britain may use words like 'pub,' 'bingo hall,' and 'underground,' in French, because these words have no French equivalent. Such words and phrases are called 'loans' or 'borrowings' (see p. 167.), when they become established and in frequent use in the other language. However, there is no clear distinction between a codeswitch and a borrowing.

Codeswitching may **reinforce** a request. For example, a teacher repeats a command to emphasize it: '*Taisez-vous, les enfants!*. Be quiet, children!' In a majority/minority language situation (see p. 53), the majority language may emphasize authority. In a study conducted at a hospital in Mid-Wales (Roberts, 1994), it was found that nurses repeat or amplify commands to patients in English to emphasize their authority: *'Peidiwch a chanu'r gloch Mrs. Jones* – Don't ring the bell if you don't need anything!' A Spanish-speaking mother in New York may use English with her children for short commands like 'Stop it! Don't do that!' and then return to Spanish.

Repetition of a phrase or passage in another language may also **clarify** a point. Some teachers explain a concept in one language then explain it again in another, believing that repetition adds reinforcement and completes understanding.

Codeswitching may **communicate friendship** or family bonding. Moving from the common majority language to the home or minority language both the speaker and listener understand well, may communicate common identity and friendship. Similarly, codeswitching may indicate the need to be accepted by a peer group. Someone with a rudimentary knowledge of a language may inject words of that new language into sentences to indicate a desire to identify and affiliate. The use of the listener's stronger language may indicate deference, wanting to belong or to be accepted.

In relating an earlier conversation, the speaker may report it in the language(s) used. Two people may be speaking Spanish. When one reports a previous conversation with an English speaker, the conversation is **reported authentically** in English, as it occurred.

Codeswitching is sometimes a way of **interjecting** into a conversation. A person attempting to break into a conversation may introduce a different language. Changing languages may signal interruption, with the message, 'I would like to join this conversation.'

Codeswitching may ease tension and inject humor into a conversation. If committee discussions become tense, the use of a second language signals a change in the 'tune being played'. Just as in an orchestra, where different instruments in a composition may signal a **change of mood** and pace, a language switch may indicate a change of mood within the conversation.

Codeswitching often reflects a **change of attitude or relationship**. When two people meet, they may use the common majority language (in Kenya, thus, Swahili or English). As the conversation proceeds and roles, status and ethnic identity are revealed, a change to a regional language may indicate the crossing of boundaries. A codeswitch signals lessening of social distance, with growing solidarity and rapport. A study of Italian immigrants to the United States at the turn of the 20th century (Di Pietro, 1977) showed that they would tell a joke in English but give the punch line in Italian. Not only was it better expressed in that language, but the shared values and experiences of the group were emphasized. This is a common feature across many languages and cultures, East and West.

Conversely, a change from minority language or dialect to majority language may indicate the speaker's wish to elevate status, **create a distance** from the listener, or establish a more formal, business relationship. Myers-Scotton and Ury (1977) describe a conversation between a Kenyan shopkeeper and his sister. After exchanging greetings in their own Luyia dialect, the brother switches to Swahili in front of the other customers and says:

> 'Dada, sasa leo unahitaji nini?' (Sister, what do you need today?) For the rest of the conversation, the brother speaks Swahili and the sister Luyia dialect. The brother's codeswitch to Swahili, the business language, indicates that he must maintain a business relationship with his sister. She should not expect any favors or gifts.

Codeswitching can also **exclude people** from a conversation. When traveling on the subway (metro, underground), two people may switch from English to their minority language to talk about private matters. Bilingual parents may use one language to exclude their monolingual children. A doctor at a hospital may make an aside to a colleague in a language not understood by the patient.

In some situations, codeswitching occurs regularly when certain **topics** are introduced. Spanish–English bilinguals in the south western United States regularly switch to English to discuss money.

> 'La consulta era (the visit costs) eight dollars'. (Valdés-Fallis, 1976)

This reflects the fact that English is the language of commerce and often the dominant language of the mathematics curriculum.

Kegl (1975) describes how a Slovenian–English bilingual adult, speaking to her mother on the telephone, switched languages with topics. Matters to do with the Slovenian neighborhood, where the mother lived (food, friends, acquaintances) were discussed in Slovenian. Matters concerning the daughter's suburb were in English.

Familiarity, projected status, the ethos of the context and the perceived linguistic skills of the listeners affect the nature and process of codeswitching. Codeswitching is not 'just' linguistic; it indicates **important social and power relationships**.

### Further Reading

Myers-Scotton, C. (1991) Making ethnicity salient in codeswitching. In J.R. Dow (ed.) *Language and Ethnicity. Focusschrift in Honor of Joshua Fishman*. Amsterdam/Philadelphia: John Benjamins.

Myers-Scotton, C. (1993) *Social Motivations for Codeswitching: Evidence from Africa*. Oxford: Clarendon Press.

# Chapter 4
# Bilingual Children and Families

## INTRODUCTION

The future of the world's languages, which are declining very rapidly in number, and the future of the languages of bilingual children are tied very closely to family influence. Unless families reproduce minority languages, then bilingual children and communities are in danger, apart from production through education.

This chapter examines bilingualism in different types of families, the development of bilingualism in children, trilingualism in the home, and how bilingualism affects home life. Professionals will gain an understanding of the parental role in children's bilingualism and of many key issues and necessary decisions.

The chapter themes are:

- Types of Bilingual Families
- The Development of Bilingualism in Children
- Childhood Trilingualism
- Bilingualism and Marriage

## THEME 1: TYPES OF BILINGUAL FAMILIES

### Introduction

The term **bilingual family** encompasses an almost infinite variety of situations and is difficult to define simply. Each bilingual family has its own patterns of intrafamilial language and in relation to the local community. A profile of such families involves consideration of the following factors:

- The native language of the parent(s).
- The language(s) spoken between parents.
- The language(s) spoken by the parent(s) to the children.
- The language(s) spoken by the children to the parent(s).
- The language(s) spoken between the children.
- The language(s) spoken or understood by the nearby extended family.

- The language(s) spoken or understood in the local community and/or by minority language groups.
- The language of education.
- The language of religious observance.
- The official or majority language(s) of the state or country.
- The family's geographical stability or mobility, with changing language needs.

These factors influence the nature and level of bilingualism within an individual family. They also illustrate the difficulty of neatly categorizing bilingual families. This list raises important points for a discussion of bilingualism within families.

### Bilingualism is Not Always Homegrown

A bilingual or multilingual family may speak more than one language, but use only one language, often a minority language, at home, while acquiring the dominant language of the community outside the home.

### Not Every Individual in a Bilingual Family is Bilingual

One parent may be bilingual and decide to speak a native language to the children, while the other parent may only speak the dominant language of the local community, as in a family with a Spanish-speaking mother and monolingual English-speaking father. In many immigrant North American communities, where local minority speech communities have formed, parents who stay at home may have limited command of English or be monolingual, while their partners and children become bilingual at work and in school.

### Monolingual Parents may have Bilingual Children, while Bilingual Parents may raise Monolinguals

Many first generation immigrants develop a limited command of the majority language of the host country. Their children learn the majority language at school and on the streets. Alternatively, parents who speak only the dominant language of their country may have their children educated in a second majority language, or a heritage minority language. In Canada, many anglophone parents choose French immersion education so their children may benefit from bilingualism in both Canadian majority languages.

Sometimes the opposite can happen. Minority language parents may have negative attitudes toward their language and raise their children in the majority language. Many immigrant families progress from monolingualism in the minority language to bilingualism in both majority and minority languages, then monolingualism in the majority language within two to three generations. This happened with many immigrants to the United States in the nineteenth and early twentieth centuries and continues to occur in many parts of the world today.

## There may be Different Degrees of Bilingualism within Families

Within bilingual families, language dominance and competence may vary among members and over time. Where parents speak a minority language to their children, and where the school and community share the dominant, majority language, the children may have only passive competence in the minority language. In immigrant communities, parents may have only limited command of the majority language, while children eventually become dominant in it. Moving to another area or country or switching to a minority (or majority) language school for the children may mean a change in the family language balance.

## Attitudes about Bilingualism Determine its Fate within the Family and in the Wider Society

In many parts of Western Europe and North America, bilingual communities exist as a result of immigration, such as the Latino communities in the US. Also, bilingual communities occur where an indigenous language co-exists with a prestigious international language, as Breton does in the French province of Brittany. However, bilingualism in these communities tends to be less stable. The political and economic dominance of majority language speakers, education through the majority language, increased population mobility and the mass media all lead to diminishing community use of the minority language. Minority speakers develop preferences for the dominant language, seeing it as culturally fashionable and conducive to social and economic advancement. The minority language seems inferior, old-fashioned, worthless and a hindrance. Over time, the prestigious language encroaches upon the domains and functions of the minority language at home. Eventually the minority language ceases to be reproduced within the family.

Fishman (1991) sees the **intergenerational transmission** of a language as crucial to its survival. Once a language ceases to be reproduced within the family, it is very difficult to reverse its decline. Thus the dwindling of bilingualism within families mirrors the attitudes of society to the minority language and the fate of bilingualism in the wider community.

It is a difficult task to reach families and influence them to raise their children bilingually. The Welsh Language Board has taken a novel initiative. Videotapes and booklets developed by the Board are aimed at midwives, to develop their understanding of the attractions of bilingualism and through them to reach parents. Mothers' 'Bounty Packs' contain colorful pamphlets explaining the advantages of bilingualism in children, as well as samples of baby creams, foods, and other items.

## Categories of Family Bilingualism

Many in-depth studies of the childhood development of bilingualism have been carried out recently. These studies have been organized broadly within categories according to the language(s) spoken by parents to children, and the language(s) of the community. Harding and Riley (1986) and Romaine (1995) suggest the following categories based on parental language strategies in raising children bilingually.

### One person–one language

The parents have different native languages, one the dominant community language. The parents each speak their own language to the child from birth. Literature on child bilingualism praises this strategy as an effective path to bilingualism, since the child keeps the two languages separate, realizes there are two different language codes, and that it is desirable to use one or the other without codeswitching (see p. 31). De Houwer (1995) and others have recently loosened this orthodoxy, arguing that complete separation is an ideal rather than a reality, and that some case histories show that when parents use both languages, the child still communicates effectively in both. Discrete episodes in one language before using the other, and correction when there is unacceptable language mixing, allow separation of a child's language.

### Non-dominant home language

The parents have different native languages, one the dominant community language. Both parents speak the non-dominant language to the child, who learns the dominant language outside the home, particularly through education.

### Non-dominant home language without community support

The parents have different native languages, neither one the dominant community language. The parents speak their own language to the child.

### Double non-dominant home language without community support

The parents have different native languages, neither one the dominant community language. The parents each speak their own language to the child from birth, producing family trilingualism.

### Non-native parents

The parents share a native language, dominant in the community. One parent always addresses the child in an acquired language.

### Mixed language

The parents are bilingual and the family lives in a community, which is at least partly bilingual. The parents speak both languages to the children, tending to codeswitch and mix (see p. 31).

These categories allow researchers to classify and compare family situations. However, they only represent a typology of the research already undertaken. They are simplistic and by no means exhaustive. Moreover, most studies (apart from Type 6 and Type 3 studies of language minority children) target 'prestigious bilingualism', where there is a stable bilingual environment and a commitment to bilingualism. However, in many families, bilingualism is in a state of development or decline, often reflecting the state of bilingualism in the wider speech community.

## One-parent Families and Bilingualism

Almost all case studies of bilingual children have been based on two-parent families. Books on raising children in two or more languages assume the presence of two parents in the home. By accident, rather than design, this implies that a one-parent family is unlikely to raise children bilingually. This is not true, for a number of reasons. A second language is often acquired outside the home. In parts of Africa, children learn one language at home or in the neighborhood, another one, two or three at school, in inter-ethnic communication and in urban areas. Children of Asian immigrant communities in Britain acquire Panjabi, Urdu, Bengali, Hindi or another Asian language in the home community and learn English at school. A single parent who speaks French but resides in Britain may use French as the family language, to give the children the opportunity of bilingualism. In such cases, parental absence does not necessarily hinder a child's bilingual development.

In some cases, the family's bilingualism may be challenged by parental absence. In cases where one parent speaks the dominant language of the community to the children and the other parent uses a minority language, the death or departure of the second parent may place the family in danger of becoming monolingual. However, if the remaining parent is committed to the family's bilingualism, it can be accomplished in various ways.

In cases of separation or divorce, frequent contact with the non-custodial parent may ensure continued competence in the minority language. Where one parent has died or has infrequent or no contact, the remaining parent may occasionally speak the minority language to the children, some or all of the time, to safeguard the lower status language. If this is not possible or desirable, the children may attend a school where the minority language is the medium of education. Contact with friends and relations who speak the language and trips to places where it is dominant are other ways to support children's bilingualism

Family disruption by death or divorce is extremely traumatic. At times of great mental and emotional stress, with many practical difficulties and changes to be faced, bilingualism may seem low priority. However, single-parent families are often adept at meeting challenges and may manage to maintain two or more languages without further disruption to the child's life. In addition, where a child has undergone such stress, it may be wise to avoid the added trauma of losing a language, a culture, and an intrinsic part of the child's identity.

### Further Reading

Baker, C. (2000) *A Parents' and Teachers' Guide to Bilingualism* (2nd edn). Clevedon: Multilingual Matters.
Harding, E. and Riley, P. (1986) *The Bilingual Family*. Cambridge: Cambridge University Press.
Romaine, S. (1995) *Bilingualism* (2nd edn). Oxford: Blackwell.

## THEME 2: THE DEVELOPMENT OF BILINGUALISM IN CHILDREN

### Introduction

Bilingualism in children develops in various ways. Some children are exposed to two languages from birth and learn to speak them simultaneously. This is often called **simultaneous bilingualism**. Others hear one language at home and another later, in the neighborhood or wider community, often through playgroup, nursery school and school. This has been variously called **consecutive**, **sequential** or **successive bilingualism**. Three years of age is generally regarded as a borderline between simultaneous and consecutive bilingualism.

Any distinction between the two will be artificial, because each situation is different. Children who hear both languages at home rarely hear them for equal amounts of time. One parent may spend more time with the child, or one of those home languages may also be the dominant language of the community. Children who hear one language at home may pick up a second at an early age from friends, neighbors, or television.

## Simultaneous Bilingualism

Children's language acquisition has inspired many studies, of which several have compared bilingual language development with that of monolinguals. Bilingual language development has been shown to follow the same basic steps as that of monolinguals (De Houwer, 1995). Until recently, a three-stage model of early childhood bilingual development was accepted as accurate. This model, originating from Volterra and Taeschner (1978) portrays the young bilingual mixing two languages, then moving to partial then full separation. A thorough review by De Houwer (1995) finds little basis for the three stage model, while children as young as two separate their languages rather than mixing them. Similarly, Paradis and Genesee (1996) have shown that the grammars of French and English of two- and three-year-olds in Canada are acquired separately and autonomously. Although Quay's study (1994) was based on only one case, that child had equivalent terms for objects, events and processes in both Spanish and English from the beginning of speech, that is, from about one year old.

## The Early Years

Language acquisition does not begin with the first recognizable words around the age of one. It begins at birth or even before. Some experts believe that babies in the womb not only hear sounds, but also learn to recognize them. Studies of newborns only a few hours old have shown they can recognize and respond to their mother's voice. After a few weeks, they can react to subtle consonantal differences. In their first year, children pass through several stages in language development. They engage in vocal play, like cooing and babbling, which helps them coordinate their muscles and try out different sounds. They begin to comprehend language long before speaking. They also begin to learn that language is a vehicle for interaction and communication.

At about one year, many children utter their first words and start building vocabulary, mostly naming and action words. At around eighteen months, many children begin to string together two word phrases. From then on, their utterances become progressively more complex.

During this initial stage, children are defining the boundaries of words and trying to express themselves with available vocabulary. Sometimes a child over- or under-extends the meaning of a word. For example, 'dog' may be used to refer to any four legged animal, or may instead refer only to the family's own dog.

Set out below is an average pattern of language development for monolingual children. Children in families where two languages are approximately equally developed will follow a similar sequence (Lyon, 1996). However, it must be stressed that many children, monolinguals and bilinguals, differ from these averages yet show perfectly normal development later.

| Age | Language |
|---|---|
| First Year | Babbling, cooing, laughing (dada, mama, gaga). |
| Around 1 year | First understandable words. |
| During second year | Two-word combinations, moving slowly to three and four. Three element sentences, such as 'Daddy come now.' 'That my book.' 'Teddy gone bye-byes'. With bilinguals, the combinations sometimes mix languages. |
| 3 to 4 years | Simple, but increasingly longer and more complex sentences, involving more than one clause. Conversations show turn taking, not always direct response. Increasing fluency and accuracy, still many errors. Start to join phrases with 'and' and 'but'. |
| 4 years onward | Increasingly complex sentences, structure and ordered conversation. Use of pronouns and auxiliary verbs. |

Young children learning two languages simultaneously follow much the **same pattern** as monolinguals. First, they assemble a vocabulary of elements from both, but usually with only one label for each concept, taken from one language. Later, they separate vocabularies, using equivalent terms in each language, but combining grammatical rules of both.

### Codeswitching in Young Children

There is frequently a **stage of mixing** two languages in children. Early research suggested that the child initially sees the two as a single, unified system, only gradually distinguishing between them. However, some recent studies suggest distinction between the two systems from a very early stage, and that the use of elements from both is an elementary form of codeswitching (see p. 31).

**Codeswitching** is the subtle and purposeful way in which bilinguals switch between their two languages, often because they do not know a word or phrase in one, or because they can express an idea more effectively in a second. Thus, very young children, rather than confusing their languages, may be codeswitching in a practical and purposeful way, expressing themselves with their available vocabulary and grammar. Just as the monolingual English child over-extends 'dog' to any four-legged animal, so the bilingual Spanish-English child may over-extend '*perro*' to refer to a dog in English. Codeswitching often occurs from the child's weaker languages into the stronger, dominant one. A child may also codeswitch when a word or phrase is simpler or easier to pronounce in the other language.

Children use their growing bilingual competence in other ways. Semantic transfer may occur from one language to another, for example, the Welsh verb '*gwyneud*' and the French verb '*faire*' both mean 'do' and 'make'. Thus a Welsh- or French-speaking child may announce in English, the intention to 'make homework' or 'do a cake'.

Parents are often concerned when children mix two languages and worry that they are mentally confused. This is unnecessary. Bilingual children, like their monolingual counter parts, are learning at a tremendous rate, experimenting with language, defining and refining usage.

Codeswitching is also learned behavior. In many bilingual homes, family members switch freely between languages, and the child imitates this behavior. This also happens in stable bilingual communities where codeswitching has become a norm. In families where the adults keep the languages separate, children tend to codeswitch much less. Some children in such families do not appear to codeswitch at all. By three years, most bilingual children seem to recognize the existence of two distinct languages and are beginning to use them in a separate and consistent way.

## Language Development and Language Boundaries

The pace of language development does not differ significantly in average bilingual and monolingual children. They utter their first words around the same age (approximately one year). During a bilingual child's early years, progress may be slower, with two vocabularies and language systems to learn, instead of one. However, by four or five years, many bilinguals catch up with their counterparts in one of their languages. Only as children approach formal schooling and require sufficient development in one of their languages to understand the curriculum, should most developmental language concerns begin. A separate topic deals with language-delayed children (see p. 126).

A valuable feature of bilingual development is the creation of **language boundaries**. The child learns to associate one language with certain individuals, contexts or situations. In families where two languages are spoken, many parents try to help this process by maintaining a strategy of 'one parent/one language'. Both parents may be able to speak both languages and may use either when speaking with one another. However, in their interaction with the child, each uses a separate language.

In single language homes (often a minority language), parents may seek to safeguard the development of that language by creating a geographical boundary and avoiding the use of the majority language in their home. As children grow older, this becomes more difficult. A few families use time boundaries. Both parents speak both languages to the child, at different times of the week. A family may speak English on weekdays and French on weekends. However, arbitrary change of language must be avoided, since it may confuse the child.

Children themselves often create their own language boundaries, to simplify the task of matching languages with each situation. Children sometimes generalize from specific situations, with amusing results. A child whose father is German speaking may address all men in German, explaining, 'All daddies speak German.'

A child whose mother and older sister speak Swedish may believe, 'Only ladies speak Swedish.'

In a bilingual community, geographical boundaries may become established in the child's mind: one language in the home, at Granny's house, for worship, at local shops, another in school, at the doctor's office, and in the town center. The child may also assign age boundaries. In cases where the minority language is in decline, children may associate the language with older people.

Small children often react with surprise, confusion or even embarrassment when language boundaries are crossed. If an elder attempts to address a child in a different language than the one they use generally, the child may become upset or angry. If one language is usually spoken in a neighbor's house, and the child encounters a speaker of the other language there, the child may refuse to reply. If a young person uses a language associated with older people, the child may become confused or insist on replying in the majority language.

## Consecutive Bilingualism

There are a variety of routes to **consecutive bilingualism**. Some children learn one language first in the home and another in the community. Many minority language children are first exposed to the majority language when starting school. (See p. 53, regarding minority and majority languages.) Some children learn a second language at a later age after emigration. If language is learned in a 'natural environment', as opposed to classroom foreign language instruction, there are many similarities between the simultaneous and consecutive acquisition of two languages. Children tend to pick up single and set phrases first. They concentrate on simple grammatical constructions and over-extend vocabulary and grammar, for example using the present instead of the past tense. Early in second language acquisition, transference of vocabulary and grammatical structures from the first language tends to occur.

There is **no critical age** for second language learning. Older children and adults can learn more quickly and efficiently than younger children, because their cognitive skills are more developed. It appears that there is more difficulty in achieving native-like pronunciation after early childhood, for reasons not yet fully understood. However, it is sometimes simpler for younger children to learn a second language. They have fewer time constraints, the level of language required is not so high, and they have fewer inhibitions.

While a second language can be learned at any age, it is important not to detract from command of the first language. Damage can occur when a child's home language and culture are ignored in a majority language school. The child's first language skills, home environment and culture may be devalued in this alien environment, where instruction is given in an unintelligible language, often in competition with native speakers of that majority tongue.

This is a **subtractive bilingual situation** (see p. 52). The introduction of a second language detracts from the child's developing skills in the first language. Here the first language skills fail to develop properly, yet the child struggles for the second language skills needed to cope in the classroom. In Tanzania, the introduction of English-medium instruction at the secondary level detracts from academic communication skills in Swahili, the medium of instruction at the primary level. Consequently, Swahili skills are often not properly developed and a student's English is insufficient to cope as the medium of instruction. Development of both languages suffers.

Some children survive and succeed in this subtractive environment. For many others, this situation initiates a pattern of failure throughout their school career. Current research suggests that minority language children succeed better when they are taught initially through their home language. Here the child's skills are valued and built upon. Later, when the majority language is gradually introduced, the academic skills and knowledge acquired through the first language transfer easily to the second.

For majority language children, the situation is different. Some parents, wishing their children to become bilingual, send them to **immersion schools**, where a second majority language is taught, or to a **heritage language school**, where teaching is through the medium of a minority language. Such majority language children usually cope well in the curriculum in a second language. Their home language and culture have status and prestige and will not be supplanted. This is an **additive bilingual situation** (see p. 52). In most 'immersion' situations, the children learn the language from the same point and do not compete with native speakers. Teachers may be specially trained in teaching second languages. Children in this situation not only learn another language, but their proficiency in the first approaches that of native speakers educated monolingually.

## The Reality of Childhood Bilingualism

Parents often worry that their child will not 'cope' with bilingualism, that it will have an adverse effect on general mental development. A popular assumption in countries where monolingualism is the norm is that the brain can only cope with one language, and that two will overload the mind. According to this view, the bilingual child learns neither language properly and becomes mentally confused. However, much research has shown that this is not the case, provided that the child does not acquire the second language in a totally subtractive situation. Where both languages are relatively well developed, a bilingual child may have some **thinking advantages** over a monolingual (see Bilingualism and Thinking, p. 66).

It is important, however, that parents do not have unrealistic expectations of their children's bilingual development. A bilingual is not two monolinguals inside a single person. Bilinguals rarely achieve the same level of proficiency as monolinguals in both their languages. Most adult bilinguals have one dominant language, which can change with circumstances, such as a move to another country.

Bilingual children often have a **dominant language**, which may change during childhood. Unequal exposure may cause one language to develop faster than the other, as when the home and neighborhood language becomes secondary to the language of school and the wider community. Over time, the second language may become dominant.

Adult bilinguals may not achieve monolingual competence in either of their two languages. This does not indicate inferiority in ability or intelligence, but merely use of the languages in different contexts, for different purposes. Similarly, a child may feel more comfortable discussing religion, special festivals or family relationships in the home language, but be more competent in the outside language when discussing computers, sports, or a school project.

A bilingual individual's vocabulary in either language may be smaller than a monolingual's, but the total bilingual vocabulary will be considerably larger, for both children and adults. Language development depends on many factors, the amount and quality of home, school and community exposure, or the mass media. If contact with the language is minimal or confined to the home, the child will not achieve the same level of competence as monolingual peers. Progress may be limited to **passive, or receptive, bilingualism**. However, bilingualism must not be viewed as 'all or nothing', success or failure. Any degree of bilingualism is valuable, and competence may increase with exposure to a language.

Imagine a child who is always spoken to in English by one parent and German by the other. The parents speak English together. The child speaks English with friends and neighbors and in all other social situations. The school language is English. Competence in German may lag behind that of German speakers of the same age, not much beyond receptive bilingualism. However, with more opportunities for German language contact, prolonged visits from German speaking relatives and friends, trips to the home country, cassettes, books and videos, contact with other German–English families in the same area, the child's German will improve. With a family move to a German-speaking country, the child would probably catch up quickly with monolingual peers.

### Further Reading

Baker, C. (2000) *A Parents' and Teachers' Guide to Bilingualism* (2nd edn). Clevedon: Multilingual Matters.
De Houwer, A. (1995) Bilingual language acquisition. In P. Fletcher and B. Macwhinney (eds) *The Handbook of Child Language*. London: Blackwell.

## THEME 3: CHILDHOOD TRILINGUALISM

Since the larger part of the world's population is bilingual, approximately six out of every ten children grow up speaking two languages. Many acquire at least a passive competence in several languages. In **multilingual communities** in Africa and Asia, children may learn one or more home languages and others in their neighborhood, school and wider community.

One documented route to trilingualism is parents' speaking two different languages at home. The children then are educated through a third language. The majority language of the community influences the relative strengths of the languages, and relative proficiency in each of them may also change over time. Stable trilingualism seems less likely than stable bilingualism. Establishing trilingualism early is usually easier than maintaining it over the teenage years. A school where policies are positive towards multilingualism and multiculturalism is needed to ensure a favorable attitude about language ability in children (particularly adolescents).

Specific references are given below to case studies of raising trilinguals. Charlotte Hoffmann studied children trilingual in Spanish (mostly from the father and *au pairs*), German (mostly from the mother and visits) and English (mostly among peers and in school). The one parent/one language rule was followed. English came to be dominant, as school experience and peer relationships developed. Equal facility in all three languages is much less likely than diminished competence in grammar or breadth of vocabulary in one or two of them.

One proviso about trilingualism is the necessity, for cognitive growth, of fully developing at least one language at age-appropriate levels. The child will need sufficient competence to operate in the increasingly abstract nature of the school curriculum. A low level of development in all three languages, a worry usually avoided by parents of trilinguals, would impede academic development and requires extra vigilance within the 'trilingual family.'

### Further Reading

Cenoz J. and Genesee, F. (1998) Psycholinguistic perspectives on multilingualism and multilingual education. In J. Cenoz and F. Genesee (eds) *Beyond Bilingualism: Multilingualism and Multilingual Education*. Clevedon: Multilingual Matters.

Helot, C. (1988) Bringing up children in English, French and Irish: Two case studies. *Language, Culture and Curriculum* 1 (3), 281–287.

Hoffmann, C. (1985) Language acquisition in two trilingual children. *Journal of Multilingual and Multicultural Development* 6 (6), 479–495.

## THEME 4: BILINGUALISM AND MARRIAGE

Marriages between people from different ethnic groups, clans and languages have been present since the dawn of history. However, the 20th century, with its changes in transportation, increased social and geographical mobility of populations, industrialization and urbanization has increased the chances of marriages involving bilingualism and also has affected the place of languages within those marriages. More partners find themselves in the situation where two or more languages and cultures are in contact. Sometimes both languages survive, sometimes one is gradually lost, and occasionally languages are revived within the partnership. Language can become an issue between people in a marriage or partnership, in the same ways as in the outer society, where increasing inter-language contact can sometimes produce conflict, issues of language maintenance, shift, vitality and revival.

Given the rise of **marriages of mixed cultures and languages**, what factors influence the relative dominance of languages within them? A number of factors determine the profile of language usage in a marriage, for example:

- The specific language(s) of each partner.
- The strength and personal dominance in ability and use of those languages.

- The relative status and prestige of the languages.
- The courtship language of the couple and their history of language use.
- The specific community in which they live, with its trends of language usage.
- The extended family and intergenerational language dynamics.
- Family policy, spoken or latent, about children and language.
- Conversation topics.

The influence of such factors shows itself in different patterns of language use in couples. In one type of bilingual marriage, for example, both partners share two or more languages, perhaps both are Spanish/English bilinguals. In these cases, where **both speak both languages**, then the early language pattern of the relationship will usually furnish the model followed in the future. The courtship language may become the home language when the partners come from a language minority background and prefer to speak in their heritage language.

Where the partners have **different dominant languages**, many factors may influence language choice: the courtship language, the language peer group where the relationship was created, extended family and community. Choice of language may involve the desire to maintain and promote a specific language, particularly where there are children involved. Imagine a native Spanish speaker and native English speaker living in the United States who decide to use Spanish exclusively at home, in order to maintain their own proficiency and transmit the language to their children.

Or again, in a second type of language partnership, one language alone is a **common denominator** while one or both of the partners also speak other languages, which are not shared. Such a relationship may provide the opportunity for a motivated partner to learn another language. In a marriage with one bilingual and one monolingual partner, both may become bilingual. When community acceptance or economic advantage in the labor market make bilingualism advantageous, the partnership provides plentiful, informal opportunities for successful learning and practice. Again, when there are children, if one parent wants the children to learn a heritage language, the other parent may also learn that language in support.

Still another model finds **both languages used** on a regular basis by both partners. Codeswitching (switching languages within a single conversation) occurs regularly in some bilingual communities. If a couple lives in such a community, such switching will tend to occur in their normal speech, in public and private. As situations change, language use by partners will respond. When guests in the house only speak one of the two languages, the host partners may converse only in that language, both with their guests and each other, to be polite. When in public, perhaps an office or school, parents may use a different language than they would at home, especially when there is a difference in language prestige or a need to conform to the norms of language behavior 'in public'. There may also be a conscious decision to avoid mixing the languages and use both, but at different times, for example reserving French for the weekend.

As these examples show, decisions about language use may be conscious or subconscious. Language policy within a marriage is not always discussed. In some cases, in cross language families, the higher status language becomes the family language without discussion.

When there are children, there may be more conscious language planning. Many alternatives are possible. Sometimes, parents may decide to separate their languages in speaking to the child, one in one language, the other in a different language. Both may speak the same chosen language to the child or the mother may feel it more natural to speak a native tongue with her child, though not with her husband.

Does bilingualism itself cause conflict in marriage? The first answer to this frequent question is that conflict in a partnership is most often due to issues other than language. Compatibility problems tend to be caused by problems of personality, attitudes, culture-specific beliefs, finance and sexual relationship, not the existence of two or more languages within the marriage. Language differences may still be blamed for marriage conflict, but usually unfairly and as an excuse, not a cause.

In bilingual marriages, communication within the extended family can become complex, especially when one partner or the children cannot communicate with relatives. When children can talk with the extended families, relationships and cultural continuity are improved. Otherwise, translation and interpretation, tolerance and imagination become necessary.

In those cases where one partner is unable to understand one of the languages of the other, discussions are valuable. Imagine the situation where one parent is talking to a child while the other is unable to understand. Such natural communication may be interpreted as exclusion. Ideally, there should be an **agreed policy** about the use of a language only one partner can speak, as well as about the possibility of the second partner becoming proficient in it. Shared understanding is required as to why one partner needs to use that language in particular circumstances, if such use might give rise to conflict. Such a family policy can allay the fear of exclusion or criticism when one partner cannot participate in a conversation.

Where both partners are bilingual or one is monolingual, there is a danger that the minority language will not survive. A subconscious personal cost–benefit analysis may drive the partnership toward the majority language. Minority languages may decay when a new partnership changes previous language patterns, without any specific conscious decision being made. Sometimes mixed language marriages mean language shift. Families play a crucial role in the transmission of minority languages to succeeding generations.

Thus marriage becomes an important life event in the history of languages within a society. Marriages may promote the maintenance and growth, or decay and death of languages and bilingualism. When there is clear language planning, bilingualism may become a valuable asset for the family. Minority languages may be reproduced in such bilingually active partnerships.

## Further Reading

Baker, C. (2000) *A Parents' and Teachers' Guide to Bilingualism* (2nd edn). Clevedon: Multilingual Matters.

# Chapter 5
# Bilingual Children in Communities

## INTRODUCTION

It is often said, there are no bilinguals without bilingual communities. Bilinguals typically live in **networks, communities and societies**, groups, which take on particular social characteristics. A professional needs to understand bilinguals within their social contexts. Societal issues surrounding monolingualism and bilingualism produce issues of ethnicity, racism, dialects, and the politics of assimilation and integration of minority groups. This chapter takes a social look at bilinguals with a necessary political viewpoint. There is no understanding of bilinguals in communities without appreciating that political preferences underlie many pressures that professionals experience when dealing with bilinguals.

The themes of this chapter are:

- Language Communities
- Language Minorities
- A Categorization of Language Minorities
- Immigration, Emigration and Language
- Ethnic Identity
- Diglossia
- Language Boundaries: The Territorial and Personality Principles
- Dialects and Bilingualism

## THEME 1: LANGUAGE COMMUNITIES

### Introduction

At its simplest, a **language community** consists of people who use one language for part, most, or all daily existence. Sometimes linguists use the term to describe groups of majority language users, however large. The 50 million people using English as their daily language in Britain can be described as 'the English language community'. However, more frequently it serves to describe minority language groups, such as the French language community in Louisiana, the Sámi community in Norway, or the Bengali language community in the East End of London. Other frequently used terms are **speech community** and **language group**, most often to describe a localized group of people with the same (minority) language. Complications in employing such terms are discussed in detail in Baker and Jones (1998).

Problems with defining a speech community, language community or language group have led some to prefer the terms **language networks** or **speech networks**. A language network posits a network of interacting speakers of a particular language. Actual patterns of daily interaction may be described and explained in great detail, referring to who interacts with whom, how often, where and when, and these patterns can be mapped in graphic format.

## Community Languages

The term **community languages** has recently become popular. In large Canadian and English cities, there are language communities, formed by Bengali, Sylleti, Panjabi, Urdu, Gujarati, Spanish, Greek and Turkish speakers. The language community may center on the local mosque, temple or Saturday school system where the heritage language and culture are taught. The community may also focus around local schools, shopping areas and recreational amenities.

The term **language community** in Britain has become particularly important for those who cannot claim the territorial principle (see p. 62). The Welsh, Irish and Gaelic speaking communities can claim that theirs is an indigenous language with territorial rights. Established immigrants, recently arrived migrants and refugees cannot. Instead they argue from the **personality principle** (see p. 62) that their language and culture have unique features with a long and strong tradition to preserve. Where the language does not belong to the land, it still belongs to the community.

## Additive and Subtractive Bilingualism

It is important to understand the distinction between **additive** and **subtractive bilingualism** before leaving the subject of communities. When the addition of a second language and culture is unlikely to replace or displace the first language and culture, the bilingual situation is additive. English-speaking North Americans who learn French or Spanish will not lose English, but gain a second language and parts of its culture. The 'value added' benefits are social and economic as well as linguistic and cultural. Positive attitudes about bilingualism may also result.

In contrast, the learning of a majority second language may undermine a minority first language and culture, thus creating a subtractive situation (e.g. many Latinos in the United States). Immigrants may experience pressure to use the dominant language and feel embarrassed to use the home language. When the second language is prestigious and powerful, used exclusively in education and employment, while the minority language is perceived as low in status and value, there is subtraction with the potential loss of the second language.

With little or no pressure to replace or reduce a first language, the acquisition of a second language and culture occurs as an additive form of bilingualism, with a positive self-concept as a component. When the second language and culture are acquired with pressure to replace or demote the first, as with immigrants, a subtractive form occurs, related to a less positive self-concept, loss of cultural identity, possible alienation and assimilation. There is also the danger of failure in education and finding work.

**Additive** and **subtractive bilingualism** are terms used with individuals, as well as with language communities. A **balanced bilingual**, who has cognitive advantages from knowing two languages, typically enjoys additive bilingualism. A bilingual whose languages are both underdeveloped may suffer from subtractive bilingualism. Another more frequent use of the terms, however, relates to the enrichment or loss of minority language, culture and ethnolinguistic identity at a community or societal level. In an additive context, a minority community uses both languages in a relatively stable diglossic manner, with ethnolinguistic vitality. In a subtractive context, the languages are used in a shifting, unstable way, with both languages used for the same purposes and a declining use of the minority language.

### Further Reading

Coulmas, F. (ed.) (1997) *The Handbook of Sociolinguistics*. Oxford: Blackwell.
Geach, J. (1996) Community languages. In E. Hawkins (ed.) *Thirty Years of Language Teaching*. London: Centre for Information on Language Teaching and Research (CILT).

## THEME 2: LANGUAGE MINORITIES

While **language minority** is a frequently used term, an exact definition is difficult. It may be used to describe many groups that differ in size, geographical distribution, status and origin.

The term 'minority' is ambiguous. Does it refer to the numbers of people who speak the language? Is the implied comparison in 'minority' at the regional or national level? Is the total number of speakers important, or only the density of speakers within a region?

'Minority' may be used to reflect less (or low) political status and power. Thus in Peru, Quechua has less power and status than Spanish, in France, Breton less status that French, and in Malaysia, Tamil is less prestigious than Malaysian. The relative status and power of a language within a country, not the number of speakers, is the preferred academic use of 'minority'.

Nevertheless, defining a majority language solely in terms of status and power runs into difficulties. In Ireland, where Irish is an official state language, it still may be perceived as a minority language, because English has a much higher perceived status in education, business and government. While Spanish is a high status language in Spain and most of Latin America, it is a minority language in comparison to English in the United States.

'Minority' can carry an additional meaning when used by sociolinguists. In one sense 'minority' evokes images of disadvantage, under privilege, oppression, discrimination and exploitation. It carries a stereotype, a label or prejudice, that 'diversity' and 'difference' translate as 'less valuable' and 'less worthwhile,' with a diminished future.

### Further Reading

McKay, S.L. and Wong, S.C. (eds) (1988) *Language Diversity: Problem or Resource?* New York: Newbury House.

Skutnabb-Kangas, T. (1981) *Bilingualism or Not: The Education of Minorities.* Clevedon: Multilingual Matters.

## THEME 3: A CATEGORIZATION OF LANGUAGE MINORITIES

Ogbu (1978, 1983), distinguishes between **caste-like**, **immigrant** and **autonomous** minority groups. **Autonomous minorities** are not subordinate to the dominant majority group and have distinct separate identities. Some Jews in the United States have a distinct racial, ethnic, religious, social, linguistic or cultural identity and are generally not politically or economically subordinate. Such minorities are unlikely to be characterized by disproportionate or persistent failure in school.

**Caste-like minorities** are often poorly educated, fill the least paid jobs, and are regarded as inferior to the dominant majority. They are sometimes labeled negatively as 'culturally deprived,' 'limited in English proficiency,' 'with low innate intelligence'. 'Bilingual' becomes pejorative. In the United States, Ogbu (1978) classes African Americans, Puerto Ricans, Mexican Americans, Native Americans and many Latino groups as caste-like minorities. The 'outcastes' of India and some Caribbean immigrants in Great Britain share these characteristics. Such minorities see themselves as relatively powerless, immobile in status, and confined to subservience. Most have been permanently, often involuntarily, incorporated into the host society. Such groups experience disproportionate failure at school, which confirms the low expectations they have of themselves and the negative attributions by majority groups. A sense of inferiority joins low levels of motivation to succeed in the wider society.

Generally speaking, Ogbu's **immigrant minorities** moved relatively willingly to the United States, and may be motivated to succeed at school and prosper. Cubans, Filipinos, Japanese, Koreans and Chinese were included in this group. As a generalization these immigrants are eager to succeed, positive about schooling and optimistic about improving their lot. Some individuals are educated in the home country and arrive literate and motivated to achieve (Ogbu, 1987).

**Immigrant minorities** tend to lack power and status. They will often be low on the occupational ladder. However, their self-image is not necessarily the same as the dominant hosts' perception. 'As strangers, they can operate psychologically outside established distinctions of social status and relations' (Ogbu, 1983, p. 169). Such immigrant minorities, although suffering racial discrimination and hostility, are less intimidated and paralyzed than are caste-like minorities. Parents have relatively strong aspirations for their children in school, as well as expectations of vocational and social mobility for them. Parents whose reference group lies in the homeland or their immigrant neighborhood preserve pride in ethnic identity

Ogbu's (1978) distinction between autonomous, caste-like and immigrant minorities does not allow easy classification. The criteria are imprecise. They also are not validated by research studies. Moreover, there is a danger in stereotyping different language groups, when there is much variability within them. However, the differences between caste-like and immigrant minorities help explain why equally disadvantaged groups, facing discrimination from the dominant majority, perform differently at school. Poverty, poor quality housing, and powerlessness do not fully explain language minority failure in education. Beyond socioeconomic class and language differences, academic and economic success or failure may be due, in part, to cultural differences. Caste-like minorities seem locked into a system that perpetuates inequalities and discrimination. Other minorities attempt to escape the subtractive system, which confines their participation in society and confirms their powerlessness. Immigrant and autonomous minorities show less failure at school, partly through a more positive orientation to their own language and culture, partly through optimism about their likely success in the school system. Therefore, language minority education ('strong' forms of bilingual education) becomes highly important for caste-like minorities in the attempt to counteract both the discrimination of the dominant majority and their own acceptance and internalization of discrimination and economic deprivation.

### Further Reading

Ogbu, J. (1978) *Minority Education and Caste: The American System in Cross-Cultural Perspective.* New York: Academic Press.

Ogbu, J. (1983) Minority status and schooling in plural societies. *Comparative Education Review* 237.2, 168–190.

Ogbu, J. (1987) Variability in minority school performance: A problem in search of an explanation. *Anthropology and Education Quarterly* 18, 312–334.

## THEME 4: IMMIGRATION, EMIGRATION AND LANGUAGE

### Introduction

Most often, immigrants lose their language between the first and third generations, through the melting pot processes of employment, schooling, mass media and other influences. Most countries expect immigrants to shed their languages and culture soon after settling in.

When headlines talk about overwhelming 'floods,' 'waves,' or 'influxes' of immigrants, the pressure is on new residents to lose their heritage language. The host country may actively invite immigration, as Canada did between 1992 and 1995, calling for 250,000 immigrants per year to adjust for an aging population and augment the workforce, but pressure is still on for new residents to abandon their language. Assimilation is a common political demand, with language a visible sign of the extent of individual and group assimilation. Language often takes on a symbolic value as a highly visible **mark of group identity**.

Yet language is not essential to the maintenance of ethnic identity. Various groups of immigrants in different cultures have retained their ethnicity despite losing their language, such as Dutch immigrants in Australia, Greeks and Turks in London, and some French communities in the Unites States. Over the last few decades in the United States, there has been a revived interest and pride in ancestry, roots, and the maintenance of ethnic identity, despite the loss of original languages.

## The Speed of Assimilation

Whether an immigrant will assimilate rapidly or slowly, or integrate, is influenced by many factors (see also pp. 153f), for example:

- Was the move **chosen or forced**? When emigration is voluntary, assimilation may be more expected and desired. It may be resisted when the move is forced. For employment or economic reasons, some people choose to emigrate, others are refugees with little or no choice. However, even an apparent free choice is often made with 'loaded dice', as in the choice between material poverty and potential affluence.
- The amount of emotional and financial preparation and support affect transition and integration. **Refugees** often have little preparation and may be very vulnerable emotionally and financially.
- The amount of **separation** from the nuclear and extended family has an effect in integration. Immigrant families often arrive in stages. Reunification is difficult and often occurs after a long period of time. During stressful periods, extended family support is missing, at least short-term, and often on a long-term basis. Immigrants often feel isolated, helpless and rootless.
- **Large cities**, where many newcomers settle, are not easy environments for adjustment. For immigrants from rural backgrounds, where patterns of interaction with neighbors are very different, settling into a new culture, living conditions, and styles of relationships may be difficult.
- When newcomers cannot speak the language of the host country, both linguistic and cultural **isolation** can result. Without the host language, it is difficult to acquire the culture, rules of social interaction, cultural rituals, values and beliefs. Social and racial integration can be difficult, not only because of language barriers, but because of hostility from certain members of the host country.
- Many immigrants **lose status**. They are often unable to find immediate employment, or they work for a minimal salary. They are discriminated against in employment applications. Their self-esteem and positive self-identity may be affected. If parents must take employment well below their standard of qualification, poorly paid and 'dead end' jobs may affect the children's view of them. Some children will then be more motivated to assimilate, learn the language and culture, and improve their material conditions and identity. When immigrants are placed in conditions of poverty, deprivation and prejudice, their children may be less successful in school and drop out early, with low expectations of themselves and their families.

- Immigrants often do not get involved in parent-teacher and school activities, thus missing that valuable **home–school** link. This link is widely recognized as an important factor in children's academic success. Parents who cannot speak the language of the school, who work long evening hours or have no tradition of interaction with children and their school work, may not take advantage of school outreach to create relationships. Many parents are limited by lack of fluency in the host country language.

At other times, there is a **cultural mismatch** or conflict between home and school. Some parents expect particular gender roles appropriate to their religious beliefs. Some insist on immediate respect for elders, or cling to patterns of dating and hetero-sexual relationships, which differ from those of the host nation. When school teachers differ in their cultural values, there may be problems for immigrant children, in particular. Muslim families often find Western school culture alien and degenerate. When courses are offered on sex education, drugs, Christianity or Women's Studies, the home–school relationship may become one of conflict and culture clash.

Immigrant children have to **navigate between cultures**. Somehow they must remain loyal to both their parents and their school, to their heritage culture and the host culture. A middle path, however ambiguous and contradictory, must be steered, lest there be isolation from the parents or the school. Sometimes such isolation becomes a means of survival and security.

**Refugees** often have experienced the trauma of wars and witnessed brutal killings, even the deaths of family and close friends. They have flown from horrors in the home country, experienced refugee camps and suffered through a period of stress, anxiety and depression as they waited for immigration recognition. Once in the new country, there is often a period of elation and relief at their final escape from persecution, murder and refugee camps. Sometimes there is guilt over those people left behind, particularly close relatives and friends. A phase of depression may follow, with the realization there is little or no chance of returning to the home country, that exile will be permanent. Withdrawal, sometimes aggression may result from such a realization and sense of desperation.

## Further Reading

Dicker, S.J. (1996) *Languages in America: A Pluralist View.* Clevedon: Multilingual Matters.
Parrillo, V.N. (1994) *Strangers to these Shores* (4th edn). New York: Macmillan.
Parrillo, V.N. (1996) *Diversity in America.* Thousand Oaks, CA: Pine Forge Press.
Takaki, R. (ed.) (1994) *From Different Shores: Perspectives on Race and Ethnicity in America* (2nd edn). New York: Oxford University Press.

## THEME 5: ETHNIC IDENTITY

### Introduction

Ethnic groups and ethnic cleansing are active contemporary topics. There are clearly distinct ethnic groups – Mongolians and Maori, Somalians and Sámi, Walloons and Welsh, each with internally similar sociocultural patterns of behavior. Ethnic groups tend to live in defined communities, such as the Pennsylvania Amish, in regions such as Brittany, in nations such as Wales, or are distributed across neighboring countries as are Latinos and the Basques. Within an ethnic group, there are differences of politics, social class, occupation, age and subculture, yet usually there are unifying elements.

Ethnicity, **ethnic identity**, even an ethnic group, all are concepts whose definition is problematic. One danger lies in using only 'objective' criteria in describing an ethnic group. Dress, hair styles, manners, eating habits, religion, architecture, art, literature, music, patterns of trade and child rearing serve as the observable traits of an ethnic group. However, such attributes are outward signs, and often superficial. They may change across generations, leaving ethnic identity intact.

Ethnic identity is continuous; it lives across generations. **Ethnicity** describes a group of people whose coherence and solidarity are based on common origins, common self-consciousness, shared understandings, meanings to life and experiences. Ethnic identity may be historically deep, collectively felt with a sense of roots and togetherness. Such an understanding of ancestry and history may be real, embedded in historical fact, or it may be mythical, part of a legend. What is important, is that there is a collective belief in the historic depths of the roots, that tradition is continuous across generation. At times, the emotive is more potent than the rational in ethnic identity.

People risk presuming that 'ethnic groups' or 'ethnic identity' refer to minorities only. It is rare to refer to 'white English-speaking Americans' or 'French speakers in France' as ethnic groups. In the United States, for example, it is not uncommon for white English-speaking monolinguals to think of 'ethnics' as Puerto Rican migrants, Cuban exiles, Mexican, Greek or Chinese immigrants. In England, 'ethnic groups' are perceived as inner-city Asians or Turks, Greeks, Italians, Chinese or Vietnamese. English speaking monolinguals in the United States or UK just don't think of themselves as an ethnic group. This is as dangerous as it is wrong. Majority groups are also ethnic groups. If the term is reserved only for minorities, it takes on connotations of disadvantage, servility, of peoples who are despised and rejected.

Having 'ethnic identity', seeing oneself as Cuban, Chinese, Latino or Latvian, is essentially a self-perception. It depends on people attributing to themselves a group identity that collectively expresses historical roots and cultural continuity. It is a belief in belonging. Genetic ancestry need not create ethnic membership, A Tamil may self-categorize and prefer to be seen as Malaysian.

It is a presumed common identity, common historical comprehension, values and understandings that define ethnicity, and thus it is subjective in nature. Ask immigrants to the United States, are they Mexican, American, Mexican-American, Latino or Aztec? Are English immigrants to Wales Welsh, English, British or European? The individual answers will reveal varied self-perceived ethnic identities, and increasingly multiple ones.

The labels for ethnic groups tend to change over time, as old labels acquire negative connotations. Labels such as 'Coloreds', 'Blacks', 'African-Americans' and 'Native Americans' are variously used, applauded, disputed and rejected. Other labels are relatively less temporary – the Welsh, Bretons, Jews – although tinged with the same associations of inequality, discrimination and material deprivation.

However, the danger of the terms 'ethnicity' or 'ethnic group' is that they become **deviance** concepts. In this normative sense, the terms refer to those who deviate from the normal, who are not part of the majority and are not accepted as the societal norm. The power of the term 'ethnicity' is that it recognizes a variety of groups in society and especially highlights those which, as entities, feel especially deprived, lack power, are of low status and less valued.

## Language Boundaries

The **boundaries** between ethnic groups are important to ethnicity (Barth, 1969). As the culture of a group evolves over time, boundaries (also changeable) serve to separate different ethnic identities. Boundaries, such as different languages, are more continuous and long standing, while cultures within an ethnic group may be more fluid. At the same time, cultures are often used to establish boundaries.

Boundaries create contrasts, and sometimes conflicts, between different ethnic identities. When distinctions such as languages between groups are endangered, heightened identity awareness may result. Sometimes internal unity is enhanced by external opposition. Also, unity from within may elicit opposition from without.

Boundaries result from a continuing sense of group identity. In turn they become important in establishing ethnic identity. **Boundary markers** such as language, culture and religion fix distinctions. Language is an important marker, but not essential, in boundary making, as other markers are available. However, ethnic groups are also divided by internal boundaries. Different communities and regions of the same group may be divided, social classes exiting within the ethnic group may be set apart, varied networks of interaction are possible. Social and cultural divisions exist within as well as between ethnic groups.

An important boundary marker for many groups is language. Speaking Spanish in the United States, Walloon in Belgium or Welsh in Wales establishes **symbolic and behavioral boundaries** between such groups and the majority language speakers in their countries. Through language, ethnic identity is expressed, enacted and symbolized.

Consider an example. Attitude surveys show that the Irish language is seen as a symbol of ethnic or national identity. The people of Ireland tend to believe the language is necessary to their ethnic and cultural integrity. It is a **symbol** of a separate culture, heritage and identity. However, only a relative minority of the Irish use the language daily. This fact highlights the distinction between language for communication, the living use of a minority language, and language as a symbol of nationhood, ethnicity or a language community.

Nevertheless, language is not essential to ethnic identity. Less than 2% of Scots speak Gaelic, English is their dominant language, and yet they hold fiercely to their Scottish allegiance. Speaking English with a Scots burr is one symbol of that identity. Thus other markers than actually speaking the language, for example, accent, sporting enthusiasms, shared history and traditions, can create an ethnic unity.

For many groups, their heritage language is much more than a symbol of heritage. The vocabulary, idioms and metaphors of the minority language best express and transmit the heritage culture. The language and culture of an ethnic group are intertwined, as are heart and mind in a flourishing body. The taste and flavor of a culture permeate its language; memories and traditions are most fully stored and expressed in it.

Recently ethnic identity has been associated with **conflict**, but the two are not directly related, an important point in considering ethnic cleansing in Eastern Europe in the 1990s. Many groups live harmoniously with their neighbors, the whole world over. Whether in large cities, on borders between countries or deep within them, the majority of ethnic groups live peacefully and cooperatively. At the same time, ethnic identity may enter into religious, economic or political conflict. Just as water is essential for life, yet can cause drowning, or electricity gives light yet can kill, so ethnic identity gives cultural light and life yet contributes to intergroup conflict, even killing.

There is no essential, direct link between ethnicity and conflict. Just as the extreme of religion is bigotry, of sexuality is sexism, of democracy is anarchy, so the extreme of ethnicity is ethnocentrism and racism. Only this extreme results in conflict, and generally it is rare, ethnic tolerance is more usual. The extremes win the glare of publicity; tolerance and civility are more common but much less newsworthy.

### Ethnicity and Racism

While ethnic identity celebrates the collective heritage of a sociocultural group, racism focuses on the difference between them. Ethnicity implies that all groups have an equal right to maintain their heritage, that cultural pluralism is valuable to individuals and groups. Racism makes judgements about what is better or worse, acceptable or not, even what should be obliterated. Inside racism, distinguished from ethnicity, is the concept of dominance of one ethnic group over another. Racism requires a belief in superior races, the superiority of skin color, ethnic origin or culture.

While groups may be more or less ethnocentric, racism arises where there is active behavioral or psychological aggression against another group. While there is sometimes little separating vigorous ethnic identity and racism, or ethnicity and ethnocentrism, at its best, ethnicity celebrates a diversity among people, which does not spill over into conflict. While there is often tension, dispute, political conflict, argument and debate, particularly between minority and majority ethnic groups, warfare is not inevitable. Polemic and protest may be essential parts of an ethnic group's life, but only in relatively rare circumstances does it change into armed aggression.

An individual's **ethnicity** will vary across time and with changing contexts. One of the increasing recent tendencies is for people to take on multiple loyalties, identities and group memberships. It becomes increasingly possible to be Welsh, British and European, or instead of Cuban or American, to be Cuban-American, or Cuban and American.

Bilingualism is one enabler of **multiple identities**. As a modern world economy, global cooperation, internationalism and the information society have grown, boundaries between ethnic groups weaken. Such international changes appear to encourage multiple group membership.

There is no certainty that internationalism will make ethnic identities wither and fade. Instead, inhabitants of the global village may discover who they are and whence they came. As the world shrinks and differences melt, the need for roots and security within a local identity may grow.

### Further Reading

Edwards, J.R. (1985) *Language, Society and Identity*. Oxford: Basil Blackwell.
Fishman, J.A. (1997) Language and ethnicity: The view from within. In F. Coulmas (ed.) *The Handbook of Sociolinguistics*. Oxford: Blackwell.
Fishman, J.A. (ed.) (1999) *Handbook of Language and Ethnic Identity*. New York: Oxford University Press.
Tabouret-Keller, A. (1997) Language and identity. In F. Coulmas (ed.) *The Handbook of Sociolinguistics*. Oxford: Blackwell.

## THEME 6: DIGLOSSIA

### Introduction

'Bilingualism' typically serves to describe an individual's two languages. When the focus changes to two language varieties co-existing in society, a common term is **diglossia** (Ferguson, 1959; Fishman, 1972, 1980). In practice, a community is unlikely to use both language varieties for the same purposes. It is more likely for one variety to serve in certain situations and functions and the other to be used in others. A language community may use its heritage, minority language in the home, for devotions and in social activity. The majority language may serve at work, in education and in the mass media.

Ferguson (1959) first defined diglossia as the use of two divergent varieties of the same language for different societal functions. Fishman (1972, 1980) extended the idea to two languages existing side by side within a geographical area. In both situations, different languages or varieties may serve varied purposes, as illustrated below.

| Context | Majority Language (H) | Minority Language (L) |
|---|---|---|
| 1. The home and family | | x |
| 2. Schooling | x | |
| 3. Mass Media | x | |
| 4. Business and commerce | x | |
| 5. Community social and cultural activity | | x |
| 6. Correspondence with family and friends | | x |
| 7. Correspondence with government departments | x | |
| 8. Religious activity | | x |

Languages may be used in different situations with the low (L) variety or minority language more frequent in informal, personal situations and the high (H), majority language in formal, official communication contexts.

The table suggests that different contexts usually make one language more prestigious than the other. Many minority language situations are diglossic. Because the majority language is used for prestigious functions, it may seem superior, more elegant and more cultured, the door to both educational and economic success. On the other hand, the low variety is often restricted to interpersonal, domestic functions, and may seem inferior, inadequate, and low class.

### Further Reading

Ferguson, C. (1959) Diglossia. *Word* 5, 325–340.
Fishman, J.A. (1980) Bilingualism and biculturalism as individual and as societal phenomena. *Journal of Multilingual and Multicultural Development* 1, 3–15.
Schiffman, H.F. (1997) Diglossia as a sociolinguistic solution. In F. Coulmas (ed.) *The Handbook of Sociolinguistics*. Oxford: Blackwell.

## THEME 7: LANGUAGE BOUNDARIES: THE TERRITORIAL AND PERSONALITY PRINCIPLES

The **territorial principle** can be defined as the granting of a measure of recognition, rights or official status to a language based on its use in a certain geographical area. Where the territorial principle exists, as in Wales and Switzerland, geography serves to define language boundaries, with inhabitants of a region classified as a distinct language group. The survival, maintenance and spread of the language are justified by its historic existence within the region. As the indigenous regional speech, its rights may be enshrined in law. Welsh speakers have certain language rights in Wales, such as the use of Welsh in a court of law, but not when they cross the English border. The territorial principle benefits the Welsh, but has unfortunate implications for other immigrant language minorities in Britain. If Welsh is the language of Wales, is English the only rightful language of England? Do languages belong to regions and territories, but not to the people who speak them, wherever they may be found? Do Panjabi, Urdu, Bengali, Hindi, Greek and Turkish only belong in the home country? Do such languages have no home in Britain? Do the users of sign languages have any rights, since they are unconnected with any geographical community?

Under the territorial principle, should language minorities speak either the majority official language of the territory or return to their home country? The territorial principle benefits some, as it does the Welsh. For others, it is unacceptable and unfair. In Europe there are many indigenous, or autochthonous languages for which preservation status is being sought in the European Community. But little or no formal status is accorded the immigrant languages of Europe, such as the various Asian languages.

The term **personality principle** is particularly helpful to describe minority groups unprotected by a language territory principle. The 'personality' of each language is the sum of its more or less distinctive attributes, as revealed in its uses and functions, communication styles and literature, as well as the customs and rituals, culture and meanings enshrined in it. The Pennsylvania Amish decided to ensure the continuity of their heritage language by reserving an exclusive place for it at home, reserving English for school and contacts with the outer secular world. One language is reserved for particular societal functions, another for distinctly separate functions. This compartmentalization is relatively stable. Such separation of identity for each language exists within the psyche of each group member. There cannot be diglossia without bilingualism, if diglossia is based on the personality principle. In contrast, there can be diglossia without bilingualism where the territorial principle exists.

The personality principle can be an attribute of those claiming the territorial principle. However, the personality principle is especially supportive for immigrant groups, such as Asians in Europe and the many immigrant language minorities in Canada and the United States. People who can not claim territorial rights for their languages can assert that their heritage language has 'personality' and serves particular functions, which need safeguarding and separation from the majority language. Such groups can argue that their right to use their language is fully portable across national borders because it has its own **personality of uses**.

## THEME 8: DIALECTS AND BILINGUALISM

### What is a Dialect?

**Dialect** is a term frequently used in common speech. It may describe a low status language form, often spoken in rural areas, by people with relatively little education. 'Dialect' contrasts unfavorably with **standard** or **correct speech** or **writing** used by educated people. By implication, it is inferior, cruder and more primitive, less able to express a wide range of meanings.

This common use of 'dialect' is limited and implies a negative value judgement. Linguists prefer to use it in a more general, neutral sense to describe any variety of language. By this definition, every individual speaks a dialect, a slightly different language variety from everyone else. No two people speak a language identically; they differ in their accent, pronunciation, syntax and vocabulary. Such individual speech is an **ideolect**. A dialect is really a collection of ideolects, similar varieties of language with common features, spoken by a number of individuals. Linguists often call dialects **speech varieties** to avoid the negative connotations and value judgements of the term 'dialect'.

A dialect may be regional, used in a certain geographical location, such as Bavarian German or Parisian French. Alternatively, it may be urban, reflecting a particular employment or social class. Every language variety can be described as a dialect, even the standard form. No one variety is linguistically superior to others. The person who says 'I ain't done nothin' yet,' conveys meaning just as effectively as the person who says 'I haven't done anything yet.' Standards of correctness in language are arbitrary, not decided by linguistic factors, but by social, political and cultural ones.

If a substantial number of people speak a language over a wide geographical area, there are typically **dialectal differences** between different communities or networks of speakers. Dialects are subdivisions of a language. Within the English spoken in the British Isles, we can talk about Yorkshire English, Somerset English, Cockney English, Cardiff English and standard, spoken English. In the United States, because of immigration, westward expansion and general population mobility, dialectal variation is not as widespread or clear cut as in Britain. However, there are broad regional variations, with obvious differences between the varieties of English spoken in Texas and Pennsylvania, for instance, or Los Angeles and Washington. As in Britain, there are many urban dialects in the United States, such as the famous Brooklyn dialect of New York City.

All these and countless other **world English** dialects come under the heading of 'English'. We tend to talk about these dialects as if they were discrete and separate entities. We can describe their main features in general linguistic terms, drawing attention to differences between them from the point of view of accent, pronunciation, vocabulary, grammar and verb forms.

However, dialects are not separate entities but merge into one another. We may notice the broad difference between the German of North Germany and that spoken in the South. However, throughout Germany, there is a geographical continuum of speech variations, each slightly different from its nearest neighbor. Natural boundaries such as forests, rivers and mountains may separate neighboring dialects. The dialects farthest apart are obviously the most different from one another, even mutually unintelligible. Urban dialects tend to differ according to social class or employment, not geography.

## What is a Language?

Dialects are invariably defined in relation to a language: Parisian French is perceived as a dialect of French, Nurembergerisch is a dialect of German. However, when we try to define what is a language, as opposed to a dialect, and the relationship between them, we find a linguistic definition impossible to achieve. The concept of separate languages has more to do with cultural, historical and political realities than with linguistic boundaries.

When people attempt to define the parameters of a language such as French, Spanish, Norwegian, German, Japanese, one possible answer is 'A language is a collection of mutually intelligible dialects' (Chambers & Trudgill, 1980). However, this answer is not always sufficient. In Japan, the geographical nature of the country, with its scattered islands and high mountains, has meant that dialects have developed in isolation, and many are mutually unintelligible. Many dialects of German are mutually unintelligible.

**Boundaries** between languages often result from historical processes and conscious decisions based on ethnicity and nationalism. The Catalan language, spoken in Catalonia, Valencia, Andorra and the Balearic Isles is one of the official languages of Catalonia and has a standardized norm. This norm is not accepted by Valencians, who want their language to be recognized as separate, not a dialect of Catalan.

The definition of what constitutes a language cannot be made on linguistic grounds, but is caused by **social, cultural and political factors**. Therefore, boundaries between languages may change over time, as the history of peoples changes. The modern concept of language is closely linked to the emergence of the modern nation, in which political autonomy is tied to national solidarity, ethnic identity and cultural and linguistic unity. The autonomous variety has its own standard norms, established or evolved as a result of social, political and cultural factors. The standard autonomous variety represents the nation and all the **heteronomous varieties** look towards it as a norm.

## Conclusion

The famous statement, 'A language is a dialect with an army and a navy' underlines the important idea that boundaries between languages in the modern world are largely determined by **political power** and sovereign nations. The modern concept of a language is closely associated with the autonomous standard norm. The existence and form of such a standard is decided mainly by cultural, social and political factors rather than linguistic considerations.

## Further Reading

Hudson, R.A. (1996) *Sociolinguistics* (2nd edn). Cambridge: Cambridge University Press.
Trudgill, P. (1983) *On Dialect: Social and Geographical Perspectives*. Oxford: Blackwell.

# Chapter 6
# Bilingual Children and Thinking

## Introduction

This chapter focuses on the style of thinking and **cognitive advantages of bilingualism**. It begins by examining the key historic debate – whether bilingual children suffer or gain in their 'intelligence' due to ownership of two languages. A wider view of bilingual cognitive advantages in metalinguistic awareness and creativity is then explored. Finally, highly influential theories, which have been widely accepted as explaining the thinking benefits of bilingual children, are shared.

The themes of this chapter are:

- Bilingualism and Intelligence
- Bilingualism and Creative Thinking
- Bilingualism and Metalinguistic Awareness
- Common Underlying Proficiency and Separate Underlying Proficiency
- Thresholds Theory

## THEME 1: BILINGUALISM AND 'INTELLIGENCE'

In the 20th century, parents and teachers are sometimes advised by well meaning doctors, counselors, speech therapists and psychologists to use only one language with their children, to avoid mental confusion. Just as oil and water mixed cause an engine to malfunction, so mixing two languages would make the mental engine run more slowly, with coughs and splutters.

One intuitive belief of the 20th century is that two languages inside an individual's thinking 'quarters' leave less room to store other knowledge. Therefore, the ability to speak two languages diminishes mental efficiency. Fortunately for bilinguals, such beliefs are now known to be naive and incorrect. Throughout this section, the relationship between ownership of two languages and thinking will be explored, starting with a focus on a dominant concept in psychology and in everyday language, the concept of intelligence. Are bilinguals less intelligent, equally or more intelligent than monolinguals?

There are three approximate, overlapping periods in the 20th century which reflect changes in research findings regarding this question: the period of negative effects, the period of neutral effects, and the period of positive effects. Each will be considered in turn.

## The Period of Negative Effects

From the 19th century until the 1960s, both the public and academics believed that bilingualism had a negative effect upon intelligence. Professor Laurie, when lecturing at Cambridge University in 1890, stated that intellectual growth would not be doubled by bilingualism. On the contrary, intelligence would be halved. If language is the soil in which intelligence grows, two languages produce a thin soil and monolingualism a much more rich and fertile one.

Some of the earliest research on bilingualism compared the scores of monolinguals and bilinguals on intelligence (IQ) tests, especially on verbal IQ measures. Much of this early research came from Wales and the United States. The typical result was that monolinguals were found to have a higher IQ than bilinguals.

For example, an enterprising head teacher from Wales, D.J. Saer (1923), compared 1400 children aged 7 to 14. He found a ten-point difference in IQ between bilinguals and monolinguals in favor of monolingual English speakers. Saer's conclusion was that bilinguals were mentally confused and at a disadvantage compared with monolinguals.

In a later study, this same author found that the same difference in IQ existed between university monolinguals and bilinguals. Saer concluded that bilinguals' mental disadvantage was permanent, since it existed from the age of 7 through university. If the IQ disadvantage existed among university students, the most able in society, the problem of bilinguals' diminished intelligence would be as great or greater among people of lower IQ.

However, we now know that such early research had a series of flaws and **limitations**, which cast doubt on individual studies and on all such studies taken cumulatively. Saer did not compare like with like. His bilinguals were mostly of lower socioeconomic status, while monolinguals came from a higher social class. Hence his result may be due to differences between higher and lower social classes, rather than, or as well as, bilingualism.

A fair comparison requires matching on all the factors which might otherwise explain the result. Groups must match on variables such as sociocultural class, gender, age, type of school attended, and urban/rural as well as subtractive/additive environments.

A second problem in the early studies was that bilinguals were often given an IQ test in their **weaker language**. Many verbal IQ tests were administered in English only. This tended toward the disadvantage of bilinguals, because English was their second or weaker language. Had they been given the IQ test in their first or dominant language, different scores might well have resulted.

The proficiency in two languages of the bilinguals is a third issue. There are not simply two categories, bilinguals and monolinguals. Rather a whole range of different language skills and proficiencies may be used to classify bilinguals and monolinguals. Were all four basic language abilities, reading, writing, speaking and listening, used for classification? What was the degree of fluency in each language of the bilinguals? Were the bilinguals classified by their use of languages or by their ability in languages? Were the bilinguals relatively balanced in their language proficiencies, or were there considerable imbalances? Such criteria are crucial in fair comparisons between bilinguals and monolinguals.

Furthermore, there is a general problem in using IQ tests to measure 'intelligence'. The concept is hotly debated and highly **controversial** in psychology and education. What is intelligence or intelligent behavior? Who is intelligent, a thief who cracks a bank vault? A famous football coach? A pauper who becomes a billionaire? A chairperson who manipulates the board members? Is there social intelligence, musical intelligence, military intelligence, marketing intelligence, motoring intelligence, political intelligence, sporting intelligence, financial intelligence? Are all, or indeed, any, of these forms of intelligence measured by a simple pencil and paper IQ test with a single, acceptable and correct solution to every question?

Definitions of intelligent behavior, or of what constitutes an intelligent person, will differ from psychologist to psychologist, teacher to teacher, person to person. A value judgement must be made about what kind of behavior and what kind of person are more valuable in a particular society. IQ tests tend to target a very narrow set of skills, a middle class, 'white' and Western view of academic intelligence. Early bilingual research used such IQ tests. Such tests measure only a small sample of everyday intelligence. Whatever relationship is found between IQ tests and bilingualism refers only to 'pencil and paper intelligence' where only correct, not creative answers are demanded.

## The Period of Neutral Effects

In the late 1950s and early 1960s, a series of studies on bilingualism and IQ reported **no difference** between bilinguals and monolinguals. In the United States, when comparing Yiddish/English bilinguals with English monolinguals, IQ scores were comparable. In Wales, in the 1950s, research found that there was no difference on non-verbal IQ, once the socioeconomic class of bilinguals and monolinguals was taken into account.

This period of neutral effects was valuable, because it highlighted the inadequacies and methodological mistakes of earlier research. Bilingualism was not necessarily an intellectual disadvantage. In the 1960s, such a conclusion was a boost to parents who supported bilingualism in the home and bilingual education in schools. As a short transitional period, it led to the questioning of the fashionable perception of bilingualism as cerebral confusion and ushered in the current period of positive effects.

## The Period of Positive Effects

A study by Peal and Lambert (1962) in Canada proved a turning point and signpost for future research on bilingualism and cognitive functioning. It proved valuable because it rectified many of the methodological weaknesses of the earliest research. Moreover, the study found that bilingualism need not be negative, or even neutral in its effects, but might indeed have **cognitive advantages for bilinguals**, or at least a specific group of balanced bilinguals. Furthermore, the results of this study were subsequently widely quoted to support bilingual policies in different educational contexts. In Canada, the political implication was that French/English bilingualism would not be the source of a national intellectual inferiority, but rather, intellectual advantage. Finally, this study, even though it used IQ tests, moved to a much broader look at processes and products in cognition. Other areas of mental activity than the narrow concept of IQ stimulated continuing decades of research into bilingualism and cognitive functions.

Peal and Lambert (1962) found that **balanced bilinguals** scored significantly higher on 15 out of 18 variables in measuring IQ. They concluded that bilingualism provides greater mental flexibility, the ability to think more abstractly, the capacity to think independently of words, and superiority in concept formation. Their argument was that a more enriched bilingual and bicultural experience benefits the development of intelligence. Moreover, there was a positive transfer between a bilingual's two languages, rather than interference between them. While there were criticisms of this study, more recent research using IQ tests tends to confirm the original findings.

The question of 'what affects what' remains. Which comes first? Does bilingualism enhance IQ, or does a higher IQ increase the chances of becoming bilingual? Is one both the cause and the effect of the other in a cyclical fashion? This question will be explored later in this section.

### Further Reading

Baker, C. (1996) *Foundations of Bilingual Education and Bilingualism*. Clevedon: Multilingual Matters.

Hakuta, K. (1990) Language and cognition in bilingual children, bilingual education. In A.M. Padilla, H.H. Fairchild and C.M. Valadez (eds) *Issues and Strategies in Bilingual Education*. London, New Delhi: Sage Publications.

## THEME 2: BILINGUALISM AND CREATIVE THINKING

IQ tests require **convergent thinking**, that is, the test taker must converge on the one correct answer to each question. Some people seem to have a more free, open-ended, elastic, imaginative and creative form of thinking, an alternative style called **divergent** or **creative thinking**. Instead of finding the one correct answer, divergent thinkers prefer a variety of answers, all of which may be valid.

### Measuring Creative and Divergent Thinking

Simple and straightforward questions probe divergent thinking. 'How many uses can you think of for a brick?' 'How many interesting and unusual uses can you imagine for a cardboard box?' This open-ended kind of question calls for as many imaginative answers as possible.

A convergent thinker tends to produce a few, fundamental answers. Bricks can be used in building houses, walls, a barbecue. The diverger tends to fire off a large variety of responses, some quite unusual and original, perhaps 10, 12, 20 or more answers. Bricks can serve as ashtrays, boot scrapers, abstract sculpture, to weight a plumb line, prop up a wobbly table, break a window in case of fire, make a bird bath, raise a car when changing a flat tire.

In the North American tradition, it is more usual to talk about 'creative' than 'divergent' thinking. The same kinds of tests, such as unusual uses for a cardboard box, are employed. Scores for such tests are often based on the fluency, flexibility, originality and elaboration of the answers.

## Creative Thinking and Bilingualism

Studies suggest a link between the ownership of two or more languages and an increase in **fluency, flexibility, originality and elaboration** in thinking, at least when these are measured by psychological tests. Possibly because of their processing of two languages, bilinguals may have a slightly higher probability of fruitful divergent thinking. Why? Two languages mean two or more words for a single object or idea, two or more ways of referring to the same content area, concept, idea or information, and more associations due to owning a dual language system. Thus bilinguals are allowed more freedom and richness in their thinking.

Research on bilingualism and creative thinking is truly international, in Canada, Ireland, Mexico, Singapore and the United States, for example. Most studies show that bilinguals are superior to monolinguals in creative or divergent thinking, particularly among those whose two languages are both reasonably well developed. Where there is balanced bilingualism or reasonable proficiency in both languages, fluency, flexibility, originality and elaboration in thinking appear more prevalent.

## Further Reading

Baker, C. (1996) *Foundations of Bilingual Education and Bilingualism*. Clevedon: Multilingual Matters.

Bialystok, E. (ed.) (1991) *Language Processing in Bilingual Children*. Cambridge: Cambridge University Press.

## THEME 3: BILINGUALISM AND METALINGUISTIC AWARENESS

Young bilinguals sometimes have an enhanced ability to focus on the important content and meaning of language, rather than its external structure or sound. For example, a bilingual child is taught a nursery rhyme. Rather than merely learning the words by rote and concentrating on the rhyme, some young bilingual children seem to focus more (compared with monolinguals) on the meaning and story. Does this mean that bilingual children are less bound by the words, focused more on the core meaning?

An illustration comes from Leopold's famous case study (1939–1949) of the German–English development of his daughter Hildegard. Hildegard accepted very early that a word itself and its meaning were loosely connected, there was no absolute or inevitable link between them. Words were just **arbitrary labels** given to an object or idea. The name was separate from the object or idea itself. Leopold found that his stories to Hildegard were not repeated word for word. Plenty of substitutions and adjustments were made to relay the central points of the story.

One of the first to examine whether bilinguals and monolinguals are different in their attachments of word sounds and word meanings was a South African, Ianco-Worrall (1972). In a delightfully simple experiment, she compared matched groups of 30 each monolinguals and English–Afrikaans bilinguals, aged four to nine. The two groups were matched on IQ, age, gender, school grade and socioeconomic class.

In the first experiment, a typical question was: 'I have three words: 'Cap', 'Can', and 'Hat'. Which is more like 'Cap' – 'Can' or 'Hat'? A child who pairs 'Can' and 'Cap' would appear to choose by the sound of the words. That is, 'Cap' and 'Can' have two out of three sounds in common. A child who chooses 'Hat' appears to base the choice on the word's meaning, since 'Cap' and 'Hat' refer to similar objects.

Ianco-Worrall showed that, by seven years of age, there was no difference between bilinguals and monolinguals in their choices. Both groups chose HAT, the answer governed by the meaning of the word. However, with four- to six-year-olds, bilinguals tended to respond to word meaning, monolinguals more to the sound of the word. This led to the conclusion that bilinguals 'reach a stage of semantic development, as measured by our test, some two to three years earlier than their monolingual peers' (p. 1398).

In a further experiment, Ianco-Worrall (1972) asked the following types of question: 'Suppose you were making up names for things, could you call a cow "dog" and a dog "cow"?' Bilinguals mostly felt that names could be interchangeable. Monolinguals, in comparison, more often said that names for objects, such as cow and dog, could not be interchanged. For bilinguals, names and objects are separate. This seems to result from owning two languages, which give the bilingual child and adult awareness of the free, non-fixed relationship between objects and their labels.

## Further Research

One of the strongest lines of recent research in bilingual psychology studies the apparent ability of bilinguals to reflect upon the nature and functions of language. Simply stated, it appears that bilinguals have a greater awareness of language. This concept is commonly called **metalinguistic awareness**.

Metalinguistic awareness is the ability to reflect upon and manipulate spoken and written language. Language is inspected and thought about as a system to understand and produce conversations, rather than simply used. Such language awareness may include **reflection** on the intended meaning, **sensitivity** to what is implied rather than stated, and an analytical attitude towards language.

Research indicates that bilinguals, accustomed to owning and processing two languages, are better at **analyzing** them (Bialystok, 1987, 1988). They seem more able to look inwardly on each language and accumulate knowledge about the language itself, better able to **regulate**, manage and control their language processing.

One important possible outcome of the bilingual's greater metalinguistic awareness at an early age is **earlier reading acquisition**. Because bilinguals daily process two languages, they may acquire reading readiness skills faster. When this occurs, earlier reading may also relate to higher levels of academic achievement in various areas of the curriculum (see pp. 107f on literacy and biliteracy).

Not all bilinguals will have such metalinguistic awareness advantages. A study by Galambos and Hakuta (1988) found that such awareness is most developed when both languages are proficient at reasonably high levels. The effect of bilingualism on the processing of errors in Spanish sentences was found to vary depending on the level of bilingualism. The more advanced a child was in development of both languages, the better the performance on the test items.

### Further Reading

Bialystok, E. (ed.) (1991) *Language Processing in Bilingual Children*. Cambridge: Cambridge University Press.

Cummins, J. (1987) Bilingualism, language proficiency, and metalinguistic development. In P. Homel, M. Palij and D. Aaronson (eds) *Childhood Bilingualism: Aspects of Linguistic, Cognitive and Social Development*. New Jersey: Erlbaum.

Galambos, S.J. and Goldin-Meadows, S. (1990) The effects of learning two languages on levels of metalinguistic awareness. *Cognition* 34 (1), 1–56.

## THEME 4: COMMON UNDERLYING PROFICIENCY AND SEPARATE UNDERLYING PROFICIENCY

### The Separate Underlying Proficiency (SUP) Model

One erroneous visual image to represent two languages within the bilingual mind is that of a balance on weighing scales. As one side increases in weight, the other decreases proportionately, thus a second language increases at the expense of the first. This idea is part of the **Separate Underlying Proficiency** (SUP) model of bilingualism (Cummins, 1984).

Another simple visual illustration of the SUP model is that of two balloons inside the head. This idea is also incorrect, but it is an example of a common assumption about bilinguals. In contrast is a picture of the monolingual with one well-filled language balloon, with plenty of room in the thinking quarters for that one language. A well-filled balloon, full of vocabulary, grammatical rules, word associations, ideas and concepts may superficially appear as the more efficient language environment.

In the same set amount of thinking room, the erroneous view is that the worse-off bilingual has two half-filled balloons inside the head. Compared with the monolingual's larger, single balloon, two half-filled ones imply less room to store vocabulary, grammatical structures, associations and ideas in either language. The Separate Underlying Proficiency model assumes that there isn't enough room for two full language balloons. As the second increases, the first language balloon is assumed to decrease proportionately. Many teachers, politicians and members of the public instinctively assume this dual balloon image represents bilingual cognitive functioning. Furthermore, they assume that there is no interconnection nor

transfer between the balloons, that the languages operate independently. This is one case where 'common sense' is common, but not sense. There is no research evidence to support this model.

Imagine the curious predicament a bilingual would meet when 'talking internally' under this model. If it were necessary to switch languages, there might be difficulty in explaining in the second language what was heard or said in the first. Everything learned in one language would have to be relearned in the other. Clearly that is not the case. A different model is required, one called the **Common Underlying Proficiency** model of bilingualism (Cummins, 1984).

### Common Underlying Proficiency (CUP) Model

It is wrong to assume that the brain has only a limited amount of room for languages. Firstly, evidence suggests that there are enough **cerebral living quarters** for not only two languages, but others as well. The amount of thinking space available seems vast, nearly limitless. Secondly, research indicates there is easy and considerable transfer between the two language balloons. Language switching and cooperative sharing show there is substantial interaction between languages. To illustrate:

- When children are taught subtraction in one language, they do not have to relearn it in the second. Once the concept is understood, it can be applied in either language. Spanish medium lessons do not feed a 'Spanish part' of the mind, nor English-medium lessons an 'English part'. Ideas, concepts, attitudes, knowledge and skills transfer into either language.

- Children who have learned to use a dictionary or computer are able to explain their understanding to others in either language. The child does not have to be retaught in the second language. When language skills are well enough developed to understand ideas and knowledge in the second language, what is learned in the first transfers easily.

A visual image for the idea of a Common Underlying Proficiency (CUP) model is an iceberg. The picture below suggests that two icebergs are visible, above the surface level. In outward conversation, the two languages often are separate. Below the surface, the internal processing and storage of two languages occurs, there are storage, conceptual associations, and representations in words and images, which belong specifically and separately to the two languages. There is also a common area where the two icebergs are fused, the central, unified processing system, called Common Underlying Proficiency, which both languages can access, use and augment.

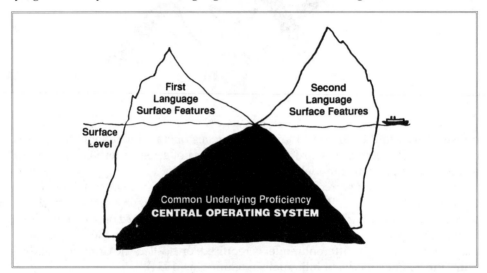

When a child learns to use a library or computer, it is this central, integrated processing system which is fed. The understandings, concepts and processing operate from common ground between the languages. This important iceberg analogy leads to these implications:

- No matter the language in which a person is operating, the thoughts accompanying speech, reading, writing and listening come from the same central 'engine'. Though a person owns two or more languages, there is one integrated source of thought.
- Bilingualism and multilingualism are possible because people have the capacity to store multiple languages. People can function in multiple languages with relative ease.
- Information processing skills and educational attainment may be developed through two languages as well as through one. Cognitive functioning and

school achievement may be fed with equal success through one monolingual channel or two well developed language channels. Both channels feed the same central processor.

- The child's school language must be sufficiently developed to process the cognitive challenges of the classroom.
- Speaking, listening, reading or writing in the first or second language helps develop the whole cognitive system. However, if children must operate in an insufficiently developed second language, such as in a 'submersion' classroom, the system will not function at its best. The quality and quantity of what is learned from complex curriculum materials and produced in written and oral form may be relatively weak and impoverished. Finnish children in Swedish schools, forced to operate in Swedish, when both languages were insufficiently developed to cope with curriculum material, tended to perform poorly in the curriculum in both Finnish and Swedish (Skutnabb-Kangas & Toukomaa, 1976).
- When one or both languages are not fully functional, perhaps because of an unfavorable attitude about learning through the second language, or pressure to replace the home language with the majority one, cognitive and academic performance made be hurt.

### Further Reading

Cummins, J. (2000) *Language, Power and Pedagogy: Bilingual Children in the Crossfire*. Clevedon: Multilingual Matters.

## THEME 5: THRESHOLDS THEORY

Research on the thinking advantages that result from bilingualism includes the important theme that not all bilinguals obtain those advantages. The term 'bilingual' includes a wide spectrum, from those who are highly proficient in both languages across a variety of dimensions, to those whose abilities are underdeveloped in both languages. Which bilinguals are advantaged and which are less so?

The key issues are:

- Under what conditions does bilingualism have positive, neutral or negative effects on thinking?
- What proficiency is necessary in both languages to obtain thinking advantages?

One influential answer is contained in the **Thresholds theory** (Cummins, 2000).

Imagine the Thresholds theory in terms of a house with **three floors**. Up the sides of the house are two language ladders, indicating that a bilingual child will usually move upward, not remain stationary on one floor. On the **bottom floor** are those whose current competence in their languages is insufficiently or inadequately developed, compared with their age group. When there is a low level of competence in both languages, there may be negative cognitive effects. A child who is unable to cope in the classroom in either language may suffer when processing curriculum information.

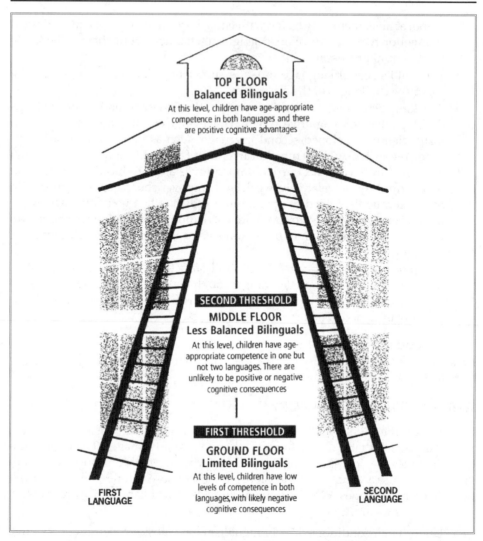

At the middle level, the **second floor**, will be those with age-appropriate competence in one language, but not both. Children can operate in the classroom in one of their languages, but not in both. At this level, a bilingual child may be little different in cognition from a monolingual.

At the **top floor** reside children who can be described as 'balanced' bilinguals. At this level, children have age-appropriate competence in two or more languages. They can cope with curriculum material in either. It is at this level that the **cognitive advantages** of bilinguals over monolinguals often appear.

Studies on thinking and bilingualism suggest two thresholds, each a level of language competence that must be attained to reach the next level. A child must reach the first threshold to avoid negative cognitive consequences. To surpass this threshold, one language at least must be proficient enough to cope with academic classroom work. The second threshold is passed when both languages are developed to the point where a child may cope in the classroom in either language. Once past this boundary, a bilingual child may have thinking advantages over monolinguals.

The Thresholds theory has important implications for bilingual education. In immersion bilingual education in Canada (see pp. 92f), there is often a temporary lag in achievement while the early curriculum is taught through the second language. Once it is sufficiently well developed for classroom tasks, immersion education seems to enable children to reach the second, then the third floor of the house.

The Thresholds image helps pinpoint why minority language children taught through a second language sometimes fail in the system, as with immigrants into the United States who do not develop sufficient competence in English (their second language) to master school work. Their lower level of proficiency in English limits their ability to cope in the curriculum. This points to the importance of strong development of the first language.

## Limitations

One problem with the Thresholds theory lies in defining the precise thresholds in language proficiency. What kind of speaking, listening, reading or writing skills must the child attain to cross each threshold? Any specification of language proficiencies will depend on the context. The relative complexity and variety of classroom academic activity will affect specification of the language threshold. In different classrooms, with different subject areas and varying ages of children, the thresholds will change.

While the Thresholds idea is important, it does not specify what language proficiency is necessary to avoid the negative effects of bilingualism and attain its advantages. In reality, movement occurs continuously along many language dimensions. Development in bilingual proficiency is gradual rather than abrupt. There is no jump from one floor to another, thus the picture shows two ladders up the sides of the house, suggesting continuous development (and occasionally decline) of a language within an individual.

A second limitation is that children who reside temporarily on the lowest floor, as limited bilinguals, may be there because they lack the linguistic abilities to perform well on cognitive tests, not because of lower cognitive abilities. Such children may not understand the test instructions or the content of the questions. Their limited language understanding masks their level of thinking ability.

The Thresholds theory can thus provide a 'Catch 22' situation. The initial argument is that a low level of language competence will produce negative cognitive effects. However, these effects are themselves tested and located by means of the language in which the child has low competence.

## Refinements

The Thresholds theory, and important ideas surrounding it, have been developed and refined in recent years (see Cummins, 2000).

A bilingual's two languages are not separate, as in the image of two language ladders, rather, they are interdependent. Cummins (1978) **developmental interdependence hypothesis** suggested that a child's second language competence is partly dependent on the level already achieved in the first language. The more proficient or developed the first, the easier it is to develop the second. When the first is at a lower stage of evolution, proficiency in the second language is more difficult.

A distinction is useful between the kind of conversational or surface fluency an individual may have in a language compared with the more advanced language competence required to learn in a formal classroom setting.

Simple communication skills, such as the ability to hold a basic conversation with a shopkeeper, may hide a child's lack of proficiency or inexperience in a language that is necessary to meet the cognitive and academic demands of the classroom. The distinction lies between **Basic Interpersonal Communication Skills** (BICS) and **Cognitive/Academic Language Proficiency** (CALP).

The distinction between BICS and CALP helps explain the relative failure within the educational system of many minority language children. In the United States, Transitional Bilingual education programs aim to give students English language skills sufficient for them to converse with peers and teachers in mainstream education and to operate in the curriculum. Having achieved basic language skills, such students may be transferred to mainstream classrooms. The children seem to have sufficient language competence (BICS) to cope. Cummins' (1984) distinction between BICS and CALP explains why such children tend to fail; their Cognitive/Academic Language Proficiency is underdeveloped to cope with the demands of the curriculum.

What Cummins (1984) regards as essential in bilingual education of language minority children is for 'common underlying proficiency' to be well developed (see p. 73). A child's fundamental, central language proficiency must be sufficiently well developed to cope with the curriculum processes. This underlying ability could be developed through either language or both languages simultaneously.

What are the crucial dimensions of language communication particularly needed in school? Different classrooms and curriculum areas, as well as varying teaching styles use different communication skills, and require different skills of their students. Compare the language demands and expectations of science, humanities, arts and crafts, sports and religious education lessons. Each differs in content, style and complexity of language.

Some teachers provide considerable support to communication with students, using plenty of body language, pointing to objects, using eye contact, head nods, hand gestures, intonation and smiles to explain and motivate. Some give plenty of clues and cues to help students understand the material. This is called **context-embedded communication**. Some teachers communicate without relying solely on words. They use objects, demonstrations, concrete examples, illustrations, pictures and graphics to convey meaning.

Other teachers tend to rely on words alone. Children are given work cards or work books and expected to rely solely on them to understand how to proceed. This is called **context-reduced communication**. There are very few cues and clues as to the meaning being transmitted. The oral or written words of the sentence stand alone in conveying its meaning. There may be a subtlety and precision of meaning in the teacher's vocabulary, which eludes the student.

The type of communication that bilingual children receive needs to be adjusted to their level of proficiency. One crucial dimension in matching proficiency with material to be taught is providing the appropriate level of context-embedded or context reduced communication. The lower a child's proficiency, the more context-embedded communication is needed. As language proficiencies grow, more context-reduced communication is possible. On the lower floors of the house, more context-embedded communication is needed. As the child climbs the ladders and reaches higher floors of the house, more context-reduced communication is possible.

A different dimension of classroom communication relates to the thinking demands made of the child in communication. Sometimes the cognitive complexity of mathematics and science, reading or writing, may be highly demanding for the child. The level of performance required is ever challenging. A child must process information quickly. This is called **cognitively-demanding communication**.

At the other end of the spectrum is **cognitively-undemanding communication**. Here language is sufficiently simple to enable understandable classroom exchanges and understanding of the curriculum. If simple instructions are given, the processing of information by the child may be relatively simple and straightforward.

The two dimensions concerning the amount of cognitive demands and the degree of contextual support can now be put together on a graph.

|  | Cognitively Undemanding Communication |  |
| --- | --- | --- |
| | **1st Quadrant** | **2nd Quadrant** |
| Context Embedded Communication | | Context Reduced Communication |
| | **3rd Quadrant** | **4th Quadrant** |
|  | Cognitively Demanding Communication |  |

The diagram is divided in four quadrants. Basic interpersonal communication skills (BICS) are context-embedded, cognitively undemanding use of a language. Cognitively and academically more advanced language (CALP) fits into the fourth quadrant. Second language competency in the first quadrant (surface fluency) develops relatively independently of first language surface fluency. In comparison, the ability to communicate and to process communication in context-reduced, cognitively demanding situations, can develop interdependently. It can be promoted through either language, or both.

## Implications

This discussion suggests that education often requires children to work in context-reduced, cognitively demanding situations. Language proficiency must be sufficient to match those demands. An elementary school child may need two years to acquire context-embedded second language fluency. However, it may take the same child five to seven years or more to acquire context-reduced fluency. Such time spans will vary with age and with the nature of the demands in different subjects.

Children with some conversational ability in their second language may appear falsely ready to be taught through their second language in the classroom. Cummins' (1981) theory suggests that children operating at the context-embedded level in the classroom language may fail to understand the curriculum content and not engage in the higher order cognitive processes of the classroom, such as synthesis, discussion, analysis, evaluation and interpretation.

This two dimensional model also helps explain various research finding:

- In the United States, minority language children may be transferred from Transitional Bilingual programs into English-only instruction when their conversational ability seems sufficient. Such students frequently perform poorly in mainstream schooling. This may be due to lack of the developed ability in English to operate in a more cognitively and academically demanding environment.
- Immersion students in Canada tend briefly to lag behind their monolingual peers in academic achievement. Once they acquire second language proficiency sufficient to operate in a cognitively demanding and context-reduced environment, they normally catch up.
- Bilingual education initiatives in the United States, Canada and elsewhere in the world show that language minority children who are allowed to use their home language for part of their elementary schooling do not experience retardation in academic achievement or in majority language proficiency. Through their minority language, they develop relatively successfully in the cognitively demanding and context-reduced classroom environment. This ability then transfers to the majority language when it is sufficiently well developed. Learning to read is an example. Children who read in their home language, be it Vietnamese, Korean or Spanish, are not just developing home

language skills. They also are developing higher order cognitive and linguistic skills that help with future development of reading in the majority language. As Cummins notes (1984), 'transfer is much more likely to occur from minority to majority language because of the greater exposure to literacy in the majority language and the strong social pressure to learn it' (p. 143).

## Curriculum Relevance

A child's previous learning is a crucial starting point in the classroom. This reservoir of knowledge, understanding and experience can provide a meaningful context on which the teacher can build. There will be occasions when the teacher reads a story, adding gestures, pictures, facial expressions and other acting skills. The story becomes more context-embedded and the child will learn more than from listening to a tape-cassette. Getting the child to talk about something familiar will be cognitively less demanding that talking about something culturally or academically unfamiliar. An extensive discussion, which relates this theory to the curriculum, is given in Cline and Frederickson (1996).

## Further Reading

Cline, T. and Frederickson, N. (eds) (1996) *Curriculum Related Assessment, Cummins and Bilingual Children*. Clevedon: Multilingual Matters.

Cummins, J. (1981) The role of primary language development in promoting educational success for language minority students. In California State Department of Education (ed.) *Schooling and Language Minority Students: A Theoretical Framework*. Los Angeles: California State Department of Education.

Cummins, J. (2000) *Language, Power and Pedagogy: Bilingual Children in the Crossfire*. Clevedon: Multilingual Matters.

Dutcher, N. (1995) *The Use of First and Second Languages in Education: A Review of International Experience*. Washington, DC: World Bank.

# Chapter 7
# The Education of Bilingual Children

## INTRODUCTION

This chapter provides an understanding of the interface of bilingual children with educational systems. It begins with the bridge between the home and school, and the importance of parents in decisions about children's education and partnerships with schools. Parental empowerment, not isolation, is central to success for bilingual children. Since this is especially true in immigrant communities, the community role in education is discussed.

Jim Cummins' framework for the empowerment of bilingual children is given. This influential and comprehensive summing-up of 'effective practice' provides central advice about quality education for bilinguals.

The chapter finishes with the varied nature and aims of bilingual education, plus a brief list of different pedagogical forms or styles.

The themes of this chapter are:

- Home and School Relationships
- Community Language Education
- Empowerment of Bilingual Children
- Nature and Aims of Bilingual Education
- Different Styles of Bilingual Education

## THEME 1: HOME AND SCHOOL RELATIONSHIPS

### Introduction

For many minority language children and their families, the relationship between school and parents is limited. Some parent–teacher relationships are marked by a lack of understanding and cooperation, alienation and even antagonism between home and school cultures. The same reasons help the failure or low achievement of many language minority students in the system.

Language minority families may be socially and educationally **isolated** from the school. There is a knowledge gap between such families and the school that must be bridged. If parents cannot speak the language of the teachers, their sense of helplessness and isolation increases. They become reluctant or unable to discuss their child's progress with the teacher, or to attend parent–teacher meetings and school events.

While there may be family discussion of school problems at home, the issues and worries remain unresolved, owing to the chasm between school and home. Some parents are intimidated by high status schools; they feel that schools do indeed know best and should act unilaterally with their children.

## Parental Empowerment

In a case study of what can be constructively accomplished to **empower parents** and resolve their isolation, Delgado-Gaitan (1990) explains how parents were encouraged to organize a leadership group and teach one another to communicate with schools. The attitudes and actions of the parents were changed as they built awareness, mobilization, motivation and commitment.

Over time, parents became convinced they had the right, responsibility and power to deal with their children's academic and social concerns, and to foster strong school relationships for their children's greater achievement. Individual parents also realized they had something to offer other parents, their children and the school. As parents became more involved, they felt more in control of their lives. They became empowered.

> 'Feelings of incompetence create isolation for parents. Those feelings must be replaced with a recognition of the ability to collaborate with others before active participation can occur.' (Delgado-Gaitan, 1990, p. 158)

However, sometimes parents are highly conservative, even reactionary. Some parents may narrowly insist on skills achievement in the core curriculum, ignoring the advances of progressive education in the 20th century. Conflicts between parents and teachers should be avoided, and cooperation sought, for the children's sake. Teachers' professionalism and expertise must be respected, as should parents' rights and interests in their children's socialization.

## Parents as Partners

'Parents as partners' is possible and desirable in education. Delgado-Gaitan (1990) reports three models of parental involvement in schooling.

Under the **Family Influence Model**, families attempt to provide the kind of home learning environment most suited to cognitive and emotional development. Parents believe children need to acquire a body of education for life skills. Teachers know this and teach it, and therefore parents need to be partners in learning. Parents assume there is a correct way to rear children (including literacy development) and that it can be learned from books or child psychologists. They believe that parents who apply this information will be successful. By extension, the Family Influence Model also includes attempts by the school to influence and change family life to fit the school's values and strategies of learning. The family is seen as a direct recipient of the school's influence, and the school–family collaboration establishes optimum learning environments.

The **School Reform Model** operates where parents try to change schools and make them more responsive. Such parents know how to pressure and interact with schools, making them more responsive to the parents' perceptions of student needs. The assumption is that the school will accommodate parental suggestions and influence. Such parents attempt to become part of the school power structure by serving on advisory committees, school governing bodies or parent–teacher organizations.

The **Cooperative Systems Model** moves one step further. Rather than collaborate or influence, parents in the third model attempt to participate directly in school activities. Parents attend workshops in the school, help teachers in the classroom and become like paraprofessionals. They see the home, school and community as interrelated and functioning as a whole. They play the roles of volunteer, employee, home teacher, adult learner and collaborator.

### Funds of Knowledge

Luis Moll (1992) develops valuable ideas for home–school relationships. He argues for the importance of identifying skills, knowledge, expertise and interests that families own, which can serve everyone in the classroom. Parents, grandparents and other community members can supplement teachers, providing what Moll calls **funds of knowledge**: 'cultural practices and bodies of knowledge and information that households use to survive, to get ahead or to thrive' (Moll, 1992, p. 21). Funds of useful knowledge include agricultural information about flowers, plants and trees, seeds, water distribution and management, animal care and veterinary medicine, ranch economy, car and bicycle mechanics, carpentry, masonry, electrical wiring and appliances, fencing, folk remedies, herbal cures and midwifery, archaeology, biology and mathematics.

Compare Moll's ideas with two other traditions of home–school relations. One traditional view is that language minority homes lack the social, cultural and intellectual stimulation and resources to enable children to progress well at school. Thus, teachers may have **low expectations** for school performance, particularly when students come from working class or materially disadvantaged backgrounds.

Another tradition is that effective teachers visit the home, to discuss particular problems with the parents, **to enlist their help** in schoolwork, and to request they help children with homework. This traditional view assumes that the school knows best and parents are valuable for the encouragement they give children to adopt school norms and values.

Moll's (1992) radically different viewpoint about language minority homes is that parents and communities possess important historically developed, accumulated knowledge, abilities, strategies, ideals, ideas, practices and cultural events. These are regarded within a household and community as important to their functioning and well-being. Whether parents are farmers or construction workers, there are prized skills, knowledge and cultural practices worth sharing in the classroom.

If parents, community leaders, workers and artists are **included in the learning experiences of children**, home notions of culture are represented, valued, and celebrated. Different forms of worthwhile knowledge, experience and expertise are shared in the classroom, raising the self-esteem of children, the language minority group and the community. Hidden talents, oral histories, household skills and latent abilities are discovered and shared. These social, cultural and intellectual resources become important curricular elements.

### Further Reading

Delgado-Gaitan, C. (1990) *Literacy for Empowerment: The Role of Parents in Children's Education*. New York: Falmer.

Moll, L.C. (1992) Bilingual classroom studies and community analysis. *Educational Researcher* 21 (2), 20–24.

Moll, L.C. *et al.* (1992) Funds of knowledge for teaching: Using a qualitative approach to connect homes and classrooms. *Theory into Practice* 31 (2), 132–141.

Multilingual Resources for Children Project (1995) *Building Bridges, Multilingual Resources for Children*. Clevedon; Multilingual Matters.

## THEME 2: COMMUNITY LANGUAGE EDUCATION

In countries such as the United Kingdom, where there has been assimilationist pressure on immigrants, sometimes language, cultural and religious education occurs outside formal schooling. In countries such as Australia, Canada and the United States, there may be no provision in schools for immigrant languages such as Spanish, Italian, Panjabi or Hebrew. When the school does not support home languages, their reproduction in the family may not suffice for language maintenance. Therefore, **local community groups** offer extra schooling for children, sometimes on Friday evenings or during vacations, and particularly in Saturday schools.

Jewish communities are often enthusiastic for Hebrew lessons to maintain a Jewish identity and support religious observance in the local synagogue. Muslims are often keen for Qur'anic Arabic to be transmitted for worship in the mosque, just as *gurdwaras* have been instrumental in the acquisition of Panjabi. The Roman Catholic Church has promoted community language teaching of Polish, Ukrainian and Lithuanian. In the United Kingdom, there has been community language teaching in Italian, Spanish, Portuguese, Greek, Turkish, Urdu, Panjabi and Bengali. In the case of European languages, High Commissions and Embassies in London have often lent support. Sometimes housed in local schools or community centers, sometimes in religious buildings, such extra schooling may attempt not only to preserve a community language but also aim at cultural and religious continuity.

Pressure from multilingual communities has risen, despite indifferent, privately antagonistic and sometimes openly hostile attitudes of education officials, administrators and politicians. This reflects a concern to combat racism and a philosophy of child centered education on the part of a few leaders in education and a growing sense of empowerment, vitality and justice among many language communities. There is often concern over children drifting away from the traditional values of their ethnic, cultural and religious groups, with a growing realization that only the community itself, not individual families or schools, can deliver continuity in values, beliefs and tradition.

### Further Reading

Edwards, V. (1995) Community language learning in the UK: Ten years on. *Child Language Teaching and Therapy* 11 (1), 50–60.
Edwards, V. and Redfern, A. (1992) *The World in a Classroom: Language in Education in Britain and Canada*. Clevedon: Multilingual Matters.

## THEME 3: THE EMPOWERMENT OF BILINGUAL CHILDREN

A framework proposed by Cummins (1986, 1996, 2000) concerns the empowerment or disablement of minority students. It starts with a fundamental point:

> 'Language minority students instructed through the minority language (for example, Spanish) for all or part of the school day perform as well in English academic skills as comparable students instructed totally through English.' (Cummins, 1986, p. 20)

Teaching through a second or minority language usually leads to the satisfactory development of English academic skills.

> 'To the extent that instruction through a minority language is effective in developing academic proficiency in the minority language, transfer of this proficiency to the majority language will occur given adequate exposure and motivation to learn the language.' (Cummins, 1986, p. 20)

This **interdependence hypothesis** posits that one common core of developed ability or 'academic proficiency' underlies the surface characteristics of both languages. Context is crucial. Community and school liaison, power and status relationships must be considered in bilingual education. Cummins suggests that minority language students are 'empowered' or 'disabled' by four major characteristics of schools.

- **The extent to which minority language students' home language and culture are incorporated into the school curriculum**. If the home language and culture are excluded, minimized or quickly reduced in school, children are likely to become academically 'disabled'. Where the school incorporates, encourages and gives status to the minority language, the chances of empowerment increase. Apart from attendant cognitive effects, curricular inclusion of minority language and culture may affect personality, self-esteem, attitude, social and emotional well being.

Bilingual education that emphasizes minority languages typically empowers children by fostering cognitive and academic proficiency, as Cummins' (2000) interdependence hypothesis suggests. Student success also comes from securing and reinforcing cultural identity, thus enhancing self-confidence and self-esteem.

- **The extent to which minority communities are encouraged to participate in their children's education**. Where parents have power and status in the partial determination of children's schooling, the empowerment of minority communities and children results. When communities and parents are relatively powerless, inferiority and lack of school progress results. The growth of paired reading programs shows the power of a parent–teacher partnership. Parents listening to their children reading on a systematic basis tend to be effective agents of increased literacy. Parental involvement has an important effect on children's progress in reading, even when the parents are non-English speaking and non-literate.

Teachers tend toward either collaboration with, or exclusion of parents. Teachers on the collaborative side encourage parents to participate in their children's academic progress through home activities or classroom involvement. Teachers on the exclusionary side maintain tight boundaries between themselves and parents. Collaboration with parents may seem irrelevant, unnecessary, unprofessional, even detrimental to children's progress.

- **The extent to which education promotes the inner desire for children to become active seekers of knowledge, not passive receptacles**. Learning can be active, independent, internally motivated, or passive and dependent on external motivation. The transmission or 'banking' model of teaching views children as buckets into which knowledge is poured, willy-nilly. The teacher controls the nature of the fluid and the speed of pouring. The hidden curriculum of the transmission model parallels and reinforces the powerlessness of language minority students. Someone is in control, someone is controlled.

The alternative model is **reciprocal interaction**, which:

'requires a genuine dialogue between student and teacher in both oral and written modalities, guidance and facilitation rather than control of student learning by the teacher, and the encouragement of student/student talk in a collaborative learning context. This model emphasizes the development of higher level cognitive skills rather than the correction of surface forms. Language use and development are consciously integrated with all curricular content rather than taught as isolated subjects, and tasks are presented to students in ways that generate intrinsic rather than extrinsic motivation.' (Cummins, 1986, p. 28)

If the transmission model is allied to the disablement of minority language students, then the reciprocal interaction model is related to their empowerment. Students are given more control over their own learning, with consequent potential positive effects for self-esteem, cooperation and motivation.

- **The extent to which the assessment of minority language students avoids locating problems in the child and seeks to find the root of concerns in the social and educational system or curriculum**. Traditional psychological and educational tests by their very nature tend to locate problems in the individual, in low IQ or motivation, backwardness in reading, and so forth. At worst, educational psychologists and teachers may test and observe a child, expressly to find the flaw *in that child* to explain poor academic attainment. Such a testing ideology and procedure may overlook the root of the issue in the social, economic or educational system. The subtractive nature of Transitional Bilingual education, the transmission model used in the curriculum, the teacher's exclusionary orientation towards parents and the community, and the relative economic deprivation of minority children could each or jointly be the origin of a minority child's language problem. Assessment and diagnostic activity must be **Advocacy** rather than **Legitimization** oriented. 'Advocacy' means the assessor or diagnostician works for the student by critically inspecting the child's social and educational context, including comments about the power and status relationships between the dominant and dominated groups, at national, community school and classroom level. 'Legitimization' in testing a child points to the cause of a problem within the student, rather than the system, which is absolved of any fault. Solution of the problem requires individual rather than societal action.

Empowerment is an important concept in transforming the situations if many language minorities. For Cummins (2000) schools must actively challenge historical patterns of disempowerment and existing language majority/ language minority power relationships. Power relationships are at the core of schooling for Cummins (2000). Such relationships exist in the classroom, between teachers and students, to either confirm powerlessness or evoke empowerment. **Coercive classroom relationships** maintain subordination and inferiority among students. Cummins (2000) argues that **collaborative power relations** between all classroom participants generate achievement, self-confidence and motivation among students. They also feel ownership of their education, their lives and their future. One aim of empowerment is to provide students with positive, values and honored identities.

'Empowerment means the process of acquiring power, or the process of transition from lack of control to the acquisition of control over one's life and immediate environment' (Delgado-Gaitan & Trueba, 1991, p. 138). Education may further empowerment, but it also needs to be realized in legal, social, cultural and particularly economic and political events. Delgado-Gaitan and Trueba (1991) add necessary sociocultural and political dimensions to the possibilities of empowerment through education.

## Empowerment and Pedagogy

When the focus is on the language minority group, and particularly individual bilinguals, differences in economic opportunity, in power, and pedagogic opportunity are evident. Language minorities generally have less power and less chance of acquiring political clout than majorities. This inability to act is enacted in the classroom (Delpit, 1988). If **classrooms transmit and reinforce power relations and powerlessness**, is this reversible? Is language minority impotence reproduced inside 'weak' forms of bilingual education? Can it be reversed by 'strong' bilingual education? It is important to ask 'how' and 'why' minority children are at a disadvantage in school. Can there be attempted reversal and empowerment?

Expecting bilingual education to right all wrongs is dangerous. Empowerment of the disadvantaged must also come from other agencies, other processes and other interventions. Yet bilingual education can provide a student with potential resources for empowerment, such as literacy, knowledge, understandings, ideals. Delpit (1988) provides some ideas of how:

(1)  The 'Culture of Power' is enacted in the classroom by:
  - teachers having power over students;
  - the curriculum determining a legitimate world view;
  - the definition of 'intelligent' behavior in terms of the majority culture, to the detriment of minority students;
  - school as the gateway to employment (or unemployment), thus to economic status (or lack of status).

(2)  The 'Culture of Power' is embedded in ways of talking, writing, dressing, manners and patterns of interaction. Compare 'upper', 'middle' and 'lower' or 'working' class children.

(3)  Success in school and employment often requires acquisition of the power culture, essentially upper and middle class culture. 'Children from other kinds of families operate within perfectly wonderful and viable cultures but not cultures that carry the codes or rules of power' (Delpit, 1988, p. 283).

(4)  Those outside of the 'Culture of Power' should be taught explicitly the rules and nature of that culture to become empowered. If styles of interaction, discourse patterns, manners and forms of dress, for example, are explained, does this empower the language minority child, or does this move the child toward cultural separation?

## Conclusion

Cummins' (1986, 1996, 2000) theoretical framework incorporates psychological function and educational attainment and includes a focus on the social, economic and political background that is crucial to understanding bilingualism and bilingual education. The theory covers research on cognitive functioning, motivation, educational success or failure in different forms of bilingual education, and includes the context of education in terms of power relationships, culture, community and parental involvement.

## Further Reading

Cummins, J. (1986) Empowering minority students: A framework for intervention. *Harvard Educational Review* 56 (1), 18–36.

Cummins, J. (1996) *Negotiating Identities: Education for Empowerment in a Diverse Society.* Ontario, CA: California Association for Bilingual Education.

Cummins, J. (2000) *Language, Power and Pedagogy: Bilingual Children in the Crossfire.* Clevedon: Multilingual Matters.

Delgado-Gaitan, C. and Trueba, H. (1991) *Crossing Cultural Borders: Education for Immigrant Families in America.* New York: Falmer.

Delpit, L.D. (1988) The silenced dialogue: Power and pedagogy in educating other people's children. *Harvard Educational Review* 58 (3), 280–298.

## THEME 4: THE NATURE AND AIMS OF BILINGUAL EDUCATION

'Bilingual education' generally describes schools where two languages are present. However, this simple label masks a complex phenomenon, which elicits the following questions:

- Are both languages used in the classroom?
- For how long are the languages used in school?
- Are two languages used by all or only some students?
- Are two languages used by the teachers or only by students?
- Is the aim to *teach* or *teach through* a second language?
- Is the aim to support the home language or to move to an alternative majority language?

Eight important aspects of the international structure of bilingual education are presented to help unravel its complexity.

**First**, a distinction between a school where there are **bilingual children** and one that promotes bilingualism is important. In many schools, there are bilingual and multilingual children, yet the educational aim is to develop one language only. A child arrives speaking fluent Spanish and a little English. The school aims to make that child fluent and literate in English only. The child's integration and assimilation into mainstream society is the teachers' primary language aim.

In other types of schools, the intention is to teach the children two languages and through the medium of two languages, to develop full bilingualism and literacy. In heritage language schools, children receive much of their instruction in the home language, with the national majority language used for 20% to 50% of the curriculum.

Alternatively, a majority language child may go to an immersion school or mainstream bilingual school and learn a second language. In Canada, an anglophone child may attend a French Immersion school where much of the curriculum will be taught through French.

The **second** aspect of bilingual education is the distinction between schools that teach a second language and schools teaching through the medium of a second language. Many schools include **foreign** or **second language teaching** within the curriculum. English or French 'as a second language' means that the language will be taught as a classroom subject, just like Social Studies, Mathematics and Science. The aim of second and foreign language instruction can range from providing 'survival skills' or basic competence in the target language, to achieving near fluency.

**Second language medium (or content) teaching** differs from second language teaching. A child learns curriculum content by way of the second language, as in the European schools movement where children in the middle years of secondary education study History, Geography and Social Sciences through a second language. In Canadian immersion schools, elementary school students learn much of the curriculum through their second language, French. If there is a useful demarcation, bilingual education may be said to start when more than one language is used to teach content, rather than being taught only as a subject by itself. However, as we will see later, many programs are called 'bilingual education' when there are merely two languages being taught, or when the students are bilingual but the medium of instruction is monolingual.

**Third**, bilingual education tends to be aligned with public-funded education, although there are exceptions, such as International Schools. In Canada, Wales, Luxembourg, Malaysia, the United States and Australia, bilingual education is part of the state system. These countries fund bilingual education to maintain and develop bilingualism in their official or widely spoken languages. Yet there is also a solid tradition of bilingual education in private schools. Elite children of various countries go to select Swiss Finishing schools. The International Schools movement is another example of fee-paying schools where bilingualism flourishes in many countries. Such private establishments aim to maintain or develop individual bilingualism for the purpose of work, travel, foreign residence or personal enrichment.

A **fourth** dimension in the structure of bilingual education is the important difference between **weak** and **strong** forms. When schools aim almost solely to transfer language minority children from the home culture and language to the majority culture and language, bilingual education is 'weak'. Such schools are basically assimilationist, called 'bilingual' because they contain bilingual children, not because they foster bilingualism.

In contrast, 'strong' bilingual education aims to give children full biliteracy and two mutually enriching languages and cultures. The intent is for children to maintain their mother tongues and become culturally pluralist. Maintenance and enhancement of language, literacy and cultural skills are a major part of the school's ambitions. This aspect of bilingual education is crucial to understanding debates, policies and practices of bilingual education.

**Fifth**, bilingual education spans **all age groups**. Young children in many countries attend bilingual nursery schools to learn a second or local language or to socialize in their mother tongue. Internationally, bilingual education exists chiefly at primary school level. However, in Canada, Wales, Catalonia and elsewhere, there are numerous examples of strong bilingual education at the secondary level as well.

Bilingual education is also found at further and higher educational levels. In Europe, university students increasingly travel around from one country to another to study. Through programs such as Erasmus (funded by the European Commission), students take part of their higher education in other lands. In Wales, arts and humanities subjects may be pursued through the medium of Welsh to undergraduate and postgraduate degree level. Courses in music, sociology, history, education, geography, communication studies, environmental studies, drama and religious studies can all be taken partly or sometimes wholly through the medium of Welsh.

Bilingual education continues beyond statutory schooling. In adult language learning classes in community and four year colleges, universities and other institutes of further and higher education, bilingual education can and does still take place. A person may learn a new language, be taught in two languages, and use curriculum resources in more than one language, such as English on the computer, Internet and computer assisted learning, while all writing on paper is in Spanish.

**Sixth**, 'bilingual education' is an umbrella term, including not only 'weak' and 'strong' forms but also **trilingual and multilingual education**, where three or more languages are used in schools, such as in the European Schools Movement, or the Luxembourg/German/French education in Luxembourg, or Hebrew/English/ French in Canada.

**Seventh, bilingual education** is a more expansive term than **bilingual schooling**. Bilingual schooling is typically formal, state-funded education for children between the ages of 5 and 16. Bilingual education encompasses the informal aspects of learning that can stretch from cradle to grave. Education involves processes such as enculturation, socialization, imparting of knowledge, skills, attitudes and beliefs, and it is practiced in the home as well as the school. When mother reads to the child in one language and father in the other, then bilingual education occurs.

**Eighth**, there are other **'contextual' factors** to include in analyzing the aims of bilingual education. What is the child's background, language minority or majority? If minority, is it a prestigious minority language within the region, or does the language lack status, as does Spanish in much of the United States or Turkish, Greek, Urdu and Bengali in Schools of the United Kingdom? It is difficult to understand bilingual education except through regional status, power and politics. This factor and others are included in a typology of bilingual education in the accompanying table (see next section).

To conclude, bilingual education is a wide, 'umbrella term' encompassing a number of dimensions:

- High and low status forms of education.
- All age groups and school levels.
- Public and private education.
- Where two languages are both used for curricular instruction.
- Where language learning begins to merge with content teaching.
- Trilingual and multilingual education.
- Schools where there is no bilingual policy but bilingual children as well as schools with a strong policy of bilingualism.
- Schools that aim at assimilation into majority language and culture, and those that foster pluralism.

### Further Reading

García, O. (1997) Bilingual education. In F. COULMAS (ed.) *The Handbook of Sociolinguistics*. Oxford: Blackwell.
García, O. and Baker, C. (eds) (1995) *Policy and Practice in Bilingual Education: A Reader Extending the Foundations*. Clevedon: Multilingual Matters.

## THEME 5: DIFFERENT STYLES OF BILINGUAL EDUCATION

The accompanying table proposes ten different styles of bilingual education. Each is considered in detail in specialist publications (see Baker & Prys Jones, 1998; Baker, 1996). Due to the intrinsic limitations of typologies, not all real-life examples will fit easily into the classification. For example, elite 'Finishing Schools' in Switzerland and classrooms in Wales where first language Welsh speakers are taught alongside 'immersion' first language English speakers make classification essentially simplistic, although necessary for discussion and understanding. This typology is extended in García (1997).

| A. Weak Forms of Education for Bilingualism | | | | |
|---|---|---|---|---|
| Type of Program | Typical Type of Child | Language of the Classroom | Societal and Educational Aim | Aim in Language Outcome |
| 1. **Submersion** (Structured Immersion) | Language Minority | Majority Language | Assimilation | Monolingualism |
| 2. **Submersion** (Withdrawal Classes/Sheltered English) | Language Minority | Majority Language with 'pull-out' L2 lessons | Assimilation | Monolingualism |
| 3. **Segregationist** | Language Minority | Minority Language (forced, no choice) | Apartheid | Monolingualism |
| 4. **Transitional** | Language Minority | Moves from minority to majority language | Assimilation | Relative Monolingualism |
| 5. **Mainstream** with Foreign Language Teaching | Language Majority | Majority Language with L2/FL lessons | Limited Enrichment | Limited Bilingualism |
| 6. **Separatist** | Language Minority | Minority Language (out of choice) | Detachment/ Autonomy | Limited Bilingualism |
| B. Strong Forms of Education for Bilingualism and Biliteracy | | | | |
| Type of Program | Typical Type of Child | Language of the Classroom | Societal and Educational Aim | Aim in Language Outcome |
| 7. **Immersion** | Language Majority | Bilingual with initial emphasis on L2 | Pluralism and Enrichment | Bilingualism and Biliteracy |
| 8. **Maintenance/ Heritage Language** | Language Minority | Bilingual with emphasis on L1 | Maintenance, Pluralism and Enrichment | Bilingualism and Biliteracy |
| 9. **Two-Way/ Dual Language** | Mixed Language Minority and Majority | Minority and Majority | Maintenance, Pluralism and Enrichment | Bilingualism and Biliteracy |
| 10. **Mainstream Bilingual** | Language Majority | Two Majority Languages | Maintenance, Pluralism and Enrichment | Bilingualism and Biliteracy |
| Notes: 1. L2 = Second Language; L1 = First Language; FL = Foreign Language. 2. Formulation of this table owes much to discussions with Professor Ofelia García | | | | |

Six of these are 'weak' forms of bilingual education, the other four are 'strong' forms of education for bilingualism and biliteracy. Generally a **weak form** program will contain bilingual children but the aim of instruction is often to produce monolingualism or limited, rather than full, bilingualism. In contrast, a **strong form** of bilingual education aims to produce proficiency and biliteracy in two languages.

**Weak forms** of bilingual education are essentially **assimilationist**, with the aim of transition from minority language and culture to the language and culture of those with most power and status. For example, Spanish speaking children in the United States may undergo submersion or transitional bilingual education which attempts to make them thoroughly competent in English, without attention to equal proficiency in their home language. The aim of such education is integration of children into mainstream society, intending to provide equality of opportunity in schooling and employment. The classroom language tends to be the majority language, although the minority language may be used for a short period of temporary acclimatization for the child. The student is expected to operate in the majority language curriculum as soon as possible.

In **strong forms** of bilingual education, the classroom language often varies. Early on in the school, the emphasis may be on one language, with a movement to a more equal use of both languages as the child proceeds. Strong forms of bilingual education generally attempt to make children **bilingual and biliterate**, while also maintaining the language minority and creating **cultural pluralism and multiculturalism** within the child and the society.

The differences between weak and strong forms of bilingual education reflect divergent monolingual and bilingual views of the world, as well as beliefs about societies. In one view, language minorities must be assimilated into the mainstream. In the other, multiculturalism and language diversity are crucial in an increasingly global village.

## Further Reading

Baker, C. (1996) *Foundations of Bilingual Education and Bilingualism*. Clevedon: Multilingual Matters.

García, O. (1997) Bilingual education. In F. Coulmas (ed.) *The Handbook of Sociolinguistics*. Oxford: Blackwell.

# Chapter 8

# The Bilingual Classroom

## INTRODUCTION

This chapter studies the use of two languages in the bilingual classroom. Some practices are inefficient, duplicating effort. They do not maximize achievement and cognitive growth. Other strategies are more promising. In particular, this chapter concentrates on language separation in the classroom, a major feature of Dual Language schools in the United States, and, paradoxically, the concurrent use of two languages to strengthen both languages and improve learning for bilingual children.

While this discussion is valuable for teachers, it is also crucial for professionals such as psychologists, speech therapists and counselors, who give help and guidance to schools and teachers.

The themes of this chapter are:

- Language Allocation in Bilingual Classrooms
- Recent Approaches to Bilingual Teaching and Learning

## THEME 1: LANGUAGE ALLOCATION IN BILINGUAL CLASSROOMS

### Introduction

There are many varied possibilities using two languages in the curriculum, rather than teaching entirely in the first language or solely in the second, as in Submersion education. For example, in the immersion strategy

in Canada, majority language children are educated through the medium of their second language, but their first is gradually introduced into the curriculum.

This chapter proposes to explore different dimensions of 'how and when' two languages can be separated and integrated in bilingual methodology. For example, when two languages are assigned to distinct curricular areas, the intention is usually to establish **clear boundaries** between their use. In the second part of this topic, an examination is made into the more integrated or **concurrent use** of two languages, as when a teacher repeats explanations in a different language. The concluding pages will investigate the problems and limitations of concurrent class-room use of two languages.

There are **different purposes** in separating and integrating languages in bilingual techniques. Such purposes are the foundation of the methodology and provide evaluative tools for different strategies. First a 'strong' form of bilingual education enables students to develop oral and literate competence in both languages. A system that results in more successful language development outcomes is usually preferred. Such a methodology may hold that language instruction must occur across the curriculum, with simultaneous targeted development through language lessons. However, success throughout the curriculum may be as strong a preference among teachers and parents, if not stronger. If strategic classroom integration of languages gives higher student performance than does language separation in Science, Mathematics, Humanities and the Arts, the chosen methodology may be valued and disseminated.

Again, a bilingual methodology may be necessary or desirable in a mixed language school. Where there is a mixture of, say, Spanish and English first language speakers in two-way education, clear policy and practice in language allocation is required.

Finally, where children in **linguistically mixed classrooms** have different levels of ability in two languages, as well as different levels of ability in tackling the curriculum, a bilingual methodology may be essential. In Wales, a class may contain relative beginners in Welsh, such as recent immigrants, some with partial second language Welsh fluency, and native Welsh speakers. Some native Welsh speakers are also fluent in English, while others have more competence in Welsh. Schools must implement a clear language allocation system in order to achieve a high standard of ability in both languages.

## Language Separation

Historically, distinct separation and clear boundaries between two languages in the classroom and curriculum have often been advocated. Sociolinguists have argued that survival for minority languages demands separate and distinct uses in society. This issue was raised in the discussion of diglossia (see p. 61). Therefore, for a minority language to have purpose and strength, it must have a distinct language allocation in transmitting the curriculum.

Moreover, child development research with bilinguals has raised the argument that 'one person, one language' is one of the most effective patterns in child bilingualism. If the mother speaks one language and the father another, there is a distinct separation. The child learns to speak one language to one parent, a second to the other. Alternatively, one language is spoken at home, another in the neighborhood or school. Successful development of both languages within the very young child results, because there are distinct boundaries and separate reception and production of language. In theory then, effective bilingual schools should attempt to mirror such 'one person one language' separation by establishing boundaries. Details of marking boundaries will be discussed later.

Also, unstable codemixing among both adults and children is a constant problem in many minority language situations. Derogatory terms such as 'Spanglish' (a mixture of Spanish and English) highlight the concern codemixing raises for minority language preservationists. Mixing languages within sentences and across sentences can be a half-way house, indicating movement away from the minority language to the majority. Therefore, educators argue the importance of school language separation, particularly to strengthen and maintain the purity and integrity of the minority language.

With three established arguments for language separation in the classroom and curriculum, we will now consider how this can be done. There are eight overlapping dimensions along which the **separation of languages** can occur in school settings.

### Subject or Topic

Different curricular areas may be taught in separate languages. Social studies, religious education, art, music and physical education may be taught through the minority language, perhaps Spanish in the United States, mathematics, sciences, technology and computer studies, through the majority language. In kindergarten and early elementary schools, allocation may be by topic rather than academic subject. A project on 'Conservation' may proceed through one language while 'Weather' is studied through the other.

In the examples so far, **content sensitive** issues are raised. That is, there is sometimes a call for arts and humanities culture to be relayed through the minority language, while science and technology material is studied in an international majority language. History and geography are often judged as best reflecting the heritage and culture of a language group. Science and technology are judged international, thus dominated by English. However, this can result in the minority language, associated only with tradition and history, losing status and appearing less relevant to technology, science and modern existence.

### Person

Languages may be separated according to individuals, different school staff members identified with different languages. Say there are two teachers in a team teaching situation. One teacher communicates with the children through the majority language, the other through the minority language. A clear boundary is established. Teachers' assistants, parent volunteers, auxiliaries and paraprofessionals may also function as alternative but separate classroom language sources for the children.

### Time

A frequent language allocation strategy is for classes to operate in different languages at different times. In many United States Dual Language Schools, one day is Spanish, the next, English. Other schools alternate by half days, Spanish in the morning, English in the afternoon, the order reversed the next day. Different lesson hours may be allocated to different languages, thus overlapping the idea of separation by subject and topic.

Time separation can be in terms of whole weeks, months or semesters rather than days, half-days and lesson hours. Policy may vary language by grade and age, so that children are taught through the minority language for their first two or three years of elementary school for 90% of the time. Over Grades 3 to 7, an increasing amount of school time is allocated to the majority tongue.

## Place

Different physical locations offer another, less used means of classroom language separation. If there are two Science laboratories in one school, one becomes the Spanish-speaking lab, the other English-speaking. Children are expected to speak the appropriate language in each space. It is assumed that a physical location provides enough cues and clues to prompt the child to adhere to different languages in different places. In reality, the teacher and other students may be more crucial influences than location, though it is a valuable 'extra' in encouraging language separation.

A consideration of 'place' in language allocation must include all areas of the school. During morning and afternoon breaks, lunch period, religious services and announcements, music and drama events, games and sports, the school language balance is affected. Sometimes teachers allocate languages, as in drama. Other times, students have a dominant influence, as on the playground. However, all informal school events create a language atmosphere and balance, and contribute to the overall language experience.

## Medium of Activity

Making a distinction between listening, speaking, reading and writing in the classroom allows for another form of separation. The teacher may give an oral explanation of a concept in one language, with a follow-up discussion in the same tongue. Then the children complete their written work in a second language. This sequence may be deliberately reversed in another lesson. Again, children may read material in one language, then write about it in the other.

The aim of such a teaching strategy is to reinforce and strengthen learning. Material initially assimilated in one language is transferred and reinterpreted in a second. By re-processing the information, greater understanding may be achieved. However, this example shows that separation soon links with a strategy to use both languages in learning. This idea of a rational, structured and sequenced use of two languages in learning is considered later, in the examination of concurrent language use.

One danger of **different medium separation** is reserving one language for oral uses and the other for literacy. Where a minority language does not have a written script, this may be a necessary boundary. When there are few or no written materials, the minority language risks being identified with oracy and the majority language with literacy. Higher status and more functions may be assigned to the majority language and its associated literacy, hence it is important for reversal to occur where the medium separation tactic is used. If oral explanations are given in one language with reading/writing in another, on the next day or in the next lesson, that situation should be reversed.

### Curriculum Material

There are varied ways in which written, audio-visual and information technology curriculum material can be delivered bilingually, ensuring clear separation and non-duplication. Textbooks and course materials may be allocated in one language only, with oral teaching in the other. This is separation 'across' curriculum material. Separation is also possible 'within' such material. In elementary schools, for example, **dual language books** with English on one side of the page and Spanish on the other, sharing the same pictures, may be useful in the early stages of biliteracy (Edwards, 1995, 1996).

In high school the teacher may allocate readings in History or Science in both languages. Duplication of information and ideas is not necessarily present. Rather, there can be a continuation and progression in themes and content. A new topic may be introduced in one language by reading selected material. When a major subtopic appears, students may do that reading in another language. Use of both languages helps understanding of the content while separation is preserved. The child does not have the choice of reading the English text or the Spanish, but must read both to gain full comprehension. Again, it is evident that language separation does not necessarily mean using two languages in isolation, or repeating the same content in different tongues. A concern for separation involves policy and practice to include more or less use of both languages. The outcome is a classroom paradox; languages separated by function but connected in a holistic language and educational development policy.

Such a **curriculum material separation strategy** is used when, and only when, both languages are relatively secure, competent and well developed. The argument is that a child in these conditions has to think more deeply about the material while moving between languages, comparing and contrasting, developing the theme of the material, assimilating and accommodating, transferring and sometimes translating in order to secure a concept and understanding.

### Function

Where there are bilingual children, classroom teaching is often in the majority language, while classroom management occurs in the minority language. In the United States, in 'Transitional bilingual education' schools with many Spanish speakers, the teacher may transmit the formal subject matter in English, while conducting 'informal' episodes in Spanish. In this way, the stipulated curriculum is relayed in the majority language, but when the teacher is organizing students, disciplining them, talking informally with individuals or small groups, supplementing explanations, a switch to the minority language is made.

## Student

The previous seven dimensions suggest that a school or teacher may develop poli-cies about language allocation in the bilingual classroom. In reality, however, students themselves help define the language in use. When a student addresses a teacher, it may not be in the language used to deliver the curriculum; the pupil may switch languages to explain something with clarity and for ease of communication. Students influence when and where languages are used and affect boundary making. Thus separate dual classroom language use can occur by varying circum-stance, student influence, and the formality or informality of particular events. For example, students may feel at ease talking to teachers in their minority language in private or in classroom conversations.

## Concurrent Use of Languages in a Lesson

In many bilingual classrooms, frequent switching between languages is customary. The concurrent use of two languages tends to be regular in practice, but rare as a predetermined teaching and learning strategy. Jacobson (1990) has argued that the integrated use of both languages, rather than separation, can be of value. Such a purposeful and structured use of both languages inside a lesson has certain problems to be considered later. Four concurrent uses will now be considered (Jacobson, 1990).

### Randomly switching languages

Bilingual children switch languages both within and across sentences. In many language minority groups, this is frequent, in the home and street, and in school. It is relatively rare for such switching to be stable across time. It is a half-way house, a sign of movement toward the majority language. For minority languages to survive as distinct and standardized languages, few would argue for such a random prac-tice to be encouraged.

### Translating

In some bilingual classrooms, teachers will repeat in another language, what they have just said. The teacher explains a concept in Spanish, then repeats it in English. Everything is said twice, aimed at students who are dominant in different languages. This practice risks that pupils will stop listening to instruction in the weaker language, since the same content is eventually given in the preferred language. Such duplication results in less efficiency, less language maintenance and less likely achievement in the curriculum.

### Previewing and reviewing

Another strategy is to give a preview in the minority language and follow with a fuller review in the majority language. The introduction in the home language gives an initial understanding. The subsequent consideration in depth uses the majority language. This may be reversed. While extension and reinforcement of ideas occurs in moving from one language to the other, there is sometimes also unnecessary duplication and loss of momentum.

### Purposeful concurrent usage

In a variety of publications, Jacobson (1990) proposed this strategy, where equal amounts of time are allocated to both languages. Teachers consciously initiate movement between them, inside the lesson, where there are discrete events and episodes. There are distinct goals for each language. There must be a conscious and planned movement from one language to the other, in a regular and rational manner. Jacobson proposes thus to strengthen and develop both languages, and to reinforce concepts by considering and processing them in both. A use of two languages contributes to a deeper understanding of the subject matter.

Jacobson (1990) suggests a variety of cues that can trigger a switch from one language to another. Examples include: reinforcement of concepts, reviewing the lesson, capturing (and recapturing) student attention, praising and reprimanding students, and change of topic.

The **amount of time** allocated to each language in the curriculum is important. Some balance between languages, perhaps 50/50, perhaps 67/33, even 90/10 is needed, but the purpose, manner and method in which the two languages are used are more important. All four language abilities need fostering in both languages. To emphasize oracy in one language and literacy in another may result in lopsided bilingualism.

As is discussed below, there are potential problems in the complexity of managing, allocating and organizing such a purposeful use of two languages. The value of the idea is that the teacher plans strategies to employ both languages in the classroom, thinks consciously about their use, reflects and reviews what is happening and attempts to cognitively stimulate students by a 'language provocative' and 'language diversified' lesson.

## Issues and Limitations

In decisions about language separation and allocation in a bilingual classroom, there are other ingredients and contexts that must be taken into account before formulating an effective dual language policy.

The **aims of the school** must be examined carefully, in terms of language preservation and second language competence. School teachers are language planners, even if subconsciously. If the children's minority language is to be preserved, then separation may be a central policy element. When teachers are more enthusiastic about majority (second language) competence, then different practices and outcomes, in terms of language allocation, will be desired. Fewer language boundaries may be maintained, since loosening them helps ensure development of the majority language.

The **nature of the students** must be considered in any policy regarding language boundaries and concurrent use, with policies and practices adjusted to age and grade level. If language development is still at an early evolutionary stage, boundary setting is more important. With older children, whose languages are relatively well developed, the concurrent use of two languages may be more viable and desirable. Older children may have more stability and separation in their language abilities.

Furthermore, this suggests that a **static policy** with regard to boundaries and concurrent use within the school is less justifiable than a progressive policy that examines different applications across years and grade levels. Early separation may be very important. Later on, in high school, a more concurrent use may encourage conceptual clarity, depth of understanding and cognitive development.

For a progressive policy it is necessary to consider **different types of classroom communication**. When the teacher speaks more informally and simply to the class, the weaker language may be appropriate. In practical activities, also, where there is context embedded help, the weaker language may serve well. Where the cognitive level is higher in transmitting the curriculum, as with more complex, abstract ideas, either the stronger language or a bilingual approach may be needed. Different types of classroom episodes, such as managerial, instruction and practical activity, constrain or allow comprehensible second language communication and concurrent usage.

Different dimensions of the school need individual discussions related to separation and integration of languages, for example, in curriculum, whole school policies, classrooms and lessons. At what **level of organization** should separation occur? Our earlier discussion of language separation by curriculum material and medium of delivery showed that language separation is not a distinct issue from rational concurrent use, but merges into a consideration of integrated use.

Another important factor in deciding language separation issues is class **language balance**. If all the children are native speakers of one language, it may be easy to determine a language allocation. With mixed classes there are differing balances of majority and minority languages. Who dominates numerically, linguistically and psychologically? When the balance is tilted against language minority children, a clear separation, with the curriculum balance toward the minority language may be desirable. Whether the student body is language minority in a subtractive or additive situation should also affect language allocation policies.

Where language minority children are the numerical majority, a **slow change**, rather than sharp shift from language separation to concurrent use is advisable. The minority language often risks perception as less powerful or useful, and lower in status, as children grow older. Therefore, the minority language must be protected and keep a constant high profile in the school.

School language policy must take into account '**out of school exposure**' to the first and second languages. Sometimes, equal time is advocated to each language within the school, half the curriculum in one, half in the other. However, if the child is surrounded by the majority language outside the school, on the street, in shops and through the media, then perhaps the separation balance ought to be adjusted toward the minority language in school. 'Out of school' exposure may also make some teachers hesitant about concurrent usage.

Replication and duplication of content threaten bilingual classroom methodology, since some pupils will not concentrate when the same subject matter is repeated in a different language. However, **repetition** is sometimes pragmatically necessary. Where there is a considerable variety of different home and preferred language, a teacher and bilingual assistant may need to repeat instruction in different languages. There are some multilingual classrooms, in New York, Toronto and London, with a diversity of home languages among the children. Replication of teaching in two or three languages may be essential for children in the early grades, so that as many as possible can comprehend. This complicates debates about concurrent use and language boundaries. One solution is small group learning, as seen in progressive British and North American primary schools. This may allow establishment of some language boundaries, with different children addressed by bilingual teachers and aides, in their preferred language.

The use of non-repetitive and non-parallel bilingual materials, built in an incremental and well sequenced and structured manner, is valuable, particularly in high schools. However, the production and **availability of materials** in many minority languages is difficult to achieve, and funding for such materials may be difficult to secure.

In a concurrent and purposeful use of two classroom languages, as advocated by Jacobson (1990), there is the danger of requiring teachers to manage an unnatural, **artificial** and highly complex language situation. Where teachers are expected to manage concurrent use of two languages in a classroom, they are assumed to have a very high level of management skill, monitoring and reflection. In reality, classrooms are busy, very fluid, often unpredictable places. Teachers must react to the moment, to individuals who don't understand, with many unpredictable and spontaneous situations. Students themselves have an important influence on classroom language uses, needing to share understanding (or lack of it) in the most appropriate way. Classroom management of learning and behavior must be fluent, accepted by students, not abrupt and unpredictable. Classroom language allocation must fit naturally, predictably, fluently and flexibly into curriculum management.

### Further Reading

Edwards, V. (ed.) (1995) *Building Bridges: Multilingual Resources for Children*. Clevedon: Multilingual Matters.

Edwards, V. (1996) *The Other Languages: A Guide to Multilingual Classrooms*. Reading: Reading and Language Information Centre.

Jacobson, R. (1990) Allocating two languages as a key feature of a bilingual methodology. In R. Jacobson and C. Faltis (ed.) *Language Distribution Issues in Bilingual Schooling*. Clevedon: Multilingual Matters.

Wong Fillmore, L. and Valadez, C. (1986) Teaching bilingual learners. In M.C. Wittrock (ed.) *Handbook of Research on Teaching* (3rd edn). New York: Macmillan.

## THEME 2: RECENT APPROACHES TO BILINGUAL TEACHING AND LEARNING

Bilingual education involves more than using two languages across the curriculum. Ideally, the four language skills should be developed in both languages following a structured plan, not just in language lessons but all curricular activities.

Cen Williams (1994) argues that the purposeful concurrent classroom use of both languages can advance the bilingual development of skills and contribute to a

**deeper understanding of the subject matter**. He maintains that it is the use of time and the activities allotted to each language in the lesson that are significant, rather than the amount of time spent. The aim should be to develop academic competence (CALP) in both languages, rather than conversational competence (BICS) (see also p. 78). Spanish-speaking staff in some schools in the United States confine Spanish to personal conversations, class announcements, praise and censure. English serves for curriculum activity. Use of both languages in the curriculum may not only produce more balanced bilinguals but also raise achievement. However, there must be a balanced program to develop the four language skills in both languages across the curriculum.

Effective bilingual curriculum activity is more than random and unsystematized use of both languages. In random use, a teacher might introduce a topic in English, making some remarks and explaining some points in Spanish. Handouts and worksheets might be in English. Class activities, discussions, experiments, might be carried out in the students' preferred language. Interaction between teacher and small student groups could be in a random mixture of two languages, with work sheets completed in English. This type of situation would not develop the students' competence in Spanish. To allow progress in skills in both languages, there must be a variety of planned and made-to-measure activities to develop the four language skills.

Beneficial methods include:

- **Purposeful codeswitching by the teacher** (see Theme 1). The teacher might switch languages during a class discussion to explain more fully in a student's stronger language or during group work or one-on-one interaction, where the teacher addresses the students in their preferred language. Alternatively, where students have switched to their stronger language during such discussion or activities, the teacher might intervene by using the weaker language, as a subtle cue to switch back.

- **Translanguaging**. This term describes the hearing or reading of a lesson, a passage in a book or a section of work in one language and development of the work in the other language by discussion, writing, work sheet activities, experiments or group work. 'Translanguaging' is a more specific term than the umbrella term **concurrent use of two languages**. In 'translanguaging', the input (hearing or reading) is in one language and the output (speaking or writing) in the other. A science work sheet in English might be read by the students, followed by a teacher-initiated discussion on the subject in Spanish. The students might then perform written work in Spanish. Translanguaging has two potential advantages. It may promote a **deeper and fuller understanding** of the subject matter. It is possible, in a monolingual context, for students to answer questions or write an essay without fully understanding the subject. Whole sentences or paragraphs can be copied or adapted from a textbook, without really understanding them. This is less easy in a bilingual situation. To read and discuss a topic in one language, and then to write about it in another, means that the subject matter has to be properly 'digested' and reconstructed. 'Translanguaging' may also help students **develop skills in their weaker language**. The main part of the work may be attempted in the stronger language, with less challenging, related tasks manipulated in the weaker language. In a class composed mainly of English learners, a topic might be introduced and discussed in Spanish. An information sheet with articles in both English and Spanish would be read. The English text should be shorter, written in a simple, straightforward fashion. The text might be discussed in groups, with the teacher circulating among them and initiating discussion in both languages. Finally, a series of simple, written questions in English might be assigned. This format would give the students the chance to develop their English reading and writing skills and express the ideas they had absorbed in their stronger language, Spanish.

- **Bilingual worksheets and text handouts**. These are valuable if used with a methodology aimed at developing and using both languages in the curriculum. If bilingual teaching means no more than translation, and if students work solely in their stronger language, then students will tend to use only half of bilingual language notes. However, if they are accustomed to working in both languages, then bilingual lesson notes can be valuable, with students checking meanings in both versions. If the teacher codeswitches for other activities during the lesson, bilingual materials ensure the relevant vocabulary is always at hand. Bilingual lesson notes also facilitate home–school cooperation, as a valuable resource for monolingual parents who wish to support their children in school work.

- **Alternating modules or units of instruction** in the two languages. This approach officially encourages the separation of languages: in practice, both languages are often used concurrently in lessons, that is, if a module is taught in English, while the students' preferred language is Spanish, Spanish may be used by teacher and students in discussion and practical work. If the course is well structured, the main points of the syllabus can be covered, and the basic technical and subject-specific vocabulary learned, in both languages. Thus their concurrent use is facilitated. This structured approach is particularly valuable with subjects that require a cumulative understanding, such as Science and Mathematics. As one High School Principal remarked, 'If the students have understood it in two languages, they've really understood it.'

- The **integration of fluent speakers and learners** at various levels of attainment. If the two groups are segregated, the tendency is for majority language speakers to be taught mainly in that language, and to use the minority language with their peers in class. If they are integrated, and if strategic use is made of both languages in class, then the majority speakers can develop their second language ability without detracting from the language balance of the lesson. Both groups improve their language skills in their weaker language in various ways:

(1) Use of a methodology that is both teacher-centered and student-centered. The teacher decides on the format and language balance of the lesson, teaches from the front, and initiates discussion and whole class work. However, students also work independently and in small groups, using both languages, according to their level of attainment.

(2) The careful selection of the type of oral and written language used with students. If a large proportion of the class is majority language learners, oral presentation should be simple and straightforward, avoiding too much colloquial and idiomatic usage. Language should be simple but also sufficiently stimulating to extend students' abilities and in a register of language appropriate for the task involved. It is important to ensure that the language does not become a barrier between the child and the subject matter.

(3) The opportunity to develop the four language skills through the medium of both languages. Students' spoken language can be subtly corrected, by the teacher repeating a statement in correct form. Students can be encouraged to use their weaker language to take notes and write essays, using terms and expressions from their stronger language if necessary, with help to redraft a final version.

(4) Co-operation between teachers to establish the attainment level of individual students in either language. This helps teachers to organize work in a way that stimulates and develops student's abilities in both languages.

Williams (1994) acknowledges that some academics have maintained that curricular separation of languages gives students the best chance to develop their language abilities. However, his research shows how the concurrent classroom use of two languages can serve positively to deepen understanding of curriculum material and facilitate development of their bilingual competence.

## Further Reading
Williams, C. (1996) Secondary education: Teaching in the bilingual situation. In C. Williams, G. Lewis and C. Baker (eds) *The Language Policy: Taking Stock*. Llangefni (Wales): CAI.

# Chapter 9
# Developing Biliterate Children

## INTRODUCTION

This chapter examines literacy and biliteracy in bilingual children. Many scholars have argued that a language without literacy has little chance of long term survival, either at the societal or individual level. Bilingual children must be biliterate for their languages to have value, uses and prospects. Also, bilingual children are likely to gain in school performance and have cognitive and cultural advantages if they are biliterate. Biliteracy aids chances of employment, achievement and enculturation.

Yet bilingual children from language minorities are often restricted to majority language literacy. Even worse, the majority language literacy they are fed sometimes carries assimilative messages, conditioning them to accept underprivileged status and servitude. This chapter opens with an exploration of the uses of literacy, to show that in bilingual children literacy is much more than reading and writing.

The themes of this chapter are:

- Literacy among Bilingual Students
- Development of Biliteracy

## THEME 1: LITERACY AMONG BILINGUAL STUDENTS

### Introduction

Throughout the world, reading and writing are regarded as central to education. In both developed and developing countries, literacy is associated with progress, social mobility and economic advancement. Anderson (1966) makes the classic, if much disputed, claim that any society requires a 40% literacy rate for economic 'take off'. This belief is embedded in many literacy programs.

Whether bilingual students are found in highly literate societies, such as the United States and much of Europe, or less literate ones, the ability to read and write is essential for **personal survival, security and status**. Literacy affects daily lives in innumerable ways. Where language minorities are relatively powerless and underprivileged, literacy is a major key to self-advancement and empowerment. Given these facts, it is important to consider the needs or uses for literacy in students and adults in bilingual and multicultural societies.

In this context, it must be noted that literacy education for language minority students is often in a majority language, that is, English literacy in the United Kingdom and United States, English or French in parts of Africa, as an 'official' or international language. However, where language minorities have access to bilingual education, literacy may be introduced in the home language. This issue is considered in the latter part of this section.

Literacy can be crucial for the survival, revival, or enhancement of a minority language. At both individual and group levels, **literacy gives a language increased functions and usage**. Survival is more likely when the language is in bureaucracy and books, newspapers and magazines, advertisements and signposts. Such uses help avoid the colonial situation, where the dominant language serves all literacy purposes and the vernacular serves only oral communication. Where oral communication is in the minority language and literacy is in the majority language, that minority language has less chance of enduring. Its survival depends on playing a role in a great number of domains, as well as on its public profile and status. If minority language speakers are not literate in that tongue, the number of domains open to it is limited, and it is confined to a low profile, domestic role.

Public perceptions of the illiterate illustrate the importance and usefulness of literacy for language minorities: inability to read and write is stigmatized as shameful, embarrassing, a symptom of low or marginal status, and subject to remedial work in school or adult classes. Reducing illiteracy is a key priority in UNESCO's aims, independent of country, continent, culture or caste.

Reading literature in the minority language may serve both education and recreation, instruction and enjoyment. Whether literature is regarded as aiding moral teaching, as art, or as vicarious experience, literacy is both an emancipator and educator.

Literacy in the minority language also enables **access to the attendant culture**. It recreates the past in the present, and both reinforces and extends the oral transmission of its culture. Minority language oracy without literacy can disempower students. Literacy provides a greater chance of survival for the language at both individual and group level and also encourages rootedness, self-esteem, the vision and world view of the heritage culture, self-identity and intellectual empathy. Literacy enables access to stories that shape and develop thinking and help children develop concepts. Stories are a strong means of interpreting the world, hence they affect the structure of human cognition. Biliteracy gives access to different and varied social and cultural worlds. Does this in turn lead to more diversified **cognitive abilities**, an increased ability to process and manipulate ideas and symbols? Swain and Lapkin (1991) point to first language literacy and then biliteracy as a strong source of cognitive and curricular advantage for bilinguals.

### The Uses of Literacy in Bilingual and Multicultural Societies

That literacy and, preferably, biliteracy are desirable for language minorities and bilingual societies may seem self-evident. However, it is not simple to define precisely what is meant by literacy, and what kind of literacy might be a desirable goal for a language minority community.

There are many possible **uses for literacy** in modern society. It can be essential for day-to-day survival, to read road signs and food labels. It is essential for education, for citizenship, for personal empowerment, to participate in local or regional government, to read newspapers or political pamphlets. It is needed for personal contacts, to write letters, for pleasure and creativity, to read magazines and novels. It is required for many kinds of higher status and better paid employment. Lastly, literacy is needed to empower the mind. Wells and Chang-Wells (1992) maintain that literate thinking is 'the building up, metaphorically speaking, of a set of mental muscles that enable one effectively to tackle intellectual tasks that would otherwise be beyond one's powers' (p. 122). Literacy is a mode of thinking, a means of reasoning, reflecting and interacting with oneself. Thus it is linked to individual empowerment and possession of a public voice.

Whether children should become literate first in the majority language or in the minority language will be discussed later, as will the question of whether majority language monoliteracy or biliteracy should be attempted. Before engaging such discussions, it is important to explore the kind of literacy that language minority individuals require.

## Approaches to Literacy

### The skills approach

In 1962, UNESCO provided a definition of a literate person as someone who 'has acquired the essential knowledge and skills which enable him to engage in all those activities in which literacy is required for effective functioning in his group and whose attainments in reading, writing and arithmetic make it possible for him to continue to use those skills towards his own and the community's developments' (cited in Oxenham, 1980, p. 87).

The concept of **functional literacy**, as in the UNESCO definition, is primarily a technical skill, neutral in its aims and universal across languages. Reading and writing skills can be categorized into vocabulary, grammar and composition. Teaching sounds and letters, phonics, and standard language is the important focus. Errors in reading and writing incur keen attention, along with a concern about achieving high scores in tests of reading and writing. Such tests tend to assess fragmented and decontextualized language skills, eliciting superficial comprehension, rather than deeper language thinking and understanding.

Underlying the skills approach, there is a belief that children need only functional or 'useful' literacy. 'Effective functioning' implies that the individual will contribute in a collaborative, constructive and non-critical manner to the smooth running of the local community. The functionally literate individual recognizes the status quo, understands and accepts a given place in society, and is a 'good citizen'.

While there are various types of literacy, it is important to remember the amount of illiteracy and low levels of literacy in many countries. Functional literacy does not mean reading print in 'quality' newspapers and books, it is at a lower lever. It is the ability to read labels on cans and road signs, to find a number in a telephone directory. Functional literacy is unlikely to suffice in advanced, technological societies, where people constantly face complex tasks, such as bureaucratic forms and written instructions which demand ever more advanced literacy skills.

### The Whole Language approach

The **Whole Language approach** to literacy is diametrically opposed to reading and writing as a set of separate decoding skills. The Whole Language approach emphasizes learning to read and write naturally, for meaningful communication and inherent pleasure. Writing means reflecting on ideas and sharing meaning with others, it can be done in partnership with others, involving drafting and redrafting.

In this approach, reading and writing involve **real, natural events**, not artificial stories or sequences, rules of grammar and spelling, or stories that are irrelevant to students' experiences. Reading and writing must be interesting and relevant, they must allow choice to the learner, giving students power and understanding of their world. In reality, a Whole Language approach and attention to literacy skills are combined eclectically by many practicing teachers.

The Whole Language approach overlaps with functional literacy in many ways. The child can be viewed as a relatively non-critical, monocultural, assimilated being. Literacy can be about socialization into customary, normative values and beliefs. In such an approach to literacy, the meaning of text can be decoded, because it has a definite, autonomous meaning. Therefore, reading involves detecting the author's meaning, writing means conveying meaning to readers. The Whole Language approach can result in an uncritical, accepting attitude by the child. For language minority students in stigmatized, racist and prejudiced contexts, this may not seem empowering.

### The Construction of Meaning approach

The **Construction of Meaning approach**, partly connected to the Whole Language approach, is a recent consideration of literacy which emphasizes that readers bring their own meanings to text. Reading and writing are essentially a construction and reconstruction of meaning. The meaning individuals give to a text depends on their culture, personal experiences and histories, personal understandings of textual themes and tone, and the particular social context where reading occurs. This has implications for language minorities, to be revealed later.

**Readers bring meaning** with them; they make sense of a text from previously acquired knowledge. Without relevant background, readers may fail to construct any meaning at all. We need to know what kind of text is in question, a folk story or 'real event', or maybe an advertisement seeking to persuade. A reader's current knowledge, family background, social and economic lifestyle and political orientation all affect how meaning is constructed from the text.

Different individuals make different meanings. When there is a mismatch between the reader's knowledge and the information assumed by the writer, the construction of meaning is difficult. Many illiterate adults face this 'vicious circle'. They are denied access to certain kinds of knowledge and understanding of the world, because they cannot read. Since they do not understand the subtext taken for granted by writers of adult material, becoming literate as an adult is difficult. Language minority groups, in particular, can be caught in this situation. Trying to make sense out of texts from a different culture, with different cultural assumptions, makes predicting the story line and understanding the text more difficult.

To help **children construct meaning** from text, teachers must be aware that classroom literacy exists in a social context, guided by culturally bound ways of thinking. In classrooms, there are adult and educational criteria of relevant and appropriate ways to respond: reading and writing. Students learn about the rules of behavior for the different literacy events the teacher creates. A typical teacher–student interaction is an initiation by the teacher, then student response, followed by evaluation by the teacher. This sequence signals expectations and rules, not only in classroom behavior, but in literacy also. There are rights and wrongs, authoritative knowledge and culturally inappropriate responses. The power relationships of the classroom shape language and literacy use. The social rules of students and teachers are taught and embedded in classroom literacy events. To promote literacy and fully meet students' needs, teachers must expand, rather than limit, students' roles. Children ought to be empowered through celebration of the different uses of literacy, including critical literacy.

The further reading and writing develop, the more text becomes socially and culturally embedded. External social forces shape the interior reading process. Dyson (1989) and Graves (1983) have shown how young writers develop and change in the midst of social influences from peers, teachers and extracurricular sources, such as the local community, political movements and ideological forces.

Writing is not just a technical process of putting correctly spelled words in correct grammatical structures down on paper, it is shared meaning. People who write have an **interpersonal purpose**. They want to be read by an audience, to inform, persuade, influence or purely delight others. Writing anticipates an audience reaction. We write with some kind of understanding of the background, knowledge and culture of our readers. We use language in different ways to meet particular purposes. Newspaper editorials try to persuade. Cookbooks inform and explain. Poets delve for deeper, fresh meanings. Textual effectiveness depends on the writer's familiarity with readers' expected conventions. Literacy is a social event, not a private, personal one. We often discuss our reading and writing with others, making the social dimension of literacy even more prominent.

Thus it is argued that literacy is not limited to information gathering and giving, it is also develops culture appropriate thought. Wells and Chang-Wells (1992) conceive of literacy as 'a mode of thinking that deliberately makes use of language, whether spoken or written, as an instrument for its own development' (p. 123).

### The Sociocultural Literacy approach

The **Sociocultural Literacy approach** is related to and overlaps the Construction of Meaning approach. It spotlights the enculturation aspect of literacy. For example, a language minority literacy program may aim to ensure each child is fully socialized and enlightened in the heritage culture.

Sociocultural literacy is the ability to construct appropriate cultural meaning while reading. In theory, one can be **functionally** literate but **culturally** illiterate, reading without meaning. In reading and writing, we bring not only previous experience, but also values and beliefs, enabling us to create meaning from what we read and insert understanding into what we write. Reading and writing are acts of construction by the individual. Cultural heritage is discovered and internalized through reading. While reading and writing have certain overt, testable skills, they also include an information processing activity, which ensures enculturation. Beyond the observable skills of reading and writing is cultural literacy. For some people, such cultural literacy may lead to assimilation and integration, through accenting the values embedded in the majority language classics. Assimilationists may argue for a **common literacy**, transmitting the majority language culture to ensure assimilation of minority groups within the wider society.

In contrast, a cultural pluralist viewpoint argues that national unity is not sacrificed by cultural, or multicultural literacy in minority languages. **Multicultural literacy** gives a wider view of the world, a more extensive outlook on human history and culture, and a less narrow perspective on science and society.

What is the importance of literacy in the mother tongue? While the educational feasibility of such literacy is discussed later, for the moment, the educational argument is that literacy is most easily and effectively learned in the home language. The cultural argument is that mother tongue literacy gives access to the wealth of local and ethnic heritage contained in the literature. However, mother tongue literacy is not without practical problems and objections. Some native languages do not yet have a formal grammar or writing system, lack educational materials for teaching purposes, and have a shortage of teachers and teacher training. Political objections are raised; native language literacy is seen as an impediment to national unity and immigrant assimilation, or as expensive to maintain for a variety of indigenous and immigrant languages in a region. Preservationists may promote mother tongue literacy in order to resist change.

Where there is a broad variety of language cultures within a region, local literacies may be supported. These are literacy practices identified with local and regional cultures, distinct from national culture. Such local literacies may be forgotten by international and national campaigns, or there may be tensions between local and national/international literacy practice. **Local literacies** (for examples, see Street, 1994, 1995) avoid the impoverishment of uniformity created by the dominance of English. They make reading and writing relevant to people's lives, their local culture and community relationships.

An important element in the social and cultural context of literacy is the relationship between an ethnic community and literacy acquisition. What counts as reading differs between cultures, subcultures and ethnic groups. As Gregory (1993, 1994) demonstrates in a study of British Bangladeshi and Chinese families, the purposes of reading, resources provided by the home, and parental help with reading vary with the school. Indeed, the varying expectations in home and school may produce a **mismatch** or conflict, causing the child uncertainty, low achievement or even failure. Gregory contrasts the differing viewpoints and practices of the school and language minority parents. The school teaches reading for recreation and enjoyment: the family wants literacy for utilitarian purposes, to avoid unemployment and poverty, for trade and business transactions. The school literacy policy aims for a child-centered, individualized approach, with teacher as facilitator, partner and guide, with a wide choice of colorful, attractive books. The ethnic group, in contrast, provides Saturday school literacy classes, at the mosque or temple, with instruction in large groups, and an authority figure teacher. The valued outcome is, for example, learning the will of Allah. A treasured Bible, the Qur'an or other highly valued, even holy, book is the focus of reading.

Gregory (1993, 1994) further compares styles of literacy teaching. In school, the child is socialized gently into the 'literary club' via book play in an uncritical, relaxed atmosphere. In ethnic Saturday schools, by contrast, children learn by rote, repeating letters, syllables and phrases until perfect. There are continual practice, testing and correction of mistakes in a fairly strict and disciplined regime, with an expectation of success.

The mismatch of school and ethnic literacy expectations and practices may be difficult for the student, caught between two literacy worlds, two versions of appropriate literacy behavior, and home and school literacy concepts. Despondence, learning paralysis, low motivation and disaffection with school may result. However, children do successfully negotiate this path between two literacy worlds. Some teachers are particularly successful in engineering such a happy rapprochement, especially when there is collaborative dialogue with parents.

### The Critical Literacy approach

Literacy can support the status quo, ensuring that people with power in society influence what the masses read and think. Propaganda, political pamphlets, newspapers and books, formal and informal education can all serve in attempts to **control popular thought**.

Thus, those in power maintain control over potential social subversives, or democratically challenge their power base. Literacy can instill certain preferred attitudes, beliefs and thoughts. Similarly, some religious traditions deliberately use literacy to ensure that their members are influenced, at the least, by texts, at the worst, by brainwashing. Watchfulness by religious leaders and parents over what children read attempts to use literacy to control and contain the mind.

Graff (1979) has shown that in 19th century Canada, literacy was used for normative, controlling purposes. Illiterates were thought dangerous to social stability, since they were alien to the dominant culture. Thus, an effort to increase literacy was a political move to maintain and further the position of the ruling elite. Since the elite realized that literacy could also lead to radical beliefs, teaching literacy was carefully controlled.

Graff (1979) also attempted to show that literacy did not necessarily improve a person's chances of acquiring employment, wealth or power. Certain ethnic groups were disadvantaged, whatever their literacy rates, while others obtained employment despite their relatively high illiteracy rate. For example, Irish Catholics in Canada did badly, whether literate or not. English Protestants fared better, in comparison. Whether literacy was an advantage depended on ethnicity. Being unemployed or holding poorly paid jobs was more a function of ethnic background than illiteracy.

People with power and dominance in society also maintain their position by their view of '**correct language**'. Ethnic minorities with little political and economic power are often taught that their very patterns of speech and writing are inferior and connected with their economic deprivation. Such groups are expected to adopt standard majority language, to speak 'proper' English, for example.

Some forms of literacy education in schools and adult classes pose literacy as a technical skill. They emphasize reading skills rather than comprehension, being able to say the words and copy them from a blackboard. Students are not allowed to ask questions, they are expected to read aloud large chunks of text and be corrected for pronunciation, stress and fluency. This restricted form of literacy is still present in many schools throughout the world.

The functional view of literacy, as evidenced in the UNESCO definition given earlier, can serve to maintain the status quo, a stable political structure, to avoid subversion or activism among the masses. National literacy may promote integration of the masses and different ethnic groups. It may promote unification and standardization of both language and culture. Literacy education always has ideological roots (Street, 1993). At its worst, this restricted, functional literacy can maintain oppression and the distance between the elite and the subservient. There is no focus on the empowering and 'critical consciousness' possibilities of literacy.

In colonization and missionary movements, a different kind of **cultural standardization** was sometimes attempted. When literacy was brought by missionaries to non-Christian regions in the 19th century, the aim was to spread the Christian gospel, control thinking and affect the moral behavior of peoples assumed to be 'primitive' and 'heathen'. In the 20th century, literacy projects have often been promoted for economic development. A literate workforce was considered essential for economic growth. However, such programs also served, consciously or not, to shore up the established order in a social system founded on injustice and inequality. Such literacy programs have sometimes conditioned the masses and consolidated existing divisions of labor.

There is an alternative to using literacy as a means of showing how to cooperate within a system from the perspective of powerful people. Literacy may be a tool of oppression, it can also be **liberating** (Hornberger, 1994). It can bar opportunity or open doors to **empowerment**. One way to empower people is through **critical**

**literacy**. Freire (1970, 1973, 1985) argued for a literacy in oppressed societies that raises social and political consciousness of their subservient role and lowly social status. The argument is that literacy must go beyond the skills of reading and writing, it must raise awareness of sociocultural context and the political environment. This effect may occur through mother tongue literacy, multilingual literacy, local–national–international 'multiple' literacies of value in differing contexts, and local literacies.

Literacy for empowerment can mean stimulating minority language activism, the demand for language rights, self-determination and an equitable share of power. Freire's literacy education in Brazil's peasant communities and with other oppressed groups around the world first teaches people consciousness of their subordinate role and inferior position in their community and society. Subsequently, they become empowered to change their own lives, situations and communities.

In the Pajaro Valley Family Literacy Project in a rural area surrounding Watsonville, California, Spanish speaking parents met once a month to discuss chosen books, write and discuss poems written by their children and themselves (Alma Flor Ada, 1988). Books were related to prior experiences, critically analyzed and applied to everyday events. Parents read to their children – including television recordings of parents reading their children's stories. This gave children (and their parents) much pride in themselves, their growing literacy, their homes and heritage. Confidence in themselves and in the power of their own self-expression increased. The community's language, culture, and personal experiences were validated, celebrated and empowered.

Through literacy, **political power and activity** can be understood, leading to collective work to change society, operating appropriately, able to challenge and complain, to assert natural rights and demand equality of access, opportunity and treatment. Through critical reflection on texts, information and propaganda, people increase their consciousness and influence over their own lives and social institutions, and strive for greater social equality.

Freire argued that as people acquire literacy, they must have their consciousness raised, enabling them to analyze the historical and social conditions, which gave rise to their particular status, position and low power-base in society. Thus literacy teaching can become a direct political challenge to the hegemony of ruling capitalist states. Many adult literacy programs have been influenced by this **critical literacy** ideology.

In radical adult literacy programs, students create their own learning material, rather than passively reading texts that propagate a centralist, dominant perspective. Through creating, binding and distributing their own books, the meaning of literacy is radically changed. Rather than a passive exercise, reading is seen as a production of ideas to be spread into the community. Students who had previously felt like failures in learning to read and write come to realize instead that the system failed them. Their illiteracy was not a personal problem but a condition imposed or allowed by those in power.

Such a radical viewpoint about literacy must be seen in contrast with the celebrated modern idea of the Whole Language approach in literacy development. Delpit (1988) argues that books within that approach can be an uncritical celebration of stories and transmission of accepted information. As such, the movement may neglect issues of **power and social justice**, and maintain the status quo.

## Conclusion

This topic has revealed that literacy in bilingual and multicultural societies is neither a simple nor a straightforward concept. While reading and writing initially seem easily understandable events, the different uses and definitions of literacy immediately spotlight complexity and controversy. The different approaches to literacy discussed here highlight variations and contrasts in literacy education. Each approach shows different expectations about bilingual children, which pervade literacy politics, provision and practices. Literacy in majority languages is contrasted with an accent on local, regional literacies, perhaps multiple literacies, with different uses in different contexts.

One expectation is that children should have 'good citizenship' skills to function in a stable society. A contrasting expectation is that children should become empowered, even politically activated, by literacy. Language minority children, for example, must read to understand propaganda, and write to defend their community, or to protest injustice, discrimination and racism. Yet another view holds that reading and writing are for sheer pleasure, celebration, creation, and self-cultivation. Biliteracy is particularly valuable for all these approaches.

The importance of the different approaches lies in their varying proposals for the role, status and self-enhancement of bilinguals. Does literacy produce cogs in the smooth running of a well-oiled machine or activists who assert their rights to equality or power, purse and opportunity? The fundamental issue of literacy and biliteracy is political. When clarity is achieved in defining the intended uses of literacy for bilinguals, the choice of approaches, methods and strategies becomes more rational.

## Further Reading

Ada, A.F. (1995) Fostering the home–school connection. In J. Frederickson (ed.) *Reclaiming Our Voices: Bilingual Education, Critical Pedagogy and Praxis*. Ontario, CA: California Association for Bilingual Education.

Edelsky, C. (1996) *With Literacy and Justice for All: Rethinking the Social in Language and Education* (2nd edn). London: Falmer.

McKay, S.L. (1996) Literacy and literacies. In S.L. McKay and N.H. Hornberger (eds) *Sociolinguistics and Language Teaching*. Cambridge: Cambridge University Press.

Perez, B., and Torres-Guzmán, M.E. (1996) *Learning in Two Worlds: An Integrated Spanish/English Biliteracy Approach* (2ond edn). New York: Longman.

Street, B.V. (1995) *Social Literacies: Critical Approaches to Literacy in Development, Ethnography and Education*. London: Longman.

Wells, G. and Chang-Wells, G.L. (1992) *Constructing Knowledge Together: Classrooms as Centers of Inquiry and Literacy*. Portsmouth, NH: Heinemann.

## THEME 2: THE DEVELOPMENT OF BILITERACY

Since literacy emancipates, enculturates, educates and is inherently enjoyable, there seems to be a strong argument for biliteracy. Pragmatically, most minority language students need to function in both the minority and majority language societies. Biliteracy is required, not literacy only in the minority language.

Parents and teachers in differing situations ask the same question. Is it better to be thoroughly literate in one language, rather than to attempt literacy (or semi-literacy) in two languages? Does literacy in one language interfere with becoming literate in a second? Typically the questions are negatively phrased. Positive questions should also be posed. Does literacy in one language aid literacy in a second? Do reading and writing skills learned in one language transfer to a second?

From reviews of research (Hornberger, 1989; Williams & Snipper, 1990) and research (Lanauze & Snow, 1989; Torres, 1991; Hornberger, 1990; Calero-Breckheimer & Goetz, 1993), the evidence tends toward the positive rather than negative questions. Academic and linguistic skills in a minority language **transfer relatively easily** to the second. A child who learns to read in Spanish does not have to start from the beginning when learning to read in English. 'Language skills acquired in a first language can, at least if developed beyond a certain point in L1, be recruited at relatively early stages of L2 acquisition for relatively skilled performance in L2, thus shortcutting the normal developmental progression in L2' (Lanauze & Snow, 1989, p. 337).

When biliteracy is encouraged, skills and strategies learned in one language appear to transfer to the other, especially if both use a similar writing system. A bilingual child learning first in French and then English has the advantage that both are written in the Roman alphabet, while many of the consonants and vowels have similar values. A child learning in French and then Russian has the added challenge that Russian is written in the Cyrillic alphabet. A child moving from a Western to an Eastern language, such as Hebrew or Arabic, will have to adjust to different orthographical conventions and a different direction of writing. However, even when the vocabulary, grammar and orthography differ, general skills in decoding and reading strategies transfer from first language literacy to second. Some such **easily transferable concepts and strategies** are scanning, skimming, contextual guessing at words, skipping of unknown words, tolerance for ambiguity, reading for meaning, drawing inferences, monitoring, recognizing textual structure, using previous learning and background knowledge about the text (Calero-Breckheimer & Goetz, 1993; Jiménez, Garcia & Pearson, 1995). This is the idea behind the Common Underlying Proficiency or Dual Iceberg concept of Cummins' interdependence principle (see p. 72).

Reading ability in a second language is partly connected with proficiency in that language, but the view that proficiency in the second language is the main factor is not generally supported by research (Calero-Breckheimer & Goetz, 1993). While sounds of letters and decoding of words have a separation in learning to read in each language, the higher cognitive abilities and strategies required in making meaning from text are common to both languages. Overall reading competence in two languages does not operate separately.

This 'transfer' rather than 'separation' viewpoint has implications for the teaching of reading among language minority students. A 'separation' view is that reading in the second language, such as English for language minority students in the United States, depends on the level of proficiency in the second language and not on first language reading ability. Therefore, students should be swiftly moved to education through the second language; maximal exposure is needed to achieve literacy in the majority language. Time spent reading in the minority language is time lost for majority language literacy. In contrast, a 'transfer' view argues for **initial command of literacy in the first language**, so that cognitive skills and reading strategies develop fully. Once well learned, these skills transfer readily to the second language.

The context in which language and literacy acquisition occurs is important. In Canadian Immersion programs, the context is additive. The child's home language of English is not being replaced but supplemented by French. Evaluations of Immersion programs show that literacy in French is acquired at no cost to English literacy. In contrast, in a subtractive environment, where the status and maintenance of the minority language is threatened, the transfer of literacy skills may be impeded. In such subtractive situations, literacy may be more efficiently acquired through the higher level of language skills in the home, heritage language, rather than through the weaker second language. When literacy is first attempted through the second, majority language, the child's oracy skills in English may be insufficiently developed for the task.

For teachers, this leaves the question of when to encourage biliteracy, given that there is some degree of literacy in one language. One model is the **simultaneous acquisition** of biliteracy with bilingualism. Some bilingual children learn to read and write simultaneously in both languages. Others learn to read and write in their second language before their first (majority) language, as in Canadian Immersion education. Both these approaches tend to produce successful biliteracy.

The third approach is acquisition of **literacy in the first (minority) language**, followed by literacy skills in the majority language. This can be a successful route to biliteracy if the minority language continues to play a strong role in the curriculum after literacy in the majority language is achieved. However, in some circumstances, first language literacy may simply be regarded as a means to majority language literacy. This tends to happen in Transitional Bilingual education, where the development of literacy skills in the minority language is temporary, gradually phased out in favor of monolingual education in the majority language. However, in Maintenance, Two-Way/Dual Language and Heritage Language education, this third approach tends to be additive, promoting literacy in both languages.

Simple answers about when to promote second language literacy are complicated by other factors, such as the educational and societal context, and the age and ability of the child. Contrast a six-year-old, just beginning to acquire pre-literacy skills in the first language, with an ten-year-old, fluent in a first language. In the first case, biliteracy might best be delayed. In the second, oracy and literacy in the second language may be mutually reinforcing. Contexts will also vary. When a language minority child is constantly bombarded with majority language written material, from advertisements to comics, computers to supermarkets, biliteracy may occur relatively easily. The accent in school can be on ensuring that first language literacy is established before introducing literacy in the second (majority) language. Such an introduction may come in the middle years of elementary school, from seven to twelve years of age, depending upon the level of literacy achievement in the first language.

## Further Reading

Edwards, V. (ed.) (1995) *Building Bridges: Multilingual Resources for Children.* Clevedon: Multilingual Matters.

Hornberger, N.H. (1989) Continua of biliteracy. *Review of Educational Research* 59 (3), 271–296.

Perez, B. and Torres-Guzmán, M.E. (1996) *Learning in Two Worlds: An Integrated Spanish/English Biliteracy Approach* (2nd edn). New York: Longman.

# Chapter 10
# Bilingual Children with Special Needs

## INTRODUCTION

Bilingual children meet problems and challenges just as do monolingual children. However, all too often, bilingualism bears the blame for problems that arise. This chapter explains why this occurs, and why there is often prejudice against bilingual children. The chapter reviews our state of knowledge when bilinguals appear to underachieve or experience learning difficulties, language delays or disorders.

The themes of this chapter are:

- Explanations of Under-Achievement in Bilinguals
- Bilingualism and Learning Difficulties
- Language Delay and Language Disorder
- Language and Speech Therapy in a Bilingual Context

## THEME 1: EXPLANATIONS OF UNDER-ACHIEVEMENT IN BILINGUALS

What may explain seeming under-achievement by language minority children when and where this occurs? When first, second or third generation immigrant children appear to fail in the classroom, where is blame popularly placed? When guest workers' children, indigenous minorities and distinct ethnic groups are shown to leave school earlier, achieve less in examinations or receive lower grades, what is the cause?

The blame may be attributed to the **child's bilingualism**, often popularly seen as causing cognitive confusion. The bilingual brain is depicted as two engines working at half throttle, while the monolingual's single, well-tuned engine runs at full throttle. Such an explanation is usually **incorrect**. Where two languages are well developed, then bilingualism is more likely to bring advantages than disadvantages. Only when a child's two languages are both underdeveloped can 'blame' be attributed to bilingualism. Even then, the blame should be on the societal circumstances that occasionally create underdeveloped languages.

Where under-achievement exists, the reason assigned may be **underexposure** to the majority language. Failure or below average performance, in the United States and the United Kingdom, is typically attributed to insufficiently developed English language skills for the curriculum. Those who use a minority language at home are sometimes perceived to struggle at school, due to a lack of competence in the dominant tongue. Thus submersion and transitional forms of bilingual education attempt to ensure a fast conversion to the majority language.

However, such a speedy conversion may do more harm than good; it denies the child's home language skills, even denies the child's identity and self-respect. Instead of using existing skills, the 'sink or swim' approach attempts to replace them. The level of English in the curriculum may be too advanced; consequently, the child under-achieves. Further English lessons become the remedy, but not the best solution.

Providing instruction through the medium of the minority language, in two-way, developmental maintenance or heritage language programs may combat under-achievement. When children are allowed to operate in the heritage language in the curriculum, evidence indicates successful results, including fluency in the majority language (Baker, 1996; Cummins, 2000). Thus underexposure to the majority language, though popular, is an **incorrect explanation** of under-achievement. It fails to note the advantages of instruction in the minority language. It inappropriately seeks an answer in increased majority language instruction, rather than increased minority language education.

Moreover, when bilingual children under-achieve, there may be a **mismatch** between home and school, based not only on language differences but also dissimilarities in culture, values and beliefs (Delgado-Gaitan & Trueba, 1991). As an extreme, this reflects an assimilationist, imperialist and oppressive majority viewpoint (see Home–School Relationships, p. 82). The child and family are expected to adjust to the school system, rather than expecting a pluralist system to incorporate variety. From such an assimilationist viewpoint, the solution lies in the home adjusting to mainstream language and culture to prepare the child for school. In the past, some educational psychologists and speech therapists advised language minority parents to raise their children in the majority, school language.

Alternatively, where practicable, the school system should be flexible enough to incorporate the home language and culture. A home–school mismatch can be positively addressed by 'strong forms' of bilingual education for minorities. By two-way, developmental maintenance and heritage language programs (see Glossary), by a multicultural classroom approach with respect for the child's value systems, culture and religious beliefs, the inclusion of parents in running the school and in partnership in their child's education, the mismatch can become a merger.

Under-achievement may also be attributed to **socioeconomic** factors surrounding a language minority group.

'Many immigrant and refugee children have a life of poverty and rural isolation in crowded dwellings where they lack privacy, toilet and shower facilities, comfort and basic medical attention. In some cases migrant life for children means abuse, malnutrition, poor health, ignorance and neglect. Uprooting a child from his/her land can lead to a life of stigma and low status.' (Trueba, 1991, p. 53)

Socioeconomic status is an umbrella term that rightly points to one cause of minority under-achievement. It provides an example of the importance of not blaming the victim, but analyzing societal features active in under-achievement: economic deprivation, poor living conditions, psychological and social factors such as discrimination, racial prejudice, pessimism and immobilizing inferiority.

Socioeconomic status is a partial explanation of under-achievement, but two cautions are necessary. Why do different language minorities of similar socioeconomic status perform differently at school? In the theme 'Language Minorities' (see p. 53), the different ideologies or orientations that vary between ethnic groups are discussed. Sociocultural factors within and between ethnic groups must be examined, as well as socioeconomic status, to begin to solve the equation of language minority achievement and under-achievement.

This raises another issue. Under-achievement is not simply related to one or several causes. The equation of under-achievement is **complex**, involving a number of factors, which interact in complicated ways. They are not simple, 'stand alone' effects. Umbrella labels, such as 'socioeconomic status' must be broken down into more definable predictors of under-achievement, such as the parents' attitudes about education. Home factors interact with school factors and provide an enormous number of different routes to varying degrees of school success. The recipes of success and failure are many, with varied, interacting ingredients. However, socioeconomic and sociocultural features are important in most equations of under-achievement.

Part of the equation is the **type of school** a child attends. This topic has highlighted the different outcomes in 'strong' forms of bilingual education, compared with 'weak'. The same child will learn more in programs using the heritage language for instruction than in programs which replace the home language as soon as possible. Therefore, under-achievement in a language minority child or group calls for scrutiny of the whole school. A system that suppresses the home language is likely to explain part of individual and ethnic group under-achievement. It tends to deny the language and cognitive achievements of children, their identity and self-esteem.

'Type of school' is a broad heading, under which a range of quality can exist, from poor to superior. Where under-achievement occurs, it is too simple to blame the type of school, rather than digging deeper and locating more specific causes. Baker (1996), Cummins (2000) and Hornberger (1991) have listed attributes that must be examined in assessing the **quality** of any educational system serving language minority children. Such factors include the supply, ethnic origins and bilingualism of teachers, classroom balance of minority and majority students, use and sequencing of languages across the curriculum over different grades, and reward systems for enriching the minority language and culture.

Under-achievement may be due to **real learning difficulties**. It is important to make a distinction. Too often, bilingual children are labeled with learning difficulties, while the causes of problems may be less in the child and more in the school or educational system. A subtractive, assimilative system typically creates negative attitudes and low motivation. In the 'sink or swim' approach, 'sinking' reflects an unsympathetic system and insensitive teaching, rather than individual learning problems. Apart from system and school generated problems, there will be children who are bilingual and have genuine learning difficulties (Cummins, 1984). Distinguishing between the real and the apparent, the system-generated and the remediable problems of the individual highlights alternatives. When under-achievement exists, do we blame the victim, blame the teacher and the school, or blame the system? When assessment tests and examinations show relatively low performance of language minority individuals and groups, will prejudices be confirmed or can we use such assessment to reveal deficiencies in the architecture of the school system and curriculum design? Under-achievement tends to be blamed on the child and the language minority group, while the explanation often lies in factors outside the individual.

A particular case of under-achievement is when students drop-out of schools. Stephen Krashen (1999) provides evidence to show that bilingual education is not the cause of **dropping-out** in United States schools, but it may be the cure. Latino students do have higher dropout rates (e.g. 30% of Latino students are classified as drop-outs compared to 8.6% of non-Latino whites and 12.1% of non-Latino Blacks). Krashen's (1999) review of evidence suggest that those who had experienced bilingual education were significantly less likely to drop-out.

There are factors (other than bilingual education) related to dropping-out such as socio-economic class, recency of immigration, family environment, and the presence of print at home. It is estimated that 40% of Latino children live in poverty compared with 15% of white non-Latino children. Latino children are more likely to have parents who did not complete High School. When these factors are controlled statistically, the drop-out rate among Latinos is the same (or virtually the same) as for other groups. Since 'strong' forms of bilingual schooling tend to produce higher standards of academic English and performance across the curriculum, then such schools become part of the cure for dropping-out.

## Further Reading

Baca, L.M. and Cervantes, H.T. (1998) *The Bilingual Special Education Interface* (3rd edn). Upper Saddle River, NJ: Prentice Hall.

Cummins, J. (1984) *Bilingualism and Special Education: Issues in Assessment and Pedagogy.* Clevedon: Multilingual Matters.

Harry, B. (1992) *Cultural Diversity, Families and the Special Education System: Communication and Empowerment.* New York: Teachers College Press.

Krashen, S.D. (1999) *Condemned Without a Trial: Bogus Arguments Against Bilingual Education.* Portsmouth, NH: Heinemann.

## THEME 2: BILINGUALISM AND LEARNING DIFFICULTIES

The previous theme disputed the link between bilingualism and under-achievement in school. The failure of some language minority children to achieve satisfactorily was argued to be potentially the result of a complex equation of factors, none of which was directly linked to bilingualism. These include an educational system that devalues the child's home language and culture and does not build on existing abilities in the home language. The social and economic difficulties that many indigenous and immigrant minorities face were shown to be another possible cause of academic under-achievement.

Another unfair assumption made by some people is that bilingualism causes specific learning disabilities. This topic argues that this assumption is usually false. **Bilingualism is rarely a cause of learning difficulties**.

Bilingual children are often wrongly assessed as having learning difficulties, because basic mistakes are made in **assessment** and categorization. A child is often tested in the weaker, second language, inaccurately measuring both language and general cognitive development. In Britain and the United States, immigrant students have often been tested through the medium of English, on English proficiency, while their level of competence in Spanish, Bengali, Cantonese or other first language is ignored. This is discussed more fully in 'Assessment and Bilingual Children' (see p. 130).

The result is that, instead of being seen as developing bilinguals, children with a good command of a first language, in the process of acquiring a second, they may be classed as 'of limited English proficiency' (LEP in the United States) or even as having general learning difficulties. Below average test scores in the second language are wrongly defined as a 'deficit' or 'disability' that can be remedied by some form of special education.

While learning difficulties occasionally occur within bilingual children, there are a variety of possible causes, almost none of them aligned to bilingualism. Six examples of causes follow, which are similar to the causes of general under-achievement in school.

- Poverty and material deprivation, child neglect and abuse, helplessness and desperation in the home, extended family and community may create personality, attitudinal and learning conditions that render assessment of learning difficulties more probable. Sometimes such assessment will reflect prejudice, misjudgments and misperceptions about the child's home experiences. The learning problem may thus lie in a mismatch between the culture, attitudes, educational expectations and values of the home and school. Different beliefs, culture, knowledge and cognitive approaches may be devalued, with the child labeled as inferior in intelligence, academically incompetent and low in potential.
- The problem may lie in the standard of education, poor teaching methods, non-motivating, even hostile classroom environment, a dearth of suitable teaching materials.

- The school may inhibit or obstruct learning progress. If a child is taught in a second language, while the home language is ignored, then failure and perceived learning difficulties may result. Some Spanish-speaking children in the United States are placed in English-only classrooms on school entry. They must sink or swim in English. Those who sink may be deemed to have a deficiency. When assessed in their weaker second language, rather than their home language, they are labeled as needing special or remedial education. The monolingual school system itself may then be responsible for specific learning difficulties as well as general underachievement. A school that promotes bilingualism would be more likely to ensure learning success for the same child.
- A lack of self-confidence, low self-esteem, fear of failure and high anxiety in the student may lead to apparent learning difficulties.
- Classroom interactions among children cause some failures. When a group of children encourage each other to play around, share a low motivation to succeed, or where there is bullying, hostility and social division rather than cohesion in a classroom, the learning ethos may hinder individual development.
- Failure is also caused by **the mismatch between the gradient of learning expected and individual ability**. Some children learn to read more slowly than others, still learning well, but after a longer period of time. Less able children can learn two languages within the (unknowable) limits of their ability. Other children experience specific learning difficulties, such as dyslexia, neurological dysfunction, short term memory problems, poor physical coordination, or problems in attention span and motivation. None of these specific learning disabilities are caused by bilingualism. At the same time, bilingual children will not escape being included in this group; bilingual families are no less likely to be affected than other families.

This list, neither exhaustive nor comprehensive, shows that there are many possible roots for a child's learning difficulties, while bilingualism has almost nothing to do with any of them, either as a secondary or primary cause. Bilingualism is unlikely to cause learning difficulties.

Almost the only case where bilingualism is associated with learning difficulty is when a bilingual child enters the classroom with **neither language sufficiently developed** to cope with the higher order language skills demanded by the curriculum. The child has simple conversational skills in two languages, but cannot keep up in either, thus implicating language in learning difficulties. In this case, bilingualism is not the true problem. The problem is insufficient language practice in the home, nursery school and outside world. It is not bilingual deprivation but deprivation in any language. This is a great rarity, but the only genuine connection, though indirect, of bilingualism with learning difficulties.

## Ability Effects

Is it the case that **less able children** will experience bilingual cognitive advantages, or would such children be better off as monolinguals? Rueda's (1983) research suggests a 'cognitive advantages' link may be found in less able children. Using children of well below average IQ (51–69 IQ points), Rueda compared bilinguals and monolinguals on three tests: a Meaning and Reference Task which examines the stability and meaning of words (the death of a 'flump', an imaginary animal), the Arbitrariness of Language Task (could we call a 'cat' a 'dog'?), and the Non-Physical Nature of Words Task (does the word 'bird' have feathers?). On each task, the bilinguals tended to score significantly higher. Although Rueda found no difference on a Piagetian conservation test, this research indicates that the cognitive advantages linked to bilingualism may not be specific to higher ability children.

If children have below average ability, there is evidence to suggest that they can **still acquire two languages** within their unknown limits. While well meaning friends, teachers and speech therapists sometimes suggest that only one language should be developed, Canadian research indicates cognitive advantages in bilingualism for these less able students. Just as their development occurs at a slower pace in mathematics, literacy and science, so also with the development of two languages. The size of vocabulary and accuracy of grammar may lag behind the average bilingual child. Nevertheless, such children, acquiring two languages early, will usually be able to communicate in both, often as well as they would in one alone.

## Further Reading

Baca, L.M. and Cervantes, H.T. (1998) *The Bilingual Special Education Interface* (3rd edn). Upper Saddle River, NJ: Prentice Hall.

Harry, B. (1992) *Cultural Diversity, Families and the Special Education System: Communication and Empowerment*. New York: Teachers College Press.

## THEME 3: LANGUAGE DELAY AND LANGUAGE DISORDER

### Language Delay

**Language delay** illustrates the erroneous link between bilingualism and developmental problems. Language delay occurs when a child is very late in learning to talk or lags well behind peers in language development. Estimates of language delay in young children vary from 5% to 20% of the child population. Such varying estimates reflect the range in delays from brief and hardly noticeable to more severe.

Language delay may have a **variety of causes**: partial hearing, deafness, autism, severe subnormality, cerebral palsy, cleft palate and other physical problems or psychological disturbance. In approximately half to two-thirds of all cases, the precise reason remains unknown. Medically normal children with no hearing loss, normal IQ and memory, who are not socially deprived or emotionally disturbed, may be delayed in starting to speak, slow in development or may have problems expressing themselves. In such cases, specialist professional help is needed, from speech therapists, clinical and educational psychologists, counselors and/or doctors.

Parents of bilingual children with such problems should not attribute them to bilingualism. Sometimes, well-meaning professionals suggest this diagnosis, when definite causes remain unknown. Raising children bilingually is sometimes believed to cause language delay, though evidence does not support this position. Raising children bilingually neither increases nor reduces the chance of language disorder or delay.

A key consideration for parents is whether removal of one language will improve, worsen, or have no effect upon language development. Since the cause of the problem may be unknown, intuition and guesswork are often substituted for 'science'. Research in this area is still in its infancy. Confronted with the suggestion of concentrating on one language only, if there is a major diagnosed language delay, parents, teachers and professionals run the risk of accenting the perceived importance of the majority language. In the United States, the advice is often to supply a steady diet of English, the language of school and employment. All too frequently, the majority language replaces the home, minority language, with painful outcomes for the child.

When someone has loved, cared for and played with the child in one language, and then suddenly only uses another tongue, the child's emotional well being may be hurt. The language used to express love and caring disappears. Simultaneously, and by association, the child may feel the love and care also are not as before. Such a language change is often drastic, with negative after-effects and consequences.

Even when parents and professionals accept that bilingualism does not cause a child's problem, some see monolingualism as a remedy. They reason that removing the 'extra demands' of bilingualism will lighten the child's burden. If the child has a language delay problem, simplifying language demands may solve or reduce the problem. The apparent complexity of a bilingual life is relieved. Is this right?

There are many cases where changing from bilingualism to monolingualism will have no effect on the problem. If the child is slow to speak, without an obvious cause, or seems low in self-esteem, dropping one language is unlikely to help. On the contrary, the sudden change in family life may exacerbate the problem, since the stability of language life is disrupted. In most cases, this move is inappropriate. However, it is dangerous to make this advice absolute and unequivocal.

To advise only 'stick with bilingualism' is simplistic and unwise. With language delay, for example, there will be a few family situations where maximal experience in one language is preferable. Where one language is much more secure and better developed than the other, it may be sensible to concentrate on developing the stronger language. If the child only hears one language from one parent, and that parent is often absent, a short-term concentration on the stronger language may help in a language delay period.

This does not mean losing the chance of bilingualism forever. If, or when, language delay disappears, the other language can be reintroduced. If a child with emotional problems really detests using a particular language, the family may sensibly decide to accede to the child's preference. Again, once problems have been resolved, the language may be reintroduced, as long as it is immediately associated with pleasurable experiences.

Any temporary move from bilingualism to monolingualism should not be judged the only solution needed. Such a focus is naive and dangerous. Emotional problems may require other rearrangements in the family's pattern of relationships, as discussed with a counselor or psychologist. Language delay may require advice from a speech therapist, including about family language interaction. Temporary monolingualism should only be seen as one component in a package of attempted solutions. However, it is important to reiterate that retaining a bilingual approach, in the great majority of cases will not exacerbate the problem of language delay.

## Language Disorder

According to Li Wei, Miller and Dodd (1997), around 5% of all children experience some form of language disorder, including: late speech development, very slow development in language competence, speaking less often and less accurately than normal, inability to produce certain sounds or remember new words, and never achieving the same language competence as peers. Bilingual children are neither more nor less likely to show problems. However, when bilinguals are inaccurate in speaking a second language (as they may be on the learning curve) or when sounds are added from one language to the other (often playful and creative), these are not language disorders.

If the child requires professional assessment and help from a psychologist or speech therapist, this professional must understand the child's bilingual background and the nature of childhood bilingualism. **Assessment** of the child must be completed in both or all languages, using tests normed on bilinguals, and avoiding comparison with monolinguals in phonology, vocabulary, syntax and fluency.

## Further Reading

Wei, L., Miller, N. and Dodd, B. (1997) Distinguishing communicative difference from language disorder in bilingual children. *Bilingual Family Newsletter* 14 (1), 3–4. (Clevedon: Multilingual Matters.)

## THEME 4: LANGUAGE AND SPEECH THERAPY IN A BILINGUAL CONTEXT

A bilingual situation adds an extra dimension to the work of language and speech therapists, since a proportion of therapy may be carried out through different languages, concurrently where feasible.

When helping young children, many language and speech therapists work with them in their first language or, in the case of children with no speech at all, in the language their parents speak to them (their potential first language). When children make progress in their first language, the work does not usually have to be repeated when the child encounters a second language at school. The language skills acquired in the first language, such as labeling objects or using verbs, transfer to the second.

Learning a second language does not pose any particular problems for a child with general learning disabilities, although the level achieved in both languages may be lower than that of peers. In fact, the stimulus of acquiring another language, with alternate labels for objects and concepts, seems to help the child progress in both languages. The careful grading of language by the teacher, the repetition of key phrases and vocabulary, the use of visual cues and stimuli, the emphasis on learning through activities, all enable the child to make good progress in the second language alongside the peer group.

The instance where there may be difficulty is when a child has a specific language related disorder (see p. 126). A child who has problems 'tuning into' or processing language may find it difficult to cope with a class where the curriculum is delivered through the medium of a second language. It may not be easy to 'pick up' the second language and the child may be shut out of classroom interaction. A preferable option for such a child might be to attend a school where the curriculum is delivered mainly through the medium of the first language, and the second language is presented only in set periods.

One situation which language and speech therapists encounter is minority language parents who speak the majority language to their children. Sometimes when a child has learning difficulties, parents believe two languages are an extra burden and adopt the useful majority language. This can also happen when the child has no particular problem, but the parents decide from the child's birth to promote the majority language to 'get a good start in life'. The result is that the child is excluded from the interaction between parents and other family and community members.

Since the parents are not native majority language speakers, sometimes the model they offer their child is impoverished and deficient. Thus the child grows up, not advantaged but deprived. A child with learning disabilities is further disadvantaged. It seems preferable, wherever possible, for parents to speak their own language to their child. If acquisition of that first language presents problems, language and speech therapy can help. The second language can be built upon the strong foundations of the first.

Many modern language and speech therapists now refute the suggestion that bilingualism is a burden, even for individuals with congenital or acquired language disabilities. Bilingualism is simply a dimension in life, to be taken into account when working with people with different kinds of language disabilities. The ability to speak two languages is a privilege and resource that should be denied to no one.

## Further Reading

Baca, L.M. and Cervantes, H.T. (1998) *The Bilingual Special Education Interface* (3rd edn). Upper Saddle River, NJ: Prentice Hall.

# Chapter 11

# The Assessment and Education of Bilingual Children with Special Needs

## INTRODUCTION

Any psychological and educational assessment of bilingual children must be fair, accurate and broad. Too often, such tests only serve to suggest 'disabilities' and 'deficits' or lack of second language proficiency, thus legitimizing the disabling of language minority students, stigmatizing them for apparent weaknesses in the majority language, with monolingual scores used as points of comparison. This chapter explores this pattern of assessment and provides more effective practices. It then discusses placement of bilinguals in Special Education and outlines policies, provision and practices for them.

The themes of this chapter are:

- Assessment of Bilingual Children
- Bilingual Special Education

## THEME 1: ASSESSMENT OF BILINGUAL CHILDREN

In the United States, legislation governs **appropriate assessment** of those for whom English is an additional language. The 1973 case in California of *Diana v. the State Board of Education* was based on nine Mexican American parents who protested that their Spanish-language dominant children were given an IQ test in English. The test revealed 'normal' non-verbal IQ scores, but ludicrously low verbal IQ scores, as low as 30 for one child. As a result of this linguistically and culturally inappropriate test, the children were placed in classes for the 'mentally retarded'. The case established that testing should be conducted in a child's native language as well as English, and that non-verbal IQ tests were usually a fairer measurement than verbal tests (Valdés & Figueroa, 1994). As a further result of this case, the collection of broader data on language minority children was required to justify placement of such children in Special Education, rather than simple test data.

In 1975, Public Law 94-142, *The Education for all Handicapped Children Act*, feder-ally mandated that all testing and assessment procedures should be **non-discriminatory**. 'Non-discriminatory' specifies tests that are culturally and linguistically appropriate. A **multi-source file of evidence** should be created with teacher recommendations, direct observations and other relevant information joined with tests. Yet in spite of legislation and discussions in academic literature and research, bilinguals in many countries meet with discrimination in testing and assessment. Therefore, it is important to review the components of such bias and suggest desirable practice. Issues in the assessment of bilingual children overlap and intersect; ten are presented here for consideration:

First, the **temporary** difficulties faced by bilinguals must be distinguished from more long-lasting impediments to everyday functioning and learning. Brief language-delays, temporary adjustment problems for immigrants and short term stammering (stuttering) are transient. Dyslexia, hearing loss and neuroticism are long term problems, which need treatment. Seemingly simple, this distinction hides complex dimensions.

Second, diagnosis must engage a diversity of **measurement and observation** devices. It must be extended over time and avoid any instant conclusion and remedy. Observation of the child in different contexts, not just the classroom, provides a more valid profile of individual language and behavior. The family and educational history must be assembled in the context of consultation with parents, teachers, doctors, counselors, speech therapists and social workers, plus samples of the child's natural communication in different roles and situations.

**Fair assessment** presupposes awareness of the child's ethnic, cultural and linguistic background, but this knowledge does not suffice. To interpret test scores and classifications meaningfully, and to make decisions on the basis of this assess-ment, require a highly sensitive and sympathetic understanding of the child's community, culture, family life and individual characteristics. Children enter school with diverse home experiences, where different kinds of ability are culti-vated. Abilities prized by parents may differ from those stressed at school.

Discovery learning and learning through play are not part of all cultures. An investigative, questioning mode of thinking may not be encouraged within a partic-ular culture. In these parent–child relationships, adults provide authoritative knowledge that must be accepted and enacted by the child. Parents may teach literacy in a similar style to a religious context, where the child is expected to memo-rize much, or all, of the holy book and repeat it, even without comprehension. Such family and community socialization practices have implications for the type of assessment of strengths and weakness in the child, for the importance of cultural evidence and the professional assessment process.

Scores on educational and psychometric **tests** tend to be decontextualized and attenuated. They are like latitude and longitude, providing a point of reference on a map of human characteristics. As a standard measurement, usable on all maps, they provide rapid and instantly comparable information. But if you imagine the most beautiful place you know, perhaps a flower-enfolded, azure lake amid green-sloped, ice-capped mountains, does the expression of latitude and longitude of that location do justice to the personality and distinctiveness of the scene? The precision of the sextant must be joined to full empathic exploration and evaluation of individual character and qualities.

Assessment of **authentic language** and behavior, not trivial, decontextualized language skills, is crucial. The child's levels of thinking and understanding through both languages must be targeted, not superficial comprehension gleaned through a 'scientific' test, with high test–retest reliability and high correlations with similar tests. 'Unauthentic language' tests relate too often to a transmission style curriculum where obtaining correct answers and 'teaching to the test' dominate teacher thinking and classroom activity. Such tests do not capture the individual's communication abilities in the playground, on the street, at the family table and in internal, solitary conversations.

Third, the **choice of assessors** will affect the results. Perception of assessors as of the same language group will affect the child's performance, and, possibly, the diagnosis. Perceived age, social class, power, and gender of the assessor will affect the child's response and, possibly, assessment outcome. The assessment process is not neutral. Who assesses, using what devices, under what conditions, all contribute to the resulting judgement. An inappropriate assessor creates an increased risk of two common, opposite judgmental errors: (1) generating a 'false positive', diagnosis of a non-existent problem or (2) generating a 'false negative', failure to locate a real difficulty.

Fourthly, children must be assessed in their **stronger language**. Ideally, assessment should be bilingual. The tests and assessment devices and the language of communication used should be in the child's stronger language. Basing assessment on tests in, and of, the child's weaker language, may lead to a misdiagnosis, a false impression of individual abilities and a partial and biased picture of the child. This sometimes occurs in the United Kingdom and the United States, where language minority children are tested in English, because of the easy availability of well-regarded psychometric tests.

Fifth, the testing language should be appropriate to the child. A **translation of the test**, say from English to Spanish, may produce inappropriate, stilted language, or be specific to one of the many different varieties of Spanish, perhaps not the one familiar to the student. Chicano Spanish speaking parents should specify tests in Chicano Spanish, not Cuban, Puerto Rican or Castilian. Once Spanish speaking children have lived in the United States for a time, their Spanish changes under the influence of English, so a test in 'standard' Spanish is also inappropriate. A monolingual standard of Spanish may accept only one 'right' answer, thus penalizing bilinguals for their United States Spanish.

Since there are language problems with tests, it is important to distinguish between a child's language and performance profiles. The performance profile is more important, as it attempts to portray underlying cognitive abilities, rather than language abilities alone. A performance profile aims at the child's overall potential, not just language proficiency.

Cummins (1984) has shown this distinction between language and performance profiles on one IQ test used in individual assessment: the Wechsler Intelligence Scale for Children – Revised (WISC-R). Language minority children tend to score significantly higher on the Performance than the Verbal subtests. As Cummins suggests (p. 30): 'The analysis of student performance on this test suggested that the majority of Verbal subtests were tapping ESL students' knowledge of the English language and North American culture in addition to, or instead of verbal/cognitive ability.'

Sixth, there are times when a test or assessment device cannot be given in the child's stronger language. Appropriate language minority professionals may not be available to join the assessment team, tests may not be available in the home language, and translations of existing tests may be unreliable.

**Interpreters** can play a necessary function in these cases. If trained in linguistic, professional and rapport-making competencies, they can make assessment more fair and accurate. They can also bring a possible bias, raising or lowering the assessment results through their interpretation.

Seventh, there is a danger of focusing the assessment solely on the child; testing assumes the 'problem' lies within the individual. At the same time, and sometimes instead, the focus should shift to **exterior causes**. Is the problem in the school? Does the school deny abilities in the first language and focus on failures in the second (school) language? Does the system deny the child's culture and ethnic character, thereby affecting academic success and self-esteem? Is the curriculum delivered at a level beyond the child's comprehension, or is it culturally strange? The remedy may lie in changing the school system not the student.

Eighth, there is a risk that assessment will disable rather than **empower** bilingual children. If the assessment separates children from powerful, dominant, mainstream groups, they may become disabled. The assessment may lead to categorization in an inferior social group and marginalization. Instead, it should work in the child's best, long-term interests, not only for short-term educational remedies, but also employment and wealth sharing opportunities. The assessment should initiate advocacy for, and not against, the child.

Ninth, the understanding and observation of **teachers**, who have seen the child in a variety of learning environments over time, are crucial. What do they identify as the root of the problem? What solutions and interventions do they suggest? Do they have a plan of action? Regular meetings of the teaching team to discuss children with problems are a valuable first stage in assessment and support. Such a team can also act as a school decision-maker for referral to other professionals, such as speech therapists, psychologists and counselors.

Finally, **norm-referenced tests** are often used to assess for entry into or exit from a bilingual program. The assessor compares the child with so called 'normal' children and indicates how different the individual is from the average. Many such tests are based on scores from 'native' language majority children, thus rendering comparisons unfair for language minority children. Tests of English proficiency may have norms (averages and scores around the average) based on native speakers of English. This biases the tests against bilinguals and leads to the stereotyping of particular language and ethnic groups

The testing of bilinguals has developed from monolingual testing practice. A bilingual is not the simple sum of two monolinguals, but a unique combination and integration of languages. A bilingual's English performance should not be compared with monolingual anglophones, as a long jumper (with dual skills of sprinting and jumping) should not be compared with a 100 meter sprinter, solely for speed. Monolingual norms are simply inappropriate for bilinguals, who use their languages in different contexts (domains) and have linguistic competence in varying curriculum areas and topics and on different language functions. Equal language facility in both tongues is rare. Comparison on monolingual terms assumes equal language facility across all domains, language functions and curriculum areas. This is unfair.

**Norm-referenced tests** are often written by white, middle-class, Anglo test producers, and test items reflect their language style and culture. Words such as 'tennis racket', 'snow man' and 'credit cards' may be unfamiliar to immigrants who have never seen snow, played tennis, or encountered the culture of plastic money.

Norm-referenced assessments are often 'paper and pencil' tests, involving multiple choice answers, one response chosen from a set of possibilities. Such tests do not measure all the different aspects of language, of 'intelligence' or of any curriculum subject. Spoken, conversational language and creative thinking, for example, cannot be adequately measured by a simple paper and pencil test.

Some norm-referenced tests, especially in the United States, report results in **percentiles**, the percentage of scores above and below the child being tested. Being in the 40th percentile means that 39% of scores are lower than those of the child being tested. Sixty percent of children score above the 40th percentile child. The child is in the 40th group from the bottom, all children being assumed to be divided into 100 equal-sized groups. Percentiles often serve in entry and exit of students in bilingual programs in the United States. A student may need to reach the 40th percentile on an English language test to exit to a mainstream class. Which 'percentile threshold' is used for entry or exit is essentially arbitrary and liable to political rather than pedagogical decisions.

Norm-referenced tests essentially compare one person against others. Is this important? Is it not what a bilingual student can and cannot do in each curriculum subject, which is the more important assessment? To say the students is in the 40th percentile in English doesn't tell the parent or teacher the child's strengths and weaknesses, capabilities and needs in English. The alternative is assessment related directly to progress in each curriculum area.

Curriculum based assessment is called **criterion referenced testing**. It seeks to establish the student's relative competence in a curriculum area, to establish what a child can do, what is the next specific step of a curriculum area where progress can be made. A diagnosis may also be made, not necessarily of a fundamental psychological or learning problem, but of remedial treatment needed to enable conceptual understanding, for example, if a child makes grapho-phono miscues. Such criterion referenced assessment gives parents and teachers more usable and important information. It profiles what an individual can do in a specific subject, and where development or accelerated learning should occur next. Such assessment enables an individualized program to be set.

However, the sequences of learning that underpin a criterion referenced test may still reflect a **cultural mismatch**. Criterion referenced assessment usually, but not necessarily, assumes a relatively linear, step by step curricular progression, in reading instruction, in number skills, in science. Such progressions may be culturally relative and culturally determined. As Cline (1993, p. 63) notes, 'because of their different prior experiences, their learning hierarchy for a particular task may follow different steps or a different sequence (e.g. in relation to phonology and orthography in learning to read)'. Therefore, it is important to use curriculum contexts and processes that are appropriate, comprehensible and meaningful to the bilingual child.

## Solutions

Valdés and Figueroa (1994) provide three **solutions** to the problems of testing bilinguals. Their first solution is to minimize the potential harm of existing tests when given to bilinguals by applying some of the guidelines given above. Their second is to temporarily ban all testing of bilinguals until more valid tests can be produced for these populations. Their third is to develop alternative approaches to testing and development. This third option may be the one most favored by teachers, educational theorists and parents. It would bring in bilingual norms, more curriculum-based and portfolio-based assessment and add greater cultural and linguistic awareness.

However, the new beginning of the third solution is insufficient. A more radical solution places change in assessment within a change in expectations about the nature and behavior of language minority students. This entails a shift in the politics and policy dimensions of assessment. Merely changing tests may alleviate symptoms, but not change root causes. The root cause is a bias against language minorities endemic in many societies, which is substantiated by tests. Since assessment is biased against bilinguals in a cultural and linguistic form, and since it fails to incorporate understanding of the cognitive constitution of bilinguals, it confirms and perpetuates discriminatory perceptions about language minorities.

Thus assessment sometimes serves, by its nature and purpose, its form, use and outcomes, to justify the perpetuation of prejudice and discrimination against language minorities. **Test results** serve to marginalize and discourage, to reveal under-achievement and lower performance in language minority children. These results often reflect the low status, inequitable treatment and poverty found among many language minorities. Assessment provides the data to justify self-fulfilling and self-perpetuating expectations. Changing assessment does not necessarily break into that cycle, unless the change is part of a wider reform.

Assessment must not, in itself, be blamed for bias against bilinguals. It is a conveyor and not a root cause of discrimination and bias. Until there is authentic acceptance of cultural pluralism in a nation, a more widespread assent for multiculturalism, a minimizing of racism and prejudice against ethnic minorities, minor modifications in the assessment of bilinguals stand the chance of merely confirming the lower status and perceived 'deficiencies' of minority children. Too often the focus in assessing bilinguals is on their language competence, or in their 'limited proficiencies', as in the test-designated 'Limited English Proficient' students in the United States, via tests such as the English Language Assessment Battery (LAB). Rarely does assessment focus on other important abilities.

In the United States, the 1991 Secretary's Commission on Achieving Necessary Skills (SCANS) recommended attention be given in high schools to work related competencies. For example, performance standards were mandated in interpreting and communicating information, thinking creatively, taking responsibility, sociability, self-management, integrity and interpersonal skills such as teamwork, negotiating, and working with people from culturally diverse backgrounds. These important life skills are essential accomplishments for employment, self-respect and building a better world.

Bilinguals may have advantages in negotiating, working with people from culturally diverse backgrounds, interpreting and communicating information and thinking creatively. If the assessment of bilinguals focused more on these outside world attributes and less on classroom linguistic skills in the majority language, a more affirmative and favorable, productive and constructive view of bilinguals might be promoted.

### Further Reading

Cline, T. (1993) Educational assessment of bilingual pupils: Getting the context right. *Educational and Child Psychology* 10, 4, 59–68.
Cummins, J. (1984) *Bilingualism and Special Education: Issues in Assessment Pedagogy.* Clevedon: Multilingual Matters.
Hamayan, E.V. and Damico, J.S. (eds) (1991) *Limiting Bias in the Assessment of Bilingual Students.* Austin, TX: Pro-Ed.
Valdés, G. and Figueroa, R.A. (1994) *Bilingualism and Testing: A Special Case of Bias.* Norwood, NJ: Ablex.

## THEME 2: BILINGUAL SPECIAL EDUCATION

### Introduction

The definition of children with special needs, who may need Special Education, is of prime importance. Categories of special need vary nationally, but are likely to include: visual and/or hearing impairment, communication disorders, learning disabilities such as dyslexia and developmental aphasia, severe subnormality in cognitive development, behavioral problems and physical handicaps. Some bilingual children will have special needs, including 'elite bilingual' children such as English–German, as well as language minority children. In the United States, the

Office of Special Education estimates that nearly one million children from language minority backgrounds need some form of special education. Why may language minority children need special education?

- Do language minority children experience special needs more frequently due to their bilingualism and communication differences from monolinguals?
- Are language minority children often wrongly assessed and categorized as 'disabled', and so incorrectly placed in special education?

Let us consider these questions. In response to the first, it seems very unlikely that bilingualism is linked with, or a direct cause of, the following special needs: visual or hearing impairment, learning disabilities such as dyslexia and developmental aphasia, severe subnormality in cognitive development, behavioral problems and physical handicaps. Membership in a language minority may **coexist** with such conditions, but does not determine them (see Explanations of Underachievement, p. 120).

There is some evidence in the United States (on a state by state analysis) that language minority children are over-represented among those in need of special education (Harry, 1992; Gersten & Woodward, 1994). If this apparently dispropor-tionate placement is true, are language minority children being wrongly assessed as disabled? Is this placement in special education incorrect?

When language minority children are assessed, **three different developmental aspects** must be kept distinct: first language proficiency, second language profi-ciency, and the existence (or not) of a physical, learning, or behavioral difficulty. This three-fold distinction allows a fairer and more accurate assessment. The child's level of functioning in a second language must not be seen as the child's level of language development. The child's development in the first language must be assessed, by observation, if psychological and educational tests are unavailable, to paint a picture of proficiency, not deficiency. Individual language proficiency is different from potential problems in capacities requiring specialized treatment, such as hearing impairment, severely subnormal cognitive development, and specific learning difficulties. Neither the home language and culture, nor socioeco-nomic and ethnic differences, should be handicaps in themselves. Social, cultural, familial, educational and personal information must be collected for a valid, reliable assessment, and an accurate placement in mainstream or special education. This is considered more fully in the previous topic, Assessment and Bilingual Children (see p. 130).

### The Example of the United States

In the United States, Public Law (94-142) mandates the right to assessment without cultural discrimination, to tests in the individual native language, to multidimen-sional 'all areas' assessment for all 'handicapped' students. The misdiagnosis of language minority students for special education has led to court cases. Such court cases reveal how language minority students were wrongly assessed. In some cases, teachers were unsure of how to cope with a student whose English was relatively weak, and on this basis alone wanted special education for the 'Limited English Proficient' child.

Such **litigation** demonstrates the importance of separating bilinguals with real learning difficulties from those whose second language proficiency is below a 'native speaker' average. The latter group should not be assessed as needing special education. This litigation also shows the wrongs done to language minority students: misidentification, misplacement, and misuse of tests and failure when paced in special education.

Unfortunately, the fear of litigation in school districts can sometimes lead to an over-referral of language minority students with a real need of special education. In the early 1980s, the trend in California, for example, was to assume that too many language minority students needed special education. When students did not appear to benefit from instruction in 'regular' classrooms, special education became the easy answer. Or again, if teachers were unsure over dealing with behavioral or learning problems, transfer to special education classes became an instant solution.

Toward the end of the 1980s, this had been reversed. The tendency moved to **underestimating** the special needs of language minorities (Gersten & Woodward, 1994). Wrongful placement of children (over-referral) in special education made administrators cautious. A fear of parental legal action, as well as a realization of the frequent low validity of assessment devices, led administrators to hesitate to place language minority students in special education. The see-saw between over-estimation and under-referral of special education need makes accurate assessment crucial. 'Assessment and Bilingual Children' (see p. 130) raises important issues about valid special needs assessment. However, accurate assessment and placement in different schools is insufficient. The development of effective instructional strategies and an appropriate curriculum is crucial. So is the need to train teachers for bilinguals in special education, and to educate the parents of special needs children.

Assessment will sometimes locate bilinguals who have a physical, neurological, learning, emotional, cognitive or behavioral difficulty. Such children may need some kind of special education or intervention. One estimate in the United States is that one in eight language minority students fits in this category. Similar figures are quoted in other countries. What form of special education should such children receive? Should such education be in their home language, where feasible, or in the majority tongue of the region? Should such children receive education that uses both home and majority languages?

A **variety of institutional arrangements** currently serve special education bilinguals. These include: special education schools (resident and non-resident), hospital based education, residential homes, special education units attached to mainstream schools, specially resourced classes in mainstream schools, withdrawal and pull out programs for extra speech and language help and behavioral management, and special help given by teachers, paraprofessionals or support staff in 'regular' classes. The extent to which such provision will be bilingual or monolingual varies within and across such institutional arrangements. Such provisions also depends upon availability of material and human resources, the types and degree of special education need or condition, proficiency in both languages, learning capacity, age, social and emotional maturity, degree of success in any previous education placements, and the wishes of the parents and child.

When bilingual or language minority children have been accurately assessed as having special needs, many educators argue only instruction in the dominant, majority language is needed. In the United States, it is sometimes advised that Latino and other language minority students with special needs be educated in monolingual, English language special schools. When there is very severe mental retardation, a child should be educated monolingually, in the minority or majority language. Such a child develops very slowly in one language. However, this would only affect a very minute proportion of children with special needs.

Many special needs children benefit considerably from specifically **bilingual special education**. A recently arrived immigrant child, who cannot speak the language of the classroom, first needs instruction mostly through the first language, with the chance to become as bilingual as possible. Most special needs children are capable of developing in two languages. Many do not reach levels of proficiency in either language, compared with mainstream peers. However, they do reach satisfactory levels of bilingual proficiency according to their abilities. Becoming bilingual does not detract from achievement in other curricular areas, such as mathematics and creative arts. Canadian research suggests that less able children share some of the cognitive advantages of bilingualism (Rueda, 1983). Just as their mathematics ability, literacy and scientific development occur at a slower pace, so the two languages develop with less speed. Vocabulary size and accuracy of grammar may be less in both languages than the average child. Nevertheless, such children will usually be able to communicate in both languages, when acquired early, often as well as they would communicate in one language.

The movement of a bilingual student into special education should occur after concluding that the child's needs cannot be met by **integration** in a regular school. This holds for those currently in bilingual education, who may need special bilingual instruction, because generally, integration is preferable to segregation. If children are placed in bilingual special education, it is important they gain the benefits found in other forms of bilingual education: dual language competence, biculturalism and multiculturalism, and other educational, cultural, self-identity and self-esteem enhancements.

Children who are failing in a mainstream school due to their language proficiency being insufficient to operate in the classroom need special attention. For example, in the United States some Spanish-speaking children are in 'submersion' programs in mainstream schools. Though of normal ability, they fail, drop out of school, repeat grades, or leave school without graduating, because their English is insufficient for the increasingly complex curriculum.

This situation creates an apparent **dilemma**. Being placed in some form of special education may stigmatize the child as having a 'deficiency' or 'language deficit'. Such special education may be a separate school or unit within a larger school that provides special (remedial) education for bilingual children. Such schools and units may not foster bilingualism. Often their emphasis is on majority language competence. Such segregation may allow more attention to the second language, but result in ghettoization of language minorities. While giving sanctuary from sinking in second language submersion in a mainstream school, special education can be a retreat, marginalizing the student. Will these children realize their potential across the curriculum? Will they enjoy increased access to employment? Will their apparent failure be accepted and validated, because they are associated with a remedial institution? Will there be decreased opportunities for success in academic achievement, employment and self-enhancement?

The ideal in this dilemma is neither mainstreaming nor special education, it is instruction which allows students to start and continue learning in their first language. The second language is nurtured as well, to ensure the development of bilinguals who can operate in mainstream society. In such schools, both languages are developed and serve in the curriculum. They avoid the remedial or compensatory associations of special education and celebrate the cultural and linguistic diversity of their students. Yet bilingual education in itself is sometimes in danger of being seen as a form of special education.

## Further Reading

Baca, L.M. and Cervantes, H.T. (1998) *The Bilingual Special Education Interface* (3rd edn). Upper Saddle River, NJ: Prentice Hall.

Cloud, N. (1994) Special education needs of second language students. In F. Genesee (ed.) *Educating Second Language Children*. Cambridge: Cambridge University Press.

# Chapter 12

# Multiculturalism, Racism and Bilingual Children

## INTRODUCTION

Bilingual populations are universally linked to language issues, cultural diversity, racism and multiculturalism. Similarly, bilingual education does not concern languages alone, but includes multiculturalism in the curriculum and sometimes in the school's overall aims and infrastructure. Just as language and culture are entwined, so bilingualism and multiculturalism are partners, a relationship to be explored in this chapter.

The themes of this chapter are:

- Multicultural Education for All
- Anti-Racism and Prejudice Reduction in School
- Immigrants and Refugee Children
- Curriculum Adaptation with Immigrants and Refugee Children

## THEME 1: MULTICULTURAL EDUCATION FOR ALL

The current movement in favor of multiculturalism and multicultural education began after the Second World War. Due partly to the revelation of atrocities during that war, concern has increased for international human rights, to oppose racism and promote equal educational opportunity. Societies began to change through economic expansion, mass migration, refugees and greater economic co-operation. Awareness of other cultures has increased, alongside mass media coverage and rapid progress in international communications and global transport. Thus multicultural education has grown as an element in educational policy, provision and practice, and the meanings ascribed to it are varied and diverse.

Lynch (1986) distinguishes between five different but overlapping approaches under the umbrella heading 'multiculturalism in education'.

(1) **Intercultural Education**. Also termed **citizenship education**, this style has often aimed at immigrants and focused on the competencies and understandings necessary to adapt to the host country, while retaining home language and culture in case of a return to the country of origin. Such intercultural education is concerned with immigrant human rights and the avoidance of discrimination. This human rights accent concerns equality, freedom and partnership, with the ideal of friendly intercommunication between cultural and linguistic groups.

(2) **International and Multicultural Education**. This style includes **development education**, the interdependence of different global communities, environmental instruction and education in human rights, cultural diversity and peace. The intent is to develop a sense of world citizenship, cultivate empathy toward different cultures and creeds, and instigate concern for the welfare of all world citizens.

(3) **Multicultural Education**. This style engages whole school policy and provision in improving race relations, ensuring total curricular inclusion of multicultural perspectives, study of other languages, cultures and religions with a concern for equal educational opportunity and respect for cultural differences. This is distinguished from multi-ethnic education.

(4) **Multi-ethnic Education**. This style focuses on **ethnic minority studies** and the revitalization of ethnic minorities, but with a strong initiative to tackle all elements of schooling involved in providing equal opportunity for all racial and ethnic groups. There is concern for raising the expectations of ethnic minority children through curriculum, tracking, assessment, and parent community involvement. The aims include combating school racism, encouraging the recruitment and promotion of staff who promote, or can act as role models, in ethnic revitalization. Students become acculturated citizens of their own cultural or ethnic communities while also becoming cohesive members of their nation and the global community.

(5) **Anti-Racist Education**. The many visible signs of racism, its enduring, stubborn existence in spite of opposition, and its role as a rudimentary cause of social inequity and injustice have led some multicultural programs to a central focus on racial prejudice and discrimination.

Doubts have been expressed about the capacity of multicultural education to combat racism in schools and wider society. Therefore, some educators have argued for a more specific focus than 'multiculturalism' to confront individual racist acts and more covert institutional racist practices. While some multicultural education programs include racism, an anti-racist program goes further and deeper, sometimes becoming an alternative to multicultural education. Supporters of anti-racist programs argue that multicultural education often derives from dominant social class members who evade central issues of inequity of power, social dominance and subordination, marginalization and deprivation, and of internal colonialism, economic exploitation and linguistic and cultural assimilation (Bullivant, 1981; Nieto, 1996; May, 1994).

The argument is that multicultural education risks overemphasizing cultural, linguistic and ethnic identity and undervaluing the struggle for social, economic and political equality for language and cultural minorities. Multicultural education risks 'inserting' minorities into the dominant order and way of understanding. Anti-racist educators argue that multicultural education should center on changing and challenging hierarchies, class disadvantages and racism. It should engage life chances, not just life styles. An anti-racist or prejudice reduction program aims to tackle basic power and status issues, as well as racist behaviors among individuals, cultures and institutions.

## The Aims of Multicultural Education

The aims and assumptions of multicultural education rest on an underpinning of politics and ideology. The assumptions of multicultural education include the following points:

- All individuals and minority groups are fundamentally equal, regardless of language and culture.
- In a democracy, there should be equality of opportunity, regardless of ethnic, cultural or linguistic origin.
- Any manifest or latent discrimination by the dominant power group against minorities must be eliminated.
- A culturally diverse society should avoid racism and ethnocentrism.
- While generalizations about cultural behavior seem a natural part of understanding the world, cultural stereotypes must be avoided.
- Minority cultural groups need awareness of their culture as a precondition and foundation for building on intercultural awareness.
- In mainstream monocultural education, language minority parents are often excluded from participation in their children's education. In multicultural education, parents become partners.
- A pluralist integration is not a mosaic; it is established by interaction and intermingling, with discovery of others to improve mutual understanding, break down stereotypes and prejudice and increase self-knowledge and self-esteem.

## Multicultural Education for Whom?

**Minority language students** in 'submersion education', for example, are educated solely through the majority language. The added danger is that only the majority culture will be transmitted in the classroom, making minority language children less confident of their culture, community, home values and beliefs, even themselves. This is also true of students in Transitional Bilingual education where the majority language gradually supersedes the minority tongue in classroom teaching. Consequently, the heritage culture, at the least, is not well represented in the curriculum.

Minority language children in 'strong' forms of bilingual education, where their language has a permanent place and high status in the curriculum, need their culture to be strongly promoted in the classroom and all school activities. This is a valuable encouragement for participation in the heritage culture. **Bilingualism does not guarantee that a child will become bicultural**. Language skills do not guarantee continued adult use of the language; enculturation is essential if the language is to be useful and used.

**Majority culture students** also need multicultural and anti-racist teaching, to help them interact with immigrants, refugees and guest workers and feel comfortable and enriched when crossing cultural and national boundaries. If ethnically diverse populations are to co-exist within one nation, it is essential to promote awareness of and respect for diversity through education. A classroom response has been to initiate programs to develop sensitivity and sympathy, understanding and awareness of diverse cultural groups. Such programs are often considered relevant solely for students attending multiracial or ethnically mixed schools. However, they are no less relevant for students in areas where the majority culture predominates.

## Types of Multicultural Programs

In a 'weak' approach, classroom multicultural programs focus on beliefs, values, eating habits, cultural activities, dress and gestures (such as greeting and non-verbal reward systems) of varying ethnic groups. This **cultural artifact** education extends the individual's cultural vocabulary and grammar. Such an approach risks accenting cultural differences and emphasizing colorful and bizarre features. It may even reinforce and extend differences. A 'weak' form of multicultural education tends to divorce language from culture, paying little or no attention to minority home languages. Since language and culture are inseparable, and since merely using a language means imparting its culture, a stronger form of multicultural education requires attention to the minority language, which is part of its culture. This is sometimes attempted through Language Awareness programs, which aim to increase understanding, consciousness and sensitivity to the nature of language in everyday life.

The language aspects of multicultural education may be presented through videos, tape recordings and live performances, where the language and the culture are both presented in an authentic, inseparable way. Just as there is a danger of teaching a language without immersion in the attendant culture, so there is a danger of teaching about cultural diversity with sparse or no reference to the attendant languages.

In Europe, another variety or constituent of multicultural education is known as **citizenship education**. Curriculum content here sometimes intersects with the aims of multicultural and anti-racist education. However, it can also have assimilation aims. Butts (1980) suggested ten topics for citizenship education in the United States: justice, freedom, equality, diversity, authority, privacy, due process, participation, personal obligation for the public good, and international human rights. Most of these concepts parallel the multicultural aims of international understanding, equality, freedom and diversity. However, participation, authority and personal obligation for the public good may potentially be taught to achieve assimilation.

The aims of a 'stronger' form of multicultural program are partly based on arousing awareness of, and sensitivity to, cultural diversity. The educational basis of one relatively 'strong' form is that all cultures are attempts to discover meaning. No one culture, including the umbrella idea of Western culture, has a monopoly on understanding. There is value in the meanings of people in a subordinate position, such as language minorities. The voices of the poor are as meaningful as the privileged; the understandings of the oppressed are as valid as those of the oppressor.

When the educational basis of a multicultural program is discussed, **political implications** are present. In the United States, multicultural programs come under fire for being governed and manipulated from within a conservative education profession, as well as by textbook companies and local and state authorities (Olneck, 1993). As such, multicultural education seems to be contained and controlled by the powerful, posing little threat to academic, cultural or bureaucratic establishments. Multiculturalism in the United States is sometimes a key battlefield for reordering political relationships and power structures. It has become a mobilization watchword for people who wish to challenge ethnic inequalities and the establishment. For conservatives, multiculturalism represents conflict over which values and ideology should be dominant in the curriculum, whose traditions and perspectives should be transmitted to students. The hidden agenda of multiculturalism is sometimes perceived as self-determination and autonomy, rather than unity, the destabilization of society, rather than equality, tribalization and separation instead of plurality.

## Multiculturalism Across the Curriculum

Multicultural education may require a global **reappraisal of the whole curriculum**, with an analysis of the subtle use and perpetuation of majority, dominant culture in seemingly neutral subjects like science and mathematics. In textbook illustrations, in the teacher's prose and 'real life' problems to be solved, majority dominant culture may prevail and minority cultures be ignored. The more common examples of monoculturalism appear in the teaching of history and geography, literature and art, music and home economics, social studies and health education.

Mexican American children are taught United States history, but not Mexican history, the annexation of Mexican territory or the role of Mexican Americans in United States history. Not only do many Mexican Americans not know the history of their country of origin, they are often not taught how their ethnic group contributes to growth in the United States. Assimilation rather than awareness is the aim, dominance rather than diversity. The seeds of fear and ignorance that breed racism may be planted unintentionally by latently conveying a view of cultural inequality rather than celebrating ethnic identity and cultural diversity. As Olneck (1993, p. 248) states:

'Marginalized and subordinated groups are represented as voiceless objects, defined by their 'apartness' and difference from, or by their inferior relationship to, those more central. In curricular representations, it is alleged, the perspectives from which history and experience occur, the actors deemed central, and the experiences, cultural expressions, and projects deemed valid and valuable are all those of dominant groups.'

One curricular approach to multiculturalism is through **content**, showing that reason is not the monopoly of any single culture, and that understanding requires cultural interdependence. The 'discovery' of North America can be taught from the perspective of indigenous peoples as well as the invaders, the Crusades from both Muslim and Christian perspectives, and heresies from the viewpoint of both the orthodox and the heretics. In curriculum areas such as music and art, there can be a genuine celebration of diversity, with African, Caribbean, Asian and Latino music, Chinese and Japanese kites, Islamic and Egyptian calligraphy, African statuary and textiles. In curriculum areas such as nuclear physics, which systematically pursue a critical approach to understanding the world, some cultures have been more active than others, but the methods and approaches of different cultures may all be worthwhile, as is competition between differing and opposing ideas. Different cultures have used science to develop diverse knowledge and belief systems, as Young (1987, p. 19) argues:

'Science is practice. There is no other science than the science that gets done. The science that exists is the record of the questions that it has occurred to scientists to ask, the proposals that get funded, the paths that get pursued and the results which lead ... scientific journals and textbooks to publicize the work ... Nature 'answers' only the questions that get asked and pursued long enough to lead to results that enter the public domain. Whether or not they get asked, how far they get pursued, are matters for a given society, its educational system, its patronage system and its funding bodies.'

Profiling African and Asian scientists, learning about inventions from Africa and India and discovering the recent rapid changes in horticulture and forestry, soil science and social science in developing countries is an alternative to the danger of stereotyping the 'Third World' as rural and rudimentary, famished and inferior.

Alternative perspectives should not be included as an appendix to the mainstream view, isolating different perspectives and presenting a sanitized or expurgated version of history. Integrated, multiple perspectives must be presented, with the distinctive contributions of varied cultural groups justly represented, and the interdependence of diverse experience faithfully told. For a school, this means avoiding the curricular presentation of isolationist ideas, such as an exclusive North American or Eurocentric world view, and eschewing cultural supremacist viewpoints, such as apartheid. Isolationism and supremacist attitudes are sometimes taught in religious education, when a particular viewpoint prevails, say fundamentalist Christian or extreme Muslim, with alternative positions forbidden or other world religions presented as inferior.

Yet **religion** is a key element in multiculturalism. In Europe, religion has re-emerged as a key social issue in relationships between ethnic and language groups. With the settlement in Europe of eight to nine million immigrants from West and North West Africa, the Indian subcontinent and South East Asia, the mixing of Muslim, Buddhist, Hindu and Sikh with different Christian denominations has made religion crucial in debates about multiculturalism (Perotti, 1994).

Attempts to provide multicultural education are varied and diverse in aim, ideology, style and delivery. The term is broad and ambiguous. It ranges from awareness programs for majorities to classroom sharing of cultural experiences among a variety of ethnic groups. Multicultural education extends from formal classroom instruction to the informal, hidden, pastoral curriculum, each working toward mutual understanding and fighting against prejudice and racism. Dialogue may center on points of difference in dress and diet, language or religion or include lip-service to diversity through a superficial 'saris, samosas and steel bands' approach. At its worst, multicultural education may unintentionally reinforce and extend differences. It ranges from one weekly lesson to radical, global reconstruction of curriculum and school/community relations (Davidman & Davidman, 1994; Nieto, 1996). It covers a spectrum from occasional, token multicultural lessons to political movement for equality of opportunity and combat under-achievement, political awareness of rights, debates over social reconstruction and redress for the domination of language and cultural minorities.

### Further Reading

Davidman, L. and Davidman, P.T. (1994) *Teaching with a Multicultural Perspective: A Practical Guide*. New York: Longman.
Lynch, J. (1992) *Education for Citizenship in a Multicultural Society*. New York: Cassell.
Nieto, S. (1996) *Affirming Diversity: The Sociopolitical Context of Multicultural Education* (2nd edn). New York: Longman.

## THEME 2: ANTI-RACISM AND PREJUDICE REDUCTION IN SCHOOL

Anti-racism and prejudice reduction are often included in a 'strong' version of multicultural education, as will be considered later. However, there are multicultural programs and materials with no examination of racism or anti-racism. Students learn about other cultures and ethnic groups without confronting the racism that exists in their own ethnic groups. Such multicultural education stands accused of leaving the racist social fabric unaltered and failing to see racism as a causal need for multiculturalism. When the study of racism and anti-racism is missing from a multicultural program, the program can tranquilize anti-racist action, diverting resistance and confrontation into harmless channels.

A form of **anti-racist multiculturalism** is possible (Todd, 1991). Such a program must include analysis of the structural reasons, that is, the institutionalization of racism, social stratification, discriminatory governmental practices, why racism is perpetuated and not simply viewed as an individual attitude. Its proponents argue that sympathy is needed for the struggle to defeat racism, as well as for racism's victims, even when this means confrontation and non-violent direct action.

Language diversity in itself rarely causes poor race relations. While skin color, creed and language are the symbols of racism, its roots lie in fear and misunderstanding, and the unequal distribution of power and wealth. If schools are agents in the reproduction of social and economic differences, then schools may be perpetrators of racism. Multicultural education is therefore sometimes a way of raising consciousness in both the aggressor and the victim.

Even when bilingual education exists, there is a danger of focusing on two languages rather than on many cultures. Creating bilingual students may not be enough to reverse social inequities. Bilingual children may still be victims of racism, confined to subordinate status, unless the school system as a whole works to redress rather than reproduce inequalities.

> 'The crucial element in reversing language minority students' school failure is not the language of instruction but the extent to which educators work to reverse – rather than perpetuate – the subtle, and often not so subtle, institutionalized racism of the society as a whole. In other words, bilingual education becomes effective only when it becomes anti-racist education. Strong promotion of students' primary language can be an important component in empowering language minority students but it is certainly not sufficient in itself.' (Cummins, 1986, p. 11)

The extent of the **school influence** in combating racism and reducing prejudice is a debated point. The preconceptions and attitudes of children and teachers, of politicians and policy makers, the message of the hidden curriculum and formal curricular material may complicate the winning of hearts and minds. Racism is so widespread, brutal and ingrained in school and street that for some, training seems preferable to liberal education. Explicit racism may be combated in liberal education by conscious selection of teaching resources, pedagogical vocabulary, school organization and classroom grouping. Increased knowledge and understanding are desired outcomes. For some, a more direct, confrontational style is required. Through role-play, 'white' individuals may be confronted with their own racism and its consequences for others. Such role-play attempts to redress an inherent problem, that people who have never experienced racism cannot fully understand it.

A different, pessimistic viewpoint is that schools can do little to **reconstruct social power and racial relationships**. From this perspective, multicultural education is a token, patronizing exercise. An alternative, radical view holds that non-violent political activity is required among the victims of racism in school, particularly through extracurricular political activity. Such activity attempts to reconstruct the power, dominance and political relationships in society, seeking to eradicate prejudice, fear, victimization and racial violence.

Such a radical view indicates that multicultural and anti-racist education can be neither value-free nor politically neutral. It promotes equality of educational opportunity, the eradication of discrimination and racial dominance. It risks addressing only minorities without enlightening majorities. Multicultural education may be provided in areas where ethnic minorities live, but seen as irrelevant in many all-white, English-only schools.

---

### A Classification of Objectives in Prejudice-Reduction and Anti-Racist Education

## 1 Respect for Others

### 1.1 Cognitive (knowledge)
All students should know and understand:

- basic information on race and racial difference;
- the customs, values, beliefs and achievement of local community cultures, of their own ethnic groups, of their present country and the world;
- why different groups have immigrated and emigrated in the past, and the history of the present ethnic composition of the local community;
- the interdependence of world nations and cultures;
- the national and international context of human and civil rights.

### 1.2 Cognitive skills
All students should be able to:

- recognize racism and other forms of prejudice and discrimination;
- detect stereotyping and scapegoating and devise appropriate counter strategies;
- evaluate their own and other cultures objectively against agreed and explicit criteria.

### 1.3 Affective (attitudes, values and emotional sets)
All students should be taught:

- the unique value of each individual;
- the underlying humanity and essential core values shared by all democracies;
- the principles of equal rights and justice for all, and the value of the achievements of other cultures and nations;
- 'strangeness' without feeling threatened;
- that multicultural societies enjoy a long history, are a present reality, and a future certainty;
- that no culture is ever static, and that constant, mutual accommodation of all cultures, creating an evolving multicultural society, is customary;
- that prejudice and discrimination are as widespread as they are morally unacceptable, and that the historical social, political and economic causes which give rise to them should be examined;
- the damaging effects of prejudice and discrimination on all social groups;
- the process of multiple acculturation within a multicultural society, and the legitimacy of multiple loyalties within democratic society.

---

### A Classification of Objectives in
### Prejudice-Reduction and Anti-Racist Education (*cont.*)

## 2. Respect for Self

### 2.1 Cognitive (knowledge)
All students should know and understand:

- the history, values, distinctive features and achievement of their own culture;
- the values of their local community;
- the common values of the wider society.

### 2.2 Cognitive (skills)
All students should be able to:

- communicate competently in their mother tongue and in the majority language;
- be aware of different languages in the community, their present country and the world;
- relate creatively to members of other cultures;
- master the basic skills necessary for success at school and after;
- formulate criteria for judgement and action, compatible with the values of a multicultural society;
- analyze alternative value positions of different cultural groups;
- contribute to conflict resolution by persuasion and rational discourse.

### 2.3 Affective (attitudes, values and emotional sets)
All students should have developed:

- a positive self-image;
- confidence in the sense of their own identity;
- comfort with cultural diversity and willingness to learn from others;
- ease and pleasure in the company of people of other ethnic groups.

Adapted from: Cline, T. and Frederickson, N. (1991) *Bilingual Pupils and the National Curriculum: Overcoming Difficulties in Teaching and Learning*. London: University College London.

---

## THEME 3: IMMIGRANTS AND REFUGEE CHILDREN

Elizabeth Coelho (1994, 1998) provides sensitive advice regarding the transition of immigrant and refugee children into the classroom. A few of her wealth of procedures are listed below:

- Create welcome signs in the children's languages.
- Ensure the presence of a person or team to welcome the child and family to the school.
- Use an interpreter where possible, to facilitate transition. Interview parents

with the interpreter present, to provide basic information and begin a relationship with parents in a friendly and facilitative manner.

- Provide children with a welcome booklet of basic school information, in their own language. Include the day-to-day life, special events, role of parents.
- Encourage the home use of the first language and explain to the parents that first language development will help the child in acquisition of the majority language.
- Appoint friendly and sensitive children as official student ambassadors or student friends, to nurture newcomers and help them adjust.
- Funds should be available in the school to assist refugee and immigrant families with incidental expenses such as gym clothing or school uniforms, money for field trips and extra curriculum resources.
- Introduce newcomers positively, showing the country of origin with the aid of a world map, ensuring that all children learn to pronounce and spell new names. Make it clear the new child speaks a different language at home and is learning the majority language, avoiding the negative 'So-and-so doesn't speak English.' Display photographs of all the children to show they all belong equally to the classroom. Provide a resource corner for newcomers and ensure they understand via translation or paralinguistic language the daily activities and announcements. Communicate positive attitudes about the linguistic and cultural diversity of the classroom.
- A second (host) language program for adult learners, that encourages immigrant parents to attend, helps both parents and children. Such a program in the school can also provide information about the area and about survival and success in the new culture and employment system.
- Hire teaching and non-teaching personnel who speak the major languages of the school. They act as role models, linguistic and cultural interpreters, and inform other staff about the children's cultural backgrounds.
- Announce events in the different school languages, to spread information and raise the status of community languages.
- Select classroom and library materials with a multicultural and multiracial approach, as well as books in community languages.
- Establish heritage language programs, either in or out of school hours. Such programs promote self-esteem and cultural identity and build on first language skills.

## Further Reading

Coelho, E. (1994) Social integration of immigrant and refugee children. In F. Genesee (ed.) *Educating Second Language Children: The Whole Child, the Whole Curriculum, the Whole Community*. Cambridge: Cambridge University Press.

Coelho, E. (1998) *Teaching and Learning in Multicultural Schools*. Clevedon: Multilingual Matters.

## THEME 4: CURRICULUM ADAPTATION WITH IMMIGRANTS AND REFUGEE STUDENTS

Coelho (1994, 1998) also makes a wide variety of suggestions on taking into account the experiences, viewpoints and value systems of a variety of ethnic groups in adapting assessment and curricular content and delivery in the classroom.

- Curriculum content and materials should adapt to students' backgrounds and experiences. If materials such as reading books include concepts, lifestyles, cultural values and habits unfamiliar to the students, this will detract from learning. Unfamiliar content should appear gradually. Content should be relevant to students' real life experiences and positively depict people of all racial backgrounds and both genders.
- Differences and similarities should be highlighted and celebrated through discussion of themes such as 'Birthdays', 'Weddings' 'Coming of Age', to help children appreciate distinct and shared experiences of various cultures.
- The teacher should be aware of children's learning expectations. Newcomers from different cultures maybe unfamiliar with an approach that emphasizes student initiative and individual or group projects. They may expect guidance every step of the way. Student-centered learning should be introduced gradually.
- Classroom language should be modified to assist children not yet proficient in the language, especially with new, unfamiliar content. New content should not be introduced with new language.
- Group work and cooperative learning techniques produce student interaction and promote practice in the classroom language in smaller, less threatening groups.
- Methods of assessment should take into account that there are no tests that are equally appropriate for all cultures. If possible, tests should contain familiar tasks and content.

Coelho (1994) concludes:

'Immigrant and other language minority children come from many different backgrounds and bring with them a great variety of experience. They face a period of adjustment on entry to school systems where a new language is spoken; for some, this period is very stressful. During this period they need the support of their teachers and the acceptance of their peers. The school program itself is also required to change in order to reflect the presence of all the children in positive ways. Major initiatives in curriculum development, staff development, and community outreach have to be implemented in order to create an appropriate learning environment and home–school relationship.' (p. 325)

### Further Reading

Coelho, E. (1994) Social integration of immigrant and refugee children. In F. Genesee (ed.) *Educating Second Language Children: The Whole Child, the Whole Curriculum, the Whole Community*. Cambridge: Cambridge University Press.

Coelho, E. (1998) *Teaching and Learning in Multicultural Schools*. Clevedon: Multilingual Matters.

# Chapter 13

# The Politics Surrounding Bilingual Children

## INTRODUCTION

Bilingualism exists not only within individuals, their cognitive systems, families and local communities; it is also directly and indirectly woven into national politics. Bilingualism is not only studied linguistically, psychologically and sociologically; it is studied in relationship to power structures, political systems and basic social philosophies.

Bilingual education is not limited to educational preferences and curriculum decisions. It is surrounded and supported by basic beliefs about minority languages and cultures, immigrants, equality of opportunity, empowerment, affirmative action, individual rights and language minority group rights, assimilation and integration, desegregation and discrimination, pluralism and multiculturalism, diversity and discord, equality of recognition for minority groups and social cohesion. Education doubles as part of both the solution and problem of achieving unity in diversity.

Professionals should be aware of how their activity concerns bilingual children and fits into the overall language policy of a state or nation.

The themes of this chapter are:

- Language as a Problem, a Right and a Resource
- Assimilation of Language Minorities
- Integration and Language Minorities
- Cultural Pluralism

## THEME 1: LANGUAGE AS A PROBLEM, A RIGHT AND A RESOURCE

### Three Perspectives on Language

Ruiz (1984) suggests three basic orientations or perspectives about language: language as a problem, language as a right, and language as a resource. These three dispositions toward language planning are not necessarily at a conscious level; they may be embedded in subconscious assumptions of planners and politicians. Such orientations are fundamental, related to basic individual philosophy or ideology.

## Language as a Problem

Public discussion of bilingualism and languages in society often commences with perceived complications and difficulties caused by language. Discussions about the cognitive problems of operating in two languages illustrate this phenomenon well. Problems of bilingualism in individuals are not perceived as limited to thinking, but extended to personality and social problems, such as split identity, cultural disloca-tion, poor self-image and anomie. At a group level, bilingualism is sometimes connected with national or regional disunity and inter-group conflict. Thus, language becomes seen by some as a political problem.

'Language as problem' is based partly on the perception that perpetuating language minorities and diversity reduces integration and cohesiveness and increases social antagonism and conflict. The solution for the perceived complica-tion of minority languages is assimilation, since the majority language unifies diversity. The ability of every citizen to communicate with ease in the nation's majority language is regarded as the common leveler. Unity within a nation is seen as synonymous with uniformity and similarity, and a unified nation is a strong nation. The opposing argument, based on nations such as Singapore, Luxembourg and Switzerland, is that **national unity** is possible without uniformity; diversity and national unity can coexist.

The co-existence of languages rarely causes tension, or disunity. History suggests that economic, political and religious differences are prominent causes of war, but language seldom is. Religious crusades and jihads, rivalries between reli-gions and political parties or economic aggression spawn strife. Language, in and of itself, rarely causes unrest (Otheguy, 1982). In research on causes of conflict, Fishman (1989) found that language was not a cause. 'The widespread journalistic and popular political wisdom that linguistic heterogeneity *per se* is necessarily conducive to civil strife, has been shown, by our analysis, to be more myth than real-ity' (p. 622). Instead, deprivation, authoritarian regimes and modernization were found to lead to unrest.

A minority language is often linked with poverty, under-achievement in school, minimal social and vocational mobility, and a lack of integration with the majority culture. In this perspective, the minority language seems a partial cause of social, economic and educational problems, rather than their result. This 'language is the obstacle' attitude is summed up by the phrase, 'If only they would speak English, their problems would be solved.' The minority language becomes a handicap to be overcome by the schools. The increased teaching of the majority language, at the expense of home languages, seems to be a resolution of the problem, while devel-oping bilingualism is an irrelevant, or secondary and unimportant educational aim. Thus submersion and Transitional Bilingual education (see Glossary) aim to develop competent English language skills in minority children as quickly as possible, so they are on a par with anglophones in the mainstream classroom.

**'Strong' forms of bilingual education** are sometimes accused of causing language problems, or inspiring social unrest or disintegration, and that fostering minority languages and ethnic differences may provoke group conflict and disharmony. The general response is that 'strong' forms of bilingual education will lead instead to better integration, harmony and social peace. As Otheguy (1982, p. 314) comments, of the United States:

> 'Critics of bilingual education with a concern for civil order and social disharmony should also concern themselves with issues of poverty, unemployment and racial discrimination rather than concentrate on the use of Spanish in schools. In pledges of allegiance, it is liberty and justice – not English – for all that is to keep us indivisible.'

'Strong' forms of bilingual education should not be connected with the language-problem orientation. Indeed, evidence suggests that developing bilingualism and biliteracy within a 'strong' bilingual education is feasible and can promote:

- Higher achievement across the curriculum for minority language children.
- Maintenance of the home language and culture.
- Self-esteem, self-identity and a more positive attitude toward schooling.

These positive developments may encourage better human resource use and waste less talent, while higher self-esteem may also increase social harmony and peace.

Within the language-problem orientation, there exists the desire to remove differences between groups and achieve a common culture, but also the desire for intervention to improve the lot of language minorities.

> 'Whether the orientation is represented by malicious attitudes resolving to eradicate, invalidate, quarantine or inoculate, or comparatively benign ones concerned with remediation and 'improvement', the central activity remains that of problem-solving.' (Ruiz, 1984, p. 21)

### Language as a Right

Another orientation of language attitudes is thinking of language as a basic, human right. Just as there are individual rights in religious choice, so it is argued, there should be an individual right to language choice. People within this orientation argue for the eradication of language prejudice and discrimination in a democratic society (Skutnabb-Kangas & Phillipson, 1994).

Over time, and with a gradual growth in public acceptance, matters such as religious persecution and education develop moral force and a collective will that embeds religious and education rights in society. Increasingly, arguments for language rights have become stronger, more widespread and accepted.

Such language rights may be derived from **personal, legal and constitutional rights**. They draw on the right to freedom of individual expression. It may also be argued that there are certain natural or moral language rights in group, rather than individual, terms, based on the importance of preservation of heritage language and culture communities and expressed as 'rights to protection' and 'rights to participation'. This includes welfare rights and rights to liberty and self-determination.

A further level of language rights is international, derived from pronouncements from the United Nations, UNESCO, the Council of Europe and the European Community . Each of these organizations has declared the right of minorities to maintain their language. In directive 77/486/EEC, of July 25, 1977, the European Community announced that Member States should promote the teaching of the mother tongue and culture of the country of origin in the education of migrant workers' children. However, individual countries generally ignore such international declarations. Particular international examples, such as Sámi in Norway, Kurds in Turkey and Gikuyu speakers in Kenya are portrayed in Skutnabb-Kangas, Phillipson and Rannut (1994). Apart from language rights, minority groups may claim: protection, membership and separate existence of their ethnic group, non-discrimination and equal treatment, education and information in their ethnic language, freedom in worship, belief and movement, employment, peaceful assembly and association, political representation and involvement and administrative autonomy.

Individual rights constitute a major part of **democracy** in the United States. As Trueba (1989, p. 103) suggests, 'American democracy has traditionally attached a very high value to the right to disagree and debate, and to enjoy individual and group cultural and linguistic freedom without jeopardizing the right of others or our national unity.' Language rights are discussed in college classrooms and language communities, debated in government and federal legislatures, tested in courtrooms. This is significantly different from the European experience, where language rights have rarely been tried in court. From the early 1920s on, courts of law in the United States have continuously debated the legal status of language minority rights. Legal challenges have become an important part of the language rights movement, to gain short-term protection and a medium term guarantee for minority languages. The legal battles are not just couched in terms of minority versus majority language, but also concern children against schools, parents against school boards and states versus federal authority (Ruiz, 1984). Whereas activists among the Basques in Spain and the Welsh in Britain have been taken to court by the central government, in the United States, minority language activists have taken the central and regional governments to court.

A landmark in bilingual education was the 1970 lawsuit *Lau v. Nichols*, brought on behalf of Chinese students against the San Francisco School District. The case concerned whether non-English speaking students received equal educational opportunity, when instructed in a language they could not understand. Failure to provide bilingual education was alleged to violate both the equal protection clause of the 14th Amendment and Title VI of the 1964 Civil Rights Act. *Lau v. Nichols* was rejected by the federal district court and a court of appeals, but accepted by the

Supreme Court in 1974. The verdict outlawed English submersion programs and resulted in nationwide 'Lau remedies'. Such remedies reflected a broadening of the goals of bilingual education to include maintenance of minority language and culture. The Lau remedies created some expansion in the use of minority language programs in schools, although they rarely resulted in true heritage language, enrichment or maintenance programs. The Lau court case is representative of the dynamic, continuing contest to establish language rights in the United States, particularly through courtroom testing of laws (Casanova, 1991; Hakuta, 1986; Lyons, 1990).

Language rights are not only expressed in legal confrontations, with the chance of being legally established. They are often expressed at the **grass roots level** by protests and pressure groups, in local action and argument. Since 1982, the *Kohanga Reo* (language nests) movement in New Zealand has provided a grass roots instituted immersion pre-school for the Maori people. These 'language nests' offer a 'pre-school all-Maori language and culture environment for children from birth to school age, aimed at fostering complete development and growth within a context where only the Maori language is spoken and heard' (Corson, 1990, p. 154).

The recent Celtic resurgence in Ireland, Scotland, Wales and Brittany is another expression of 'language as right'. 'Grass roots' created pre-school playgroups, mother and toddler groups and adult language learning classes promote preservation of the heritage language in adult social interaction and especially with the young. Stronger activism and more insistent demands have led to the establishment of heritage language elementary schools, particularly in urban, mostly majority language areas. Not without struggle, opposition and antagonistic bureaucracy, parents have obtained the right of education in the indigenous tongue. Such pressure groups have included native Celtic speakers and majority language only speakers who wish their children to be taught in the heritage language of the area.

In North American and British society, no formal political or legal recognition is usually made of categories of people based on their culture, language or race. Instead, the focus is on individual rights, equality of opportunity, merit-based rewards. Policies of non-discrimination tend to be based on individual, rather than group rights. Language minority groups argue for rewards and justice based on their existence as a definable group in society. Sometimes basing their arguments on territorial rights or ethnic identity, such groups militate for rewards in proportion to their representation in society. Group based rights are often regarded as a way to redress injustices to minorities. This may be a temporary step on the way to full individual rights. Alternatively, language minorities may claim the right to some measure of individual power, decision-making and self-determination.

A note of caution must be sounded about language rights; the cause can hide preferences for coercion and conformity (Skutnabb-Kangas, 1991). Stubbs (1991) talks of government reports in England, dealing with language minorities, reports which:

'use a rhetoric of language entitlement and language rights, and of freedom and democracy ... [which] makes the correct moral noises, but it has no legislative basis, and is therefore empty. There is talk of entitlement, but not of the discrimination which many children face; and talk of equality of opportunity, but not of equality of outcome' (pp. 220–221).

The implementation of language rights depends upon public education, consciousness raising and collective will. There is a risk of seeking conformity, rather than conviction. While rights provide a valuable part of the official sanctioning of minority languages, rights do not, in themselves, mean increased language life. Language rights may extend the potential range of language functions, but retention or use of a language, once learned, cannot be legally required. Winning hearts and minds, fostering positive attitudes about a language, must join rights. At the worst, language rights may compel; at the best, rights help legitimize and institutionalize a minority language. Rights may empower a language; personal empowerment requires many other supports and rewards.

## Language as a Resource

Another orientation toward language is to see it as a personal and national resource, as in the recent movement in Britain and North America for increased second and foreign language fluency. Under the general heading of 'language as a resource' also comes a view of minority and less used languages as cultural and social resources. While people may see languages in terms of potential for building economic bridges, languages also build social bridges across different groups and promote cultural cross-fertilization.

The recent trend in the West is to expand foreign language education. Second languages are viewed as an essential resource to **promote foreign trade** and world influence. Paradoxically, while bilingual education to support minority languages is often depreciated in the United States, English speakers are appreciated for learning a second language to ensure the major role of the United States in world politics and economy. The acquisition of languages is valued, while the language minority speakers of those languages are devalued. While integration and assimilation is still the dominant ideology in internal American politics, external politics increasingly demand bilingual citizens (Kjolseth, 1983). Ovando (1990) describes the language policy of the United States as schizophrenic.

'On the one hand, we encourage and promote the study of foreign languages for English monolinguals, at great cost and with great inefficiency. At the same time, we destroy the linguistic gifts that children from non-English language backgrounds bring to our schools.' (p. 354)

In the United States, 'language as resource' refers not only to the development of a second language in monolingual speakers, it also refers to the preservation of languages other than English. Children whose home language is Spanish, German, Italian, Chinese, Greek, Japanese, Portuguese or French have a practical resource. Spanish speakers in the United States make that country the fourth largest Spanish speaking nation in the world. Water in the reservoir, oil in the oil fields, basic resources and commodities are preserved. A language such as Spanish, despite being difficult to measure and define as a resource, may be preserved for the common economic, social and cultural good. Suppression of language minorities, particularly by school systems, is economic, social and cultural wastage. Such languages are natural resources, to be exploited for cultural, spiritual and educational growth, as well as for economic, commercial and political gain.

Within the 'language as resource' orientation lies the assumption that linguistic diversity does not cause social separation nor prevent integration. National unity and linguistic diversity can co-exist; they are not necessarily incompatible. Tolerance and co-operation between groups may be as possible with linguistic diversity as they are unlikely when such diversity is repressed.

Which languages are resources? The favored languages tend to be both international and valuable in international trade. A lower status is given to small, regional minority languages and those perceived to be less valuable in the international marketplace. In England, French has traditionally been placed at the top of the first division in schools. German, Spanish, Danish, Dutch, Modern Greek, Italian and Portuguese are major European languages placed in the second division. Despite large numbers of mother tongue Bengali, Panjabi, Urdu, Gujarati, Hindi and Turkish speakers, the politics of English education relegates these languages to a very low position in the school curriculum. In the British National Curriculum, the listed languages (Arabic, Bengali, Cantonese or Mandarin Chinese, Gujarati, Modern Hebrew, Hindi, Japanese, Panjabi, Russian, Turkish and Urdu) were initially only allowed in secondary school, for 11- to 18-year-olds, if a higher division language, such as French, is first taught. Thus a caste system of languages prevails in Britain. The system is Eurocentric, culturally discriminatory, and economically short sighted, 'allowing languages already spoken in the home and community to be eroded, whilst starting from scratch to teach other languages in schools and colleges' (Stubbs, 1991, p. 225).

To conclude, while the three orientations have differences, they also share certain common aims: national unity, individual rights, the importance of majority language fluency in economic opportunities. The basic difference seems to be whether majority language monolingualism or full bilingualism should be encouraged as a means of achieving those ends. All three orientations connect language with politics, economics, society and culture. Each recognizes language as not simply a means of communication but also as connected with socialization in the local and wider community and as a powerful symbol of heritage and identity. The differences between the three orientations lie in the socialization and identity to be fostered, assimilation or pluralism, integration or separatism, monoculturalism or multiculturalism.

### Further Reading

Crawford, J. (1999) *Bilingual Education: History, Politics, Theory and Practice*. Los Angeles: Bilingual Educational Services.

Ruiz, R. (1984) Orientations in language planning. *NABE Journal* 8 (2), 15–34.

Skutnabb-Kangas, T., Phillipson, R. and Rannut, M. (eds) (1994) *Linguistic Human Rights*. New York: Mouton de Gruyter.

## THEME 2: THE ASSIMILATION OF LANGUAGE MINORITIES

### Introduction

The social and political questions surrounding bilingualism and bilingual education tend to revolve around two contrasting ideological positions.

> 'At one extreme is assimilation, the belief that cultural groups should give up their 'heritage' cultures and take on the host society's way of life. At the opposite pole is multiculturalism, the view that these groups should maintain their heritage cultures as possible.' (Taylor, 1991, p. 1)

Between these two extremes, lie many 'middle ground' viewpoints: pluralistic integration, participationist pluralism, modified pluralism, liberal pluralism, multivariate assimilation, social accommodation, integrationism and others (see John Edwards, 1994). Even the two extremes hide many different dimensions, such as racism, inter-culturalism, different conceptions of citizenship, identity, individualism, and collectivity (see below and in the multicultural education topic, p. ###).

Zangwill's play, *The Melting Pot* (1908), introduced the idea of diverse immigrant elements merging to make a new homogenized whole, the key image for **assimilationism**. The melting pot idea immediately raises two different perspectives.

First is the idea that the final product results from all the cultural groups in the pot. No one ingredient dominates in the unique combination, where each group contributes to the final taste. However, this is not the usual association with this image. In the second perspective, cultural groups in the melting pot give up their heritage and adopt the host culture, conforming to the dominant national norms.

The rationale for this assimilationist perspective is that equality of opportunity, meritocracy and the individual potential for economic prosperity due to personal effort are each incompatible with the separate existence of different racial and cultural groups. When the emphasis is on individual rights, freedom, effort and affluence, the argument for assimilation is that groups should not have separate rights and privileges from the rest of society. Advantage and disadvantage associated with language minority groups are to be avoided, so individual equality of opportunity can reign.

The umbrella term 'assimilationist ideology' shelters a **variety of types of assimilation**: cultural, structural, marital, identificational, attitudinal, behavioral, social and civic (Gordon, 1964). The distinction between economic-structural assimilation and cultural assimilation is important (Skutnabb-Kangas, 1977). Some immigrant and minority individuals may wish to assimilate into the cultural mainstream, other language minorities may wish to avoid it. However, economic-structural assimilation may be sought by language minorities, in the case of equality of access, opportunity, and treatment (Paulston, 1992). Equal access to jobs, goods and services, in voting rights and privileges, equal educational opportunities and treatment, health care and social security, law and protection may be desired by language minorities. Therefore, structural incorporation tends to be more desired and cultural assimilation more resisted (Schermerhorn, 1970; Paulston, 1992).

Assimilation may be explicit, implicit or concealed (Tosi, 1988). **Explicit assimilation** occurs when language minority children are required to be educated solely in the majority language, as with submersion education in the United States. **Implied assimilation** occurs when such children are diagnosed with 'special needs' and offered compensatory forms of education, such as Sheltered English and Transitional bilingual education in the United States. **Concealed assimilation** may be found in some multicultural education programs where language minorities are instructed in racial harmony, national unity and individual achievement, using majority language criteria to gauge success. Such programs are designed to achieve hegemony and ethnic harmony.

Since assimilation appears in a variety of forms, measuring the extent of its occurrence is difficult. Is it measured by segregation and integration, in terms of housing for immigrants, by their position within the economic order, by the extent of intermarriage between different cultural groups or by the attitudes they exhibit? Assimilation is multidimensional and complex, neither defined nor quantified easily.

Assimilationists may have mildly differing views. A few may accept that students should maintain their home languages and cultures, while arguing this to be the responsibility of the home, not the school. Most will maintain that bilingual programs are low priority when resources are scarce and school budgets are stretched, particularly if program costs exceed regular mainstream programs.

Since the 1960s, with an increased accent on ethnicity, assimilation assumptions have been challenged, and 'new ethnicity' born. Ideologies surrounding the terms 'integration', 'ethnic diversity', 'pluralism' and 'multiculturalism' challenge assimilationist philosophy. More recently, the debate over assimilation and pluralism has sharpened. A re-emphasis on personal endeavor, individual success, less reliance on welfare and collectives (that is, positive discrimination for ethnic groups), has been joined by ethnic conflicts in Bosnia, Croatia, Serbia and Russia. Increased arguments and disputes over the merits of assimilation and pluralism have resulted (Takaki, 1993).

## Assimilation and Immigrants

The expectation was that immigrants to the United States, Canada and Great Britain would be pleased to escape political oppression or economic disadvantage and jubilant to embrace equality of opportunity and personal freedom. Individuals would happily relinquish the past and commit to a new national identity. Yet heritage cultures and identities have persisted, resisted and insisted. Assimilation has often failed. Is this deliberate or difficult, desired or not?

Immigrants may seek assimilation, but find themselves in segregated neighborhoods and schools, prevented by social and economic factors outside their own wishes. Some immigrant groups may wish to be classified as citizens of the United States, but are categorized and treated as different, separate and non-American by the mainstream society. Living conditions may create the negative labels and social barriers to integration. As Otheguy remarks of the United States, 'Because of their experience with racism in this country, many Hispanics have long ago given up hope of disappearing as a distinct group' (1982, p. 312). The result may be the prevention of assimilation and integration, with a consequent need to embrace some form of multiculturalism for survival, security, status, and self-enhancement.

### Further Reading

Crawford, J. (1999) *Bilingual Education: History, Politics, Theory and Practice*. Los Angeles: Bilingual Educational Services.

Dicker, S.J. (1996) *Languages in America: A Pluralist View*. Clevedon: Multilingual Matters.

Paulston, C.B. (1994) *Linguistic Minorities in Multilingual Settings*. Amsterdam/Philadelphia: John Benjamins.

## THEME 3: INTEGRATION AND LANGUAGE MINORITIES

A distinction between language minority assimilation and integration is valuable. As the word suggests, **assimilation** is about becoming similar or the same. In this sense, an assimilated minority language speaker will become similar to majority speakers through socialization practices of schools and the mass media.

The **distinction between cultural assimilation and structural integration** is also important. Often, immigrant groups are expected to acquire a cultural similarity to majority residents but not allowed structural integration, in economic and social terms, because of racism, unequal opportunity, and the reproduction of advantages by privileged groups in society.

In contrast to assimilation, **integration** refers to situations where ethnic groups are able to remain distinct and establish boundaries with the majority, while having relatively equal access to employment, affluence, power and self-promotion. In integration, an ethnic group is able to maintain its separate vitality while having equal opportunity in the political, economic, social and educational systems. Such integration allows language minority individuals to become as empowered, employed and effective members of society as majority language speakers.

If assimilation is symbolized by the '**melting pot**', where individuals from different ethnic groups and languages are melted down by the socialization process to produce a homogeneous people, integration is a **salad bowl**, where each ingredient, separate and distinguishable, is no less valuable than another. The final taste is more than the simple sum of the individual parts. Canada uses yet another metaphor, the concept of an **ethnic mosaic**, of different pieces of society, Quebecois, native Indian language communities, English speakers and newer immigrant language groups, joined in one overall political and economic arrangement.

Assimilation aims to shape everyone into the same characteristics. Integration affirms the value of societal diversity, with equal opportunity in a mutually tolerant and respectful atmosphere. Assimilation absorbs one culture and language into another. Integration retains ethnic, cultural and linguistic differences and celebrates variety for the common good.

Integration tends to be an aim and an ideal, with reality falling below that ideal; it implies cultural pluralism and equality of cultures and languages within society.

The ideal is cohesion between different language minority groups. The reality is often competition and occasionally conflict. A mutual respect for ethnic, cultural and linguistic differences is an important aim, rarely achieved in a stable way in society. Such integration is often identified with Belgium, Canada and Switzerland, where cultural differences are protected and some equality in distribution of resources is attempted.

Integration at one level implies peaceful co-existence. At a higher level it implies active participation of language minority groups with the majority group inside a stable framework that allocates fairly power, privileges, rights, goods and services.

### Further Reading

Crawford, J. (1999) *Bilingual Education: History, Politics, Theory and Practice*. Los Angeles: Bilingual Educational Services.

Dicker, S.J. (1996) *Language in America: A Pluralist View*. Clevedon: Multilingual Matters.

Ghuman, P.A.S. (1994) *Coping with Two Cultures: British Asian and Indo-Canadian Adolescents*. Clevedon: Multilingual Matters.

## THEME 4: CULTURAL PLURALISM

### Introduction

At the heart of the assimilationist ideology is the belief that an effective, harmonious society can be achieved only if minority groups are absorbed into mainstream society. Harmony and equal opportunity depend on a shared language and culture. At the other end of the spectrum are cultural pluralism and multiculturalism, embracing the ideal of equal, harmonious, mutually tolerant existence of diverse languages and religious, cultural and ethnic groups in society. A cultural pluralist viewpoint is partly based on the idea that individuals can hold two or more cultural identities, Ukrainian and Canadian, Chinese and Malaysian, Cuban or Puerto Rican or Mexican and North American. In a different sense, it is possible to be a Ukrainian-Canadian, a Chinese-Malaysian or a Cuban-North American; identities are merged and the parts become a new whole. A redefined ethnicity creates a person who is not a replica of a Cuban in Cuba, nor a stereotypical 'white' North American, but an integrated combination of parts of both.

### The Nature of Cultural Pluralism

'**Multiculturalism**' is used in a broad, sometimes vague, manner, but tends to include the following basic beliefs:

- Two languages and cultures provide dual or multiple perspectives in society.
- People who speak more than one language and own more than one culture are more sensitive and sympathetic, more likely to build bridges than barricades and boundaries.
- Whereas assimilation produces a subtractive situation, multiculturalism is additive.
- Ideally, a multicultural person has more respect for other people and cultures

than monocultural people who are stereotypically more insular and culturally introspective.

- Assimilation leads ethnic minorities to adopt a positive attitude toward the majority culture and a negative attitude toward their own heritage.
- Pluralism and multiculturalism may lead to a positive attitude, not only toward the host and heritage cultures, but to the equal validity of all cultures.
- Multiculturalism promotes empathy and sensitivity and helps eradicate prejudice and racism.

## Cultural Pluralism versus Assimilation

In England and the United States, movements toward language and cultural pluralism have seldom received official blessing or encouragement. The assimilationist viewpoint has continued, while in parts of Canada, Scandinavia and New Zealand, in contrast, a more multicultural approach has been taken, although with much dispute and debate.

The difference between assimilationists and multiculturalists is rooted in basic human needs and motives, and is affected by the economic reward system. Both assimilation and heritage cultural maintenance can be promoted by the need to earn a living and the desire for affluence. Assimilation may help secure a job or vocational success, abandoning the minority language and culture in order to prosper in the mainstream. At the same time, language planning can ensure jobs and promotion within the minority community.

The dominant social group may sometimes prefer heritage cultural maintenance to assimilation. Minority groups may not be permitted to assimilate, thus exploiting their members through poorly paid employment by the dominant group. The economic interests of the majority can be served by internal colonialism, instead of assimilation, while economic motives and decisions occur without reference to heritage language and culture.

Fluency in the majority tongue is often an economic necessity, thus promoting assimilation, since people must function in it to find work and compete with members of the majority. Bilinguals may also perceive the possibility of functioning economically in both language communities, of being economically viable in either and forking a bridge between their communities. However, becoming bilingual through learning the majority language is no guarantee of economic improvement. Otheguy (1982, p. 306) provides a warning from experience in the United States.

'English monolingualism has meant little in terms of economic advantages to most blacks and to the masses of poor descendants of poor European immigrants. Hispanics who now speak only English can often be found in as poor a state as when they first came. English monolingualism among immigrants tends to follow economic integration rather than cause it.'

Between these two opposing views, intermediate positions are tenable. It is possible to participate in mainstream society and maintain heritage language and culture. For many individuals, there will be both a degree of assimilation and heritage preservation. Total assimilation or isolation is less likely than some maintenance within partial assimilation. Within multiculturalism and pluralism, an aggressive, militant pluralism may be seen as a threat to social harmony. A more liberal pluralistic viewpoint allows membership in the wider community as well as identification with the heritage cultural community.

Research is unlikely to resolve this debate. While research may inform and refine opinions, the ideologies of assimilation and pluralism differ so fundamentally that simple solutions are impossible. When evidence for the maintenance of heritage languages and cultures is produced, assimilationists argue that attitudes and behavior are still changing, and that, over time, people will move away from heritage cultural maintenance and prefer majority language and cultures. Assimilationists tend to believe that bilingualism and biculturalism are temporary and lead to a preferable, unifying monolingualism. When evidence, after the second or third generation after immigration, favors assimilation having taken place in society, multiculturalists will argue in two different ways, that the change has only occurred on certain dimensions (language rather than economic assimilation) and that sometimes the wheel turns full circle. Revival and resurrection in futures generations may respond to repression and renunciation by their forebears.

## Further Reading

Delgado-Gaitan, C. and Trueba, H.H. (1991) *Crossing Cultural Borders: Education for Immigrant Families in America*. New York: Falmer.
McKay, S.L. and Wong, S.C. (eds) (1988) *Language Diversity: Problem or Resource?* New York: Newbury House.
Nieto, S. (1996) *Affirming Diversity: The Sociopolitical Context of Multicultural Education* (2nd edn). New York: Longman.

# Glossary

**Acculturation:** The process by which an individual or group adapt to a new culture.

**Active Language:** The production of language in speaking and writing. This is distinguished from passive language which refers to listening, understanding and reading. The distinction between productive and receptive language is the same.

**Active Vocabulary:** This refers to the actual number of words that people use as opposed to a passive vocabulary which is words they understand. Native language speakers often have an active vocabulary of between 30,000 and 50,000 words. Their passive vocabulary may extend up to 100,000 words or more. In foreign language learning, reasonable proficiency is achieved when someone attains an active vocabulary of between 3000 and 5000 words with a passive vocabulary of up to 10,000 words.

**Additive Bilingualism:** A situation where a second language is learnt by an individual or a group without detracting from the maintenance and development of the first language. A situation where a second language adds to, rather than replaces the first language. This is the opposite of subtractive bilingualism.

**Affective Filter:** Associated with Krashen's Monitor Model of second language learning, the affective filter is a metaphor which describes a learner's attitudes that affect the relative success of second language acquisition. Negative feelings such as a lack of motivation, lack of self-confidence and learning anxiety are like a filter which hinders and obstructs language learning.

**Agraphia:** Difficulty in writing, connected with Aphasia.

**Alexia:** Difficulty in reading, connected with Aphasia.

**Anomie:** A feeling of disorientation and rootlessness, for example in in-migrant groups. A feeling of uncertainty or dissatisfaction in relationships between an individual learning a language and the language group with which they are trying to integrate.

**Aphasia:** Damage to the brain which causes a loss of ability to use and understand language. This may be partial or total and affect spoken and/or written language.

**Artificial Language:** (1) A language invented as a means of international communication (e.g. Esperanto, Ido). (2) A system of communication created for a specific purpose (e.g. computer language).

**Assimilation:** The process by which a person or language group lose their own language and culture which are replaced by a different language and culture.

**Authentic Texts:** Texts taken from newspapers, magazines, tapes of natural speech from radio and television. They are not created by the teacher but already exist in the world outside the classroom.

**Autochthonous Languages:** A term particularly used in Europe to describe indigenous languages or languages resident for a considerable length of time in a territory or region.

**Autonomous Variety of Language:** A standard language that has its own established norms, as opposed to a heteronomous variety. See 'heteronomous variety'.

**Auxiliary Language:** (1) A language used as a means of communication between different language groups. See also lingua franca, pidgin, language of wider communication. (2) An artificial language invented as a means of communication between different language groups.

**Back Translation:** A translation is translated back into the original to assess the accuracy of the first translation.

**Balanced Bilingualism:** Approximately equal competence in two languages.

**Basal Readers:** Reading texts that use simplified vocabulary and grammar, carefully graded and structured.

**BEA:** Bilingual Education Act (United States legislation: part of ESEA – see below).

**BICS:** Basic Interpersonal Communicative Skills. Everyday, straightforward communication skills that are helped by contextual supports.

**Bicultural:** Identifying with the culture of two different language groups. To be bilingual is not necessarily the same as being bicultural.

**Biliteracy:** Reading and writing in two languages.

**Black English:** The variety of English spoken by some black people in the United States, for example in cities such as New York, and Chicago. Black English is regarded as a language variety in its own right with its own structure and system. It is not regarded in any way as a second class variety of English.

**Borrowing:** A word or a phrase from one language that has become established in use in another language. When borrowing is a single word, it is often called a loan word.

**BSM:** Bilingual Syntax Measure (attempts to establish the dominant language of a bilingual).

**CABE:** California Association for Bilingual Education.

**CALL:** Computer Assisted Language Learning.

**CALP:** Cognitive/Academic Language Proficiency. The level of language required to understand academically demanding subject matter in a classroom. Such language is often abstract, without contextual supports such as gestures and the viewing of objects.

**Caretaker Speech:** A simplified language used by parents to children to ensure understanding, also called Motherese. Caretaker Speech usually has short sentences, is grammatically simple, has few difficult words and much repetition with clear pronunciation. Caretaker speech is also used by teachers with children in Immersion classrooms.

**Circumstantial Bilingual:** Someone who, by force of circumstances, becomes a bilingual.

**Classroom Discourse:** A special type of language used in the classroom. Such language is governed by the different roles that students and teachers assume and the kind of activities that occur in classrooms. The kind of 'open' (many different answers possible) or 'closed' questions (only one or a few correct answers possible) that teachers ask is one particular area of interest in Classroom Discourse.

**Cloze Procedure:** A technique for measuring students' reading comprehension. In a Cloze test, words are removed from a reading passage at specific intervals, and students have to fill in the blanks. The missing words are guessed from the context.

**Code:** A neutral term used instead of language or speech or dialect.

**Codemixing:** The mixing of two languages within a sentence or across sentences.

**Codeswitching:** Moving from one language to another, inside a sentence or across sentences.

**Codification:** A systematic description of a variety of a language (e.g. vocabulary, grammar). This may occur when a language is being standardized, or when an oral language is being written down for the first time.

**Cognate:** A language or linguistic form, historically derived from the same source as another (e.g. French, Catalan and Spanish are cognate languages derived from Latin).

**Cognition:** The acquisition, storage, retrieval and use of knowledge. Mental processes of perception, memory, thinking, reasoning and language.

**Cognitive/Academic Language Proficiency (CALP):** The level of second language proficiency needed by students to perform the more abstract and cognitively demanding tasks of a classroom. Little support is offered in many classrooms from the context. CALP is distinguished from Basic Interpersonal Communication Skills (BICS), that are relatively undemanding cognitively and rely on the context to aid understanding.

**Common Underlying Proficiency (CUP):** Two languages working integratively in the thinking system. Each language serves one underlying, central thinking system.

**Communal Lessons:** Lessons in which students of different first languages are mixed for common activities, such as working on projects, doing art or physical education. The European Hours in the European Schools are Communal Lessons.

**Communicative Approach:** A second language teaching approach that accents the acquisition of a language by use in everyday communicative situations.

**Communicative Competence:** Proficiency in the use of a language in everyday conversations. This term accents being understood rather than being 'correct' in using a language. Not only knowing the grammar and vocabulary of a language, but also knowing the social and culturally appropriate uses of a language.

**Community Language:** A language used by a particular community or in a particular area, often referring to ethnic minority groups. The term has been used in Britain to refer to the language of Asian and European groups which are resident in particular areas.

**Community Language Learning:** A second language teaching methodology based on Rogerian counseling techniques and responding to the needs of the learner 'community'.

**Competence in Language:** A person's ability to create and understand language. This goes further than an understanding of vocabulary and grammar requiring the listener to understand sentences not heard before. The term is often used in association with Chomsky's theory of transformational grammar, describing a person's internalized grammar of the language, which enables the person to create new sentences and interpret sentences never heard before. Competence is often used to describe an idealized speaker/hearer with a complete knowledge of the whole language, and is distinguished from performance which is the actual use of the language by individuals.

**Compound Bilingualism:** One language is learnt at the same time as another, often in the same contexts. Therefore, the representation in the brain was thought to be fused and interdependent.

**Comprehensible Input:** Language delivered at a level understood by a learner.

**Consecutive Bilingualism:** see Simultaneous Bilingualism

**Content-Based Instruction:** A term particularly used in the United States. Such a program teaches students the language skills they will need in mainstream classrooms. The focus is on the language skills needed for content areas such as mathematics, geography, social studies and science.

**Content Reading:** The reading of books to learn particular curriculum areas as separate from reading for enjoyment only.

**Context:** The setting in which communication occurs, and which places possibilities and constraints on what is said, and how it is said. The context can refer to the physical setting or to the language context in which a word or utterance occurs.

**Context-Embedded Language:** Communication occurring in a context that offers help to comprehension (e.g. visual clues, gestures, expressions, specific location). Language where there are plenty of shared understandings and where meaning is relatively obvious due to help from the physical or social nature of the conversation.

**Context-Reduced Language:** Language where there are few clues as to the meaning of the communication apart from the words themselves. The language is likely to be abstract.

**Contrastive Analysis:** The comparison of the linguistic systems of two languages.

**Co-ordinate Bilingualism:** Two languages learnt in different and separate environments. The two languages were therefore thought to be independent (e.g. in representation in the brain).

**Core Language Class:** Teaching the language as a subject. Used mostly to describe foreign language instruction.

**Corpus Language Planning:** Language planning which centers on linguistic aspects of language, vocabulary and grammar for example, to try and ensure a normative or standardized system of language within an area. See also Language Planning.

**Creole:** A pidgin language which has been adopted as the native language in a region. A creole tends to be more complex in grammar with a wider range of vocabulary than a pidgin language. There are for example, English-based, French-based Creoles.

**Creolization:** The process by which a pidgin becomes a creole by the expansion of vocabulary and the development of a more complex linguistic structure.

**Criterion-Referenced Testing:** A form of educational assessment which compares students in terms of their mastery of a subject as opposed to a norm-referenced test where a student is compared with other students. A criterion-referenced test in language requires a clear specification of the structure of the language to be learnt.

**Critical Period Hypothesis:** A genetically determined period of child development when learning must take place, otherwise it will not be learned later. In language, this is a largely discredited theory that a child best learns a first or second language between birth and up to about 13 years of age.

**Cultural Pluralism:** The ownership of two or more sets of cultural beliefs, values and attitudes. Multicultural education is often designed to encourage cultural pluralism in children.

**Culture:** The set of meanings, beliefs, attitudes, customs, everyday behavior and social understandings of a particular group, community or society.

**Culture Shock:** Feelings of disorientation, anxiety or insecurity some people experience when entering a different culture. For example when people move to a foreign country there may be a period of culture shock until they become more familiar with their new culture.

**CUP:** See Common Underlying Proficiency.

**DBE:** Developmental Bilingual Education: Also known as Two-Way Dual Language Programs and Two-Way Bilingual/Immersion Programs. Two languages are used for approximately equal time in the curriculum.

**Dead Language:** (1) A form of language that is no longer used as a medium of communication in society. Its speakers have died or have shifted to using another language. (2) The term is used inaccurately to describe a language that has evolved into a distinct new variety or varieties. For example, through a process of historical change and development, Latin is described as a 'dead language', but it did not die but evolved into different Romance languages.

**Decoding:** In learning to read, decoding is the deciphering of the sounds and meanings of letters, combinations of letters, whole words and sentences of text. Sometimes decoding refers only to being able to read a text without necessarily understanding the meaning of that text.

**Decreolization:** The process by which a creole becomes closer in its form to the base language from which it derived much of its grammar and vocabulary. During this process, many varieties develop at various distances from the base language. Among the recognized varieties are the acrolect (closest to the standard, prestige variety), the basilect (furthest from the standard, base language) and the mesolect (intermediate between acrolect and basilect). These varieties form what is known as a post-creole continuum.

**Deficit Model:** The idea that some children have a deficiency in their language – in vocabulary, grammar or understanding, particularly in the classroom. The child has a perceived language 'deficit' that has to be compensated for by remedial schooling or compensatory education. The problem is seen to be located in the child rather than in the school system or society or in the ideology of the perceiver. The opposite is an enrichment model (see Enrichment Bilingual Education).

**Diagonal Bilingualism:** Situations where a 'non-standard' language or a dialect co-exists with an unrelated 'standard' language.

**Dialect:** A language variety whose features identify the regional or social background of the user. The term is often used in relation to a standard variety of a language (e.g. a dialect of English).

**Dialect Continuum:** A chain of dialects spoken in a geographical area. Mutual intelligibility is often high between dialects in close proximity and low between geographically distant dialects.

**Diglossia:** Two languages or language varieties existing together in a society in a stable arrangement through different uses attached to each language.

**Discourse:** A term used to describe relatively large chunks of conversation or written text. Rather than highlighting vocabulary or grammar, discourse extends into understandings and meanings of conversation or written text.

**Discourse Analysis:** The study of spoken and written language particularly in terms of negotiated meanings between participants in speech, choice of linguistic forms, shared assumptions that underlie utterances, structures, strategies and symbolism in communicating, and the role relationships between participants.

**Disembedded Thinking:** Thinking that is not allied to a meaningful context but is treated as a separate, distinct task with little relevance in itself.

**Distance Learning:** Independent learning outside the classroom, by telephone, satellite, distance learning packages, for example.

**Divergent Thinking:** Thinking that is original, imaginative and creative. A preference for open-ended, multiple answers to questions.

**DL:** Dual Language (School).

**Domain:** Particular contexts where a certain language is used. For example, there is the family domain where a minority language may be used. In the work domain, the majority language may be used.

**Dominant Language:** The language which a person has greater proficiency in or uses more often.

**Double Immersion:** Schooling where subject content is taught through a second and third language (e.g. Hebrew and French for first language English speakers).

**Dual Language Program:** see Two-Way Programs.

**Early-Exit/Late-Exit Bilingual Education Programs:** Early-exit programs move children from bilingual classes in the first or second year of schooling. Late-exit programs provide bilingual classes for three or more years of elementary schooling. Both programs are found in Transitional Bilingual Education.

**EFL:** English as a Foreign Language.

**Elective bilingual:** Someone who has chosen to become a bilingual (e.g. through taking second language classes).

**ELL:** English Language Learners. This is sometimes preferred to LEP (Limited English Proficiency) as it focuses on development rather than deficit.

**ELT:** English language teaching.

**Empowerment:** The means by which those of low status, low influence and power are given the means to increase their chances of prosperity, power and prestige. Literacy and biliteracy are major means of empowering such individuals and groups.

**English-Only:** An umbrella term for federal and state legislation and organizations that aim to make English the official language of the US. This includes two national organizations: US English and English First.

**English Plus:** A US movement promoting the belief that all US residents should have the opportunity to become proficient in a language other than English.

**Enrichment Bilingual Education:** A form of bilingual education that seeks to develop additive bilingualism, thus enriching a person's cultural, social and personal education. Two languages and cultures are developed through education.

**Equilingual:** Someone who is approximately equally competent in two languages.

**ERASMUS:** A European program for students to take part of their higher education at one or more European universities or colleges as well as their 'home' University or College.

**ESEA:** Elementary and Secondary Education Act (United States).

**ESL:** English as a Second Language. An ESL program (e.g. in the US) usually involves little or no use of the first language, and occurs for part of the school time-table.

**ESOL:** English for Speakers of Other Languages.

**ESP:** English for Special Purposes. For example, English may be taught for its use in the Science and Technology curriculum, or English for business, specific vocational needs and professions.

**Ethnic Identity:** Those aspects of an individual's thinking, feelings, perceptions, and behavior that are due to ethnic group membership, as well as a sense of belonging and pride in the ethnic group.

**Ethnic Mosaic:** In-migrants of different geographical origins co-existing in a country (e.g. United States) and retaining colorful constituents of their ethnicity.

**Ethnocentrism:** Discriminatory beliefs and behaviours based on ethnic differences. Evaluating other ethnic groups by criteria specific to one's own group.

**Ethnography of Communication:** The study of the place of language in different groups and communities. Language is particularly studied for its social and cultural purposes.

**Ethnolinguistic:** A set of cultural, ethnic and linguistic features shared by a cultural, ethnic, or sub-cultural social group.

**Expanded Pidgin:** See Pidgin.

**Faux Amis:** (false friends). Cognate words in different languages that have developed different meanings.

**FEP:** Fluent English Proficient.

**Field Dependency:** A learning style where the whole of the learning task is focused on, rather than component parts.

**Field Independence:** Field independence occurs when the learner is able to focus on particular components distinguished from the whole.

**First Language:** This term is used in different, overlapping ways, and can mean (a) the first language learnt (b) the stronger language (c) the 'mother tongue' (d) the language most used.

**FLAP:** The Foreign Language Assistance Program authorized under Title VII of the Improving America's Schools Act of 1994, that awards grants to US states and local educational agencies to promote programs that improve foreign language learning.

**Foreign Language:** A language taught in school which is not normally used as a mean of instruction in schools or as a language of communication within the country, in the community or in bureaucracy.

**Foreigner Talk:** The kind of speech used by native speakers when talking to foreigners who are not proficient in their language. Foreigner talk is often slower, with clear pronunciation, simplified vocabulary and grammar with some degree of repetition. This makes the speech easier for foreigners to understand.

**GAO:** General Accounting Office (United States).

**Gastarbeiter:** (German term) An in-migrant or guestworker.

**Gemeinschaft:** A society based on close community bonds, kinship, close family ties; an emphasis on tradition and heritage. Sometimes portrayed stereotypically as village life.

**Geolinguistics:** The study of language or dialects as spoken in different geographical areas and regions. Sometimes referred to as Areal Linguistics.

**Gesellschaft:** A society with less emphasis on tradition and more on rational goals; duty to organizations with many secondary relationships. Sometimes portrayed stereotypically as one type of urban existence.

**Graded Objectives:** Objectives in a language curriculum which describe levels of attainment at different stages. These provide short-term, immediate goals for learners who are required to gain mastery of these goals before moving on to higher objectives.

**Graded Reader:** A simplified book or set of children's books, carefully graded in terms of increasingly difficult vocabulary and complexity of grammar. Such books are written for first language learners, adult second language learners and students learning a second language. In order to control the linguistic features precisely, authenticity may be sacrificed on occasions.

**Grammar:** The structure of a language; the way in which elements are combined to make words and the way in which words and phrases are combined to produce sentences.

**Graphology:** The study of systems of writing and the way a language is written.

**Guest Workers:** People who are recruited to work in another society. Also known as Gastarbeiter.

**Hegemony:** Domination; the ascendance of one group over another. The dominant group expects compliance and subservience from the subordinate group.

**Heteronomous Variety of a Language:** A language variety (e.g. a dialect) that is perceived as dependent on an autonomous language or standard variety, and which gains its norms from that standard variety.

**Heritage Language:** The language a person regards as their native, home, ancestral language. This covers indigenous languages (e.g. Welsh in Wales) and in-migrant languages (e.g. Spanish in the United States).

**Hispanics:** Spanish speakers in the United States. The term is officially used in the United States Census.

**Horizontal Bilingualism:** Situations where two languages have similar or equal status.

**Immersion Bilingual Education:** Schooling where some or most subject content is taught through a second language. Pupils in immersion are usually native speakers of a majority language, and the teaching is carefully structured to their needs.

**Incipient Bilingualism:** The early stages of bilingualism where one language is not strongly developed. Beginning to acquire a second language.

**Indigenous Language:** A language relatively native to an area, contrasted with an in-migrant language.

**In-migrants:** Encompasses immigrants, migrants, guest workers and refugees. The term in-migrant is sometimes used to avoid the negative connotations of the term 'immigrant' and to avoid the imprecise and loaded distinctions between migrant workers, guest workers, short-stay, long-stay and relatively permanent in-migrants.

**Input:** A distinction is often made in second language learning between input and intake. Input is what the learner hears but which may not always be understood. In contrast, intake is that which is assimilated by the learner.

**Input Hypothesis:** Language in the second language classroom should contain elements that are slightly beyond the learner's present level of understanding. Using contextual clues to understand, the learner will gradually increase in language competence.

**Instrumental Motivation:** Wanting to learn a language for utilitarian reasons (e.g. to get a better job).

**Integrated Approach:** The integration of listening, speaking, reading and writing in language teaching and language assessment.

**Integrative Motivation:** Wanting to learn a language to belong to a social group (e.g. make friends).

**Interactionism:** A position which argues that language cannot be understood without reference to the social context in which language occurs.

**Interference:** Interference (or transfer) in second language learning is said to occur when vocabulary or syntax patterns transfer from a learner's first language to the second language, causing errors in second language performance. The term interference has been decreasingly used because of its negative and derogatory connotations. See language transfer.

**Interlanguage:** An intermediate form of language used by second language learners in the process of learning a language. Interlanguage contains some transfers or borrowing from the first language, and is an approximate system with regard to grammar and communicating meaning.

**Interlocutors:** Those who are actively engaged in a conversation as opposed to those who are silent participants.

**International Language:** A high prestige, majority language used as a means of communication between different countries speaking different languages (e.g. English, French).

**Interpreting:** The process of oral translation from one language to another. Consecutive interpreting occurs when an interpreter orally translates while a speaker pauses. Simultaneous translation occurs when the interpreter orally translates while the speaker continues to speak. For example, an interpreter sits in a sound-proof booth, receiving the speaker's words through headphones. The translation is relayed to listeners via a microphone linked to listeners' headphones.

**Intranational Language:** A high prestige language used as a medium of general communication between different language groups within a country (e.g. English in India).

**Involuntary Minorities:** Also known as 'caste-like minorities'. They differ from immigrants and 'voluntary minorities' in that they have not willingly migrated to the country.

**Isolate:** A language isolate is a language that has no apparent relationship to any other known language.

**Koine:** The spoken language of a region that has become a standard language or lingua franca.

**L1/L2:** First Language/Second Language.

**Language Ability:** An 'umbrella' term and therefore used ambiguously. Language ability is a general, latent disposition, a determinant of eventual language success. Language ability is also used to describe the outcome of language learning, in a similar but less specific way than language skills, providing an indication of current language level. Language ability measures what a person can currently do, as different from what they may be able to do in the future.

**Language Achievement:** Normally seen as the outcome of formal language instruction. Proficiency in a language due to what has been taught or learnt in a language classroom.

**Language Acquisition:** The process of acquiring a first or second language. Some linguists distinguish between language acquisition and 'language learning' of a second language, using the former to describe the informal development of a person's second language, and the latter to describe the process of formal study of a second language. Other linguists maintain that no clear distinction can be made between informal acquisition and formal learning.

**Language Across the Curriculum:** A curriculum approach to language learning that accents language development across all subjects of the curriculum. Language should be developed in all content areas of the curriculum and not just as a subject in its own right. Similar approaches are taken in writing across the curriculum and reading across the curriculum.

**Language Approach:** A term usually used in a broad sense to describe the theories and philosophies about the nature of language and how languages are learned, (e.g. aural/oral approach, communicative approach). The term 'method' is used to describe how languages are taught in the classroom, (e.g. audiolingual method), and the term 'techniques' is used to describe the activities involved (e.g. role playing, drill).

**Language Aptitude:** A particular ability to learn a language as separate from intelligence, motivation.

**Language Arts:** Those parts of the curriculum which focus on the development of language: reading, writing, spelling as well as oral communication.

**Language Attitudes:** The beliefs and values expressed by people towards different languages in terms of favorability and unfavourability.

**Language Attrition:** The loss of a language within a person or a language group, gradually over time.

**Language Awareness:** A comprehensive term used to describe knowledge about and appreciation of the attributes of a language, the way a language works and is used in society.

**Language Change:** Change in a language over time. All living languages are in a process of gradual change (e.g. in pronunciation, grammar, vocabulary).

**Language Competence:** A broad and general term, used particularly to describe an inner, mental representation of language, something latent rather than overt. Such competence refers usually to an underlying system inferred from language performance.

**Language Contact:** Contact between speakers of different languages, particularly when they are in the same region or in adjoining communities.

**Language Death:** Language death is said to occur when a declining language loses its last remaining speakers through their death or their shift to using another language. This language no longer exists as a medium of communication in any language domains.

**Language Decline:** See Language Loss.

**Language Demographics:** The distribution of the use of a language in a defined geographical area. Also called Geolinguistics.

**Language Dominance:** One language being the stronger or preferred language of an individual, or the more prestigious language within a particular region.

**Language Family:** A group of languages historically derived from a common ancestor.

**Language Laboratory:** A room with individual booths fitted with cassette recorders. Students listen to recorded tapes and practice speaking exercises which can be monitored by teachers.

**Language Learning:** The process by which a first or second language is internalized. Some authors restrict the use of the term to formal learning (e.g. in the classroom). Others include informal learning (e.g. acquisition in the home). See also Language Acquisition.

**Language Loss:** The process of losing the ability or use of a language within an individual or within a group. Language loss is particularly studied amongst in-migrants to a country where their mother tongue has little or no status, little economic value or use in education, and where language loss subsequently occurs. See also Language Decline.

**Language Loyalty:** The purposeful maintenance and retention of a language, when that language is viewed as being under threat. This is often a concern of language minorities in a region where another language is the dominant language.

**Language Maintenance:** The continued use of a language, particularly amongst language minorities (for example through bilingual education). The term is often used with reference to policies that protect and promote minority languages.

**Language Minority:** A language community (or person) whose first language is different from the dominant language of the country. A group who speaks a language of low prestige, or low in power, or with low numbers in a society.

**Language of Wider Communication:** A language used for communication within a region or country by different language groups.

**Language Performance:** A person's production of language particularly within a classroom or test situation. The outward evidence of language competence, but which is not necessarily an accurate measure of language competence.

**Language Planning:** The development of a deliberate policy to engineer the use of language varieties within a region or country on linguistic, political or social grounds. Language planning often involves Corpus Planning (the selection, codification and expansion of norms of language) and Status Planning (the choice of language varieties for different functions and purposes).

**Language Proficiency:** An 'umbrella' term, sometimes used synonymously with language competence; at other times as a specific, measurable outcome from language testing. Language proficiency is viewed as the product of a variety of mechanisms: formal learning, informal uncontrived language acquisition (e.g. on the street) and of individual characteristics such as 'intelligence'.

**Language Retention:** The opposite of Language Attrition. Language retention refers to an individual or a group who continue to use (or retain their ability) in a language.

**Language Revitalization:** The process of restoring language vitality by promoting the use of a language and its range of functions within the community.

**Language Shift:** A change from the use of one language to another language within an individual or a language community. This often involves a shift from the minority language to the dominant language of the country. Usually the term means 'downward' shift (i.e. loss of a language).

**Language Skills:** Language skills are usually said to comprise: listening, speaking, reading and writing. Each of these can be divided into sub-skills. Language skills refer to highly specific, observable, clearly definable components such as writing.

**Language Transfer:** The effect of one language on the learning of another. There can be both negative transfer, sometimes called interference, and more often positive transfer, particularly in understandings and meanings of concepts.

**Language Use Survey:** An investigation of which languages are spoken in different areas, the functions and uses of languages in different domains, and sometimes an assessment of the proficiency of different language groups in terms of their minority and the majority language.

**Language Variety:** A regionally or socially distinctive variety of language. A term used instead of 'dialect' because of the negative connotations of that term, and because 'dialect' is often used to indicate a hierarchical relationship with a standard form of a language.

**Language Vitality:** The extent to which a language minority vigorously maintains and extends its everyday use and range of functions. Language vitality is said to be enhanced by factors such as language status, institutional support, economic value and the number and distribution of its speakers.

**Latinos:** Spanish speakers of Latin American extraction. This Spanish term is now used in English, especially by US Spanish speakers themselves. Often preferred to 'Hispanics'.

**LEP:** Limited English Proficient (US term). Used to refer to students in the United States who are not native speakers of English and who have yet to reach 'desired' levels of competence in understanding, speaking, reading or writing English. Such students are deemed to have insufficient English to cope in English-only classrooms.

**Lexical Competence:** Competence in vocabulary.

**Lexis/Lexicon:** The vocabulary or word stock of a language, their sounds, spelling and meaning.

**LINGUA:** A European program to increase majority language learning across Europe. The program funds scholarships, student exchanges and teaching materials to improve language learning and teaching in the European (EU) countries.

**Lingua Franca:** A language used for communication between different language groups. A lingua franca may be a local, regional, national or international language. It may be the first language of one language group. Lingua francas are especially common in multilingual regions.

**Linguicism:** The use of ideologies, structures and practices to legitimize and reproduce unequal divisions of power and resources between language groups.

**Linguistic Purism:** A deliberate attempt to rid a language of perceived undesirable elements (e.g. dialect forms, slang, foreign loan words).

**Literacy:** The ability to read and write in a language.

**Living Language:** A language used as a medium of communication (at least for some functions) within a community.

**LM:** Language Minority.

**LMP:** Linguistic Minorities Project (Britain).

**LMS:** Language Minority Students.

**Loan Word:** An item of vocabulary borrowed by one language from another. A loan blend occurs when the meaning is borrowed but only part of the form is borrowed; loan shift when the form is nativized; and loan translation when the components of a word are translated (e.g. 'skyscraper' into 'gratte ciel' in French).

**Machine Translation:** Translation from one language to another by computer.

**Mainstreaming:** Putting a student who has previously been in a special educational program into ordinary classes. Language mainstreaming occurs when children are no longer given special support (e.g. English as a Second Language classes) and take their subjects through the majority language.

**Maintenance Bilingual Education:** A program that uses both languages of students to teach curriculum content.

**Majority Language:** A high status language usually (but not always) spoken by a majority of the population of a country.

**Marked Language:** A minority language spoken by a minority of the population in a country (as distinct from a majority language), and therefore often lowly valued in society.

**Melting Pot:** Used mainly in the US to describe how a variety of in-migrant ethnic groups have blended together to create modern US society.

**Message:** The meaning of a communication which may be conveyed in verbal form but also by non-verbal communication such as eye contact, gestures and posture. A distinction is often made between the form of message and message content. The form refers to how communication occurs and the content as to the meaning conveyed.

**Metacognition:** Becoming aware of one's own mental processes.

**Metalinguistic:** Using language to describe language. Thinking about one's language.

**Metalinguistic Knowledge:** An understanding of the form and structure of language arrived at through reflection and analyzing one's own communication.

**Minority Language:** A language of low prestige and low in power. Also used by some to mean a language spoken by a minority of the population in a country.

**Monitor Hypothesis:** A theory of second language developed by Krashen. According to this theory, language can only be acquired in a natural, unconscious manner. The consciously learned rules of language have the function of monitoring or editing communication. This involves monitoring one's own speech or writing, to ensure accuracy of form and meaning, making corrections where necessary.

**Monogenesis:** A theory that all the languages in the world derive historically from a single ancestor.

**Monoglot:** See monolingual.

**Monolingual:** A person who knows and/or uses one language.

**Morphology:** The internal structure of words (a morpheme is the smallest unit of meaning).

**Mother Tongue:** The term is used ambiguously. It variously means (a) the language learnt from the mother (b) the first language learnt, irrespective of 'from whom' (c) the stronger language at any time of life (d) the 'mother tongue' of the area or country (e.g. Irish in Ireland) (e) the language most used by a person (f) the language to which a person has the more positive attitude and affection.

**Motherese:** A simplified language used by parents to children to ensure understanding. See Caretaker speech.

**Multilingual:** A person who typically knows and/or uses three languages or more.

**Mutual Intelligibility:** A situation where speakers of two closely related or similar language varieties understand one another. The degree of mutual intelligibility depends on factors such as the proportion of shared vocabulary, similarity of pronunciation, accent and grammar, as well as non-linguistic factors such as the relative status of the languages, attitudes of speakers to the other language and extent of exposure to that other language.

**NABE:** The National Association for Bilingual Education (NABE) is a US professional association of teachers, administrators, parents, policy makers and others concerned with securing educational equity for language minority students.

**National Language:** On the surface, this refers to a prestigious, authorized language of the nation, but the term has varying and debated meanings. Sometimes it is used interchangeably with 'official language'. However, in multilingual countries, an official language (or languages) may co-exist with one or more national languages. Such national languages are not so widely used in public and official use throughout the country, but carry

symbolic status and prestige. Also, a national language may be formally recognized as such, or may be informally attributed as a national language.

**Native Language:** Language which a person acquires first in life, or identifies with as a member of an ethnic group.

**NCBE:** The National Clearinghouse for Bilingual Education is funded by the US Department of Education, Office of Bilingual Education and Minority Languages Affairs (OBEMLA) to collect, analyze, and disseminate information related to the education of linguistically and culturally diverse students.

**Negotiation:** Negotiation occurs in a conversation so that successful and smooth communication occurs. The use of feedback, corrections, exemplification, repetition, elaboration and simplification may aid negotiation.

**NEP:** Non-English Proficient.

**Network:** A group of people within a community who are regularly in communication with each other and whose manner of communication is relatively stable and enduring. Analysis of a language network examines different status relationships within the network.

**Non-Native Variety:** A language variety not indigenous to a region, but imported by in-migrants.

**Non-Verbal Communication:** Communication without words; for example, via gestures, eye contact, position and posture when talking, body movements and contact, tone of voice.

**OBEMLA:** The Office of Bilingual Education and Minority Languages Affairs in the US Department of Education, established in 1974 by Congress to provide equal educational opportunities for Limited English Proficient students.

**OCR:** Office of Civil Rights (United States).

**Official Language:** The language used in a region or country for public, formal and official purposes (e.g. government, administration, education, media).

**Orthography:** Spelling.

**Parallel Teaching:** Where bilingual children are taught by two teachers working together as a team, each using a different language. For example, a second language teacher and the class teacher planning together but teaching independently.

**Passive Bilingualism:** Being able to understand (and sometimes read) in a second language without speaking or writing in that second language.

**Passive Vocabulary:** See Active Vocabulary.

**Patois:** A derogatory term used to describe a low status language or dialect.

**Personality Principle:** The right to use a language based on the history and character of the language. Such use reflects two languages existing together in a society in a stable arrangement through different uses attached to each language.

**Phonetics:** The study of speech sounds.

**Phonics:** A method of teaching reading based on recognizing the sounds of letters and combinations of letters.

**Phonology:** The sound system of a language.

**Pidgin:** A language that develops as a means of communication when different language groups are in regular contact with one another. A pidgin usually has a small vocabulary and a simplified grammatical structure. Pidgins do not usually have native speakers although there are expanded pidgins, (for example, in Papua New Guinea) where a pidgin is the primary language of the community. If a pidgin language expands to become the native language of a group of speakers, with a larger vocabulary and a more complex structure, it is often called a creole.

**Pidginization:** (1) The evolution of a pidgin language. (2) In second and foreign language learning, the development of a simplified form of the target language (also called interlanguage). This intermediate stage is usually temporary, but according to the pidginization hypothesis, it may become permanent when learners remain socially apart from native speakers, or when the target language is infrequently used.

**Plurilingual:** Someone competent in two or more languages.

**Polyglot:** Someone competent in two or more languages.

**Post-creole Continuum:** See Decreolization.

**Pragmatics:** The study of the use of language in communication, with a particular emphasis on the contexts in which language is used.

**Preferred Language:** A self-assessment of the more proficient language of an individual.

**Primary Bilingualism:** Where two languages have been learnt 'naturally' (not via school teaching, for example).

**Primary Language:** The language in which bilingual/multilingual speakers are most fluent, or which they prefer to use. This is not necessarily the language learnt first in life.

**Process Approach In Language Teaching:** This is particularly used in teaching children to write where planning, drafting and revising are used to improve writing competence. The process rather than the product is regarded as the important learning experience.

**Process Instruction:** An emphasis on the 'activity' of a classroom rather than a creating a product. A focus on procedures and techniques rather than on learning outcomes, learning 'how to' through inquiry rather than learning through the transmission and memorization of knowledge.

**Productive Bilingualism:** Speaking and writing in the first and second language (as well as listening and reading).

**Productive Language:** Speaking and writing.

**Prosody:** The study of the melody, loudness, speed and rhythm of spoken language; apart from intonation, it includes the transmission of meaning that can be understood from different emphases.

**Psychometric Tests:** Tests to measure an individual's characteristics. The best known psychological tests are IQ tests. Other dispositions are also measured (e.g. attitudes, creativity, skills, dyslexia, personality, needs and motives).

**Pull-Out Program:** Minority language students are taken out of regular, mainstream classrooms for special instruction in the majority language. Special language classes are provided to try to raise a child's level of language in the dominant language of the classroom or of the school.

**Racism:** A system of privilege and penalty based on race. It is based on a belief in the inherent superiority of one race over others, and the maintenance or promotion of economic, social, political and educational differences based on such supposed superiority.

**Reception Classes/Centers:** For newly arrived students in a country, to teach the language of the new country, and often the culture.

**Receptive Bilingualism:** Understanding and reading a second language without speaking or writing in that language.

**Receptive Language:** Listening/understanding and reading.

**Register:** (1) A variety of a language closely associated with different contexts in which the language is used (e.g. courtroom, classroom, church) and hence with different people (e.g. police, professor, priest). (2) A variety of a language used by an individual in a certain context.

**Relexification hypothesis:** A hypothesis that all pidgin languages derive from the first widely-used pidgin which was based on Portuguese. Over time, this original pidgin developed differently in varying areas as the original vocabulary changed by substitution of words from other European languages.

**Remedial Bilingual Education:** Also known as Compensatory Bilingual Education. Uses the mother tongue only to 'correct' the students' presumed 'deficiency' in the majority language.

**SAIP:** Special Alternative Instructional Programs (USA.).

**Scaffolding Approach:** Building on a child's existing repertoire of knowledge and understanding.

**Secondary Bilingualism:** The second language has been formally learnt (see also Primary Bilingualism).

**Second Language:** This term is used in different, overlapping ways, and can mean (1) the second language learnt (chronologically); (2) the weaker language; (3) a language that is not the 'mother tongue'; (4) the less used language. The term is sometimes used to cover third and further languages. The term can also be used to describe a language widely spoken in the country of the learner (as opposed to a foreign language).

**Semantics:** The study of the meaning of language.

**Semilingual:** A controversial term used to describe people whose two languages are at a low level of development.

**Separate Underlying Proficiency:** The idea that two languages exist separately and work independently in the thinking system.

**Sequential Bilingualism:** Bilingualism achieved via learning a second language later than the first language. This is distinct from Simultaneous Bilingualism where two languages are acquired concurrently. When a second language is learnt after the age of three, sequential bilingualism is said to occur.

**Sheltered English:** Content (subject) classes that also include English language development. The curriculum is taught in English in the United States at a comprehensible level to minority language students. The goal of sheltered English is to help minority language students acquire proficiency in English while at the same time achieving well in content areas of the curriculum.

**Sight Vocabulary:** Words which a child can recognize in reading that require no decoding of letters or blends of letters. The instant recognition of basic words.

**Sign Language:** Languages used by many deaf people and by those people who communicate with deaf people that make use of non-verbal communication to communicate meaning. Sign languages are complete languages with their own grammatical systems. Various sign languages have developed in different parts of the world (e.g. American sign language; British sign language; French sign language).

**Silent Way:** A method of second language learning emphasizing independent student learning by means of discovery and problem solving.

**Simultaneous Bilingualism:** Bilingualism achieved via acquiring a first and a second language concurrently. This is distinct from Sequential Bilingualism where the two languages are acquired at different ages. When a second language is learnt before the age of three, simultaneous bilingualism is said to occur.

**Simultaneous Interpreting/Translation:** See Interpreting.

**Sister Languages:** Two or more languages historically derived from a common parent language.

**Skills-based Literacy:** Where the emphasis is on the acquisition of phonics and other language forms, rather than on ways of using those forms.

**SLT:** Second Language Teaching.

**Sociolinguistics:** The study of language in relation to social groups, social class, ethnicity and other interpersonal factors in communication.

**Speech Variety:** A neutral term sometimes used instead of 'dialect' or 'language' where a distinction is difficult.

**Standard Language:** A prestigious variety of a language that has official, formal use (e.g. in government and schooling). A standard language usually has norms for orthography, spelling, grammar and vocabulary. The standard variety is often used in literature and other forms of media (e.g. radio, television), in school text books, in centralized policies of the curriculum.

**Standardization:** The attempt to establish a single standard form of a language particularly in its written form, for official purposes, literature, school curriculum etc.

**Standard Variety:** See Standard Language.

**Status Planning:** Language planning which centers on language use and prestige within a region and within particular language domains. See Language Planning.

**Submersion:** The teaching of minority language pupils solely through the medium of a majority language, often alongside native speakers of the majority language. Minority language pupils are left to sink or swim in the mainstream curriculum.

**Substrate Language:** A language that has influenced the structure or use of a prestigious language. See Superstrate Language.

**Subtractive Bilingualism:** A situation in which a second language is learnt at the expense of the first language, and gradually replaces the first language (e.g. in-migrants to a country or minority language pupils in submersion education).

**Successive Bilingualism:** See Sequential Bilingualism.

**Suggestopedia:** A controversial language teaching methodology based on 'suggestology'. The method is concerned with subconscious and non-rational influences on the mind.

**SUP:** see Separate Underlying Proficiency.

**Superstrate Language:** (1) A prestigious language that has influenced less prestigious languages (e.g. minority languages), usually resulting in language shift. (2) The main source language, usually the language of the socially dominant group, for the lexicon and grammar of a pidgin or creole, which is also influenced by other languages known as substrate languages.

**Syntax:** The study of how words combine into sentences. Rules governing the ways words are combined and organized.

**Target Language:** A second or foreign language being learned or taught.

**TBE:** Transitional Bilingual Education. Temporary use of the child's home language in the classroom, leading to only the majority language being allowed in classroom instruction (see Early-Exit/Late-Exit Bilingual Education Programs).

**TEFL:** Teaching English as a Foreign Language.

**Terminology:** The creation, selection and standardization of terms for use in specific (e.g. school curriculum) or technical (e.g. science, medicine, computing) contexts. See Corpus Planning/Language Planning.

**Territorial Principle:** A claim to the right to a language within a territory. The right to use a language within a geographical area.

**TESFL:** Teaching English as a Second and a Foreign Language.

**TESL:** Teaching English as a Second Language.

**TESOL:** (1) Teachers of English to Speakers of Other Languages; (2) Teaching English as a Second or Other Language.

**Text:** This can refer both to spoken and written language.

**Threshold Level:** (1) A level of language competence a person has to reach to gain cognitive benefits from owning two languages. (2) The Threshold Level is used by the Council of Europe to define a minimal level of language proficiency needed to function in a foreign language. Various contexts are specified where languages are used and students are expected to reach specific objectives to attain the threshold level.

**Title VII:** The Bilingual Education Act: Title VII of the Elementary and Secondary Education Act of 1968, established US federal policy for bilingual education for language minority students. Reauthorized in 1994 as part of the Improving America's Schools Act, Title VII's new provisions increased the state role and aided applicants seeking to develop bilingual proficiency.

**Total Communication:** A method of teaching deaf and hearing impaired children based on the use of both sign language and spoken language.

**TPR:** Total Physical Response – a method of second language learning.

**Trade Language:** A language that is adopted or evolves as a medium of communication in business or commerce between different language groups. Many pidgins evolved as trade languages in ports or centers of commerce.

**Transitional Bilingual Education (TBE):** The primary purpose of these US programs is to facilitate a student's transition to an all-English instructional environment while initially using the native language in the classroom. Transitional bilingual education programs vary in the amount of native language instruction provided and the duration of the program.

**Transliteration:** The notation of one language in the writing system of another language (e.g. Chinese or Russian place names written in Roman script).

**Two-Way Programs:** Also known as Developmental Bilingual Education, Two-Way Dual Language Programs and Two-Way Bilingual/Immersion Programs. Two languages are used for approximately equal time in the curriculum. Classrooms have a mixture of native speakers of each language.

**Unmarked Language:** A majority language distinct from a minority language, and usually highly valued in society.

**US English:** An organization committed to making English the official language of the United States.

**Vernacular:** A indigenous or heritage language of an individual or community. A vernacular language is used to define a native language as opposed to (1) a classical language such as Latin and Greek, (2) an internationally used language such as English and French, (3) the official or national language of a country.

**Vertical Bilingualism:** Situations where two languages of different status (or a language and a dialect) co-exist, particularly within the individual.

**Wanderarbeiter:** A nomadic, seasonal worker, usually from a 'foreign' country. An itinerant worker in a 'foreign' country.

**Whole Language Approach:** An amorphous cluster of ideas about language development in the classroom. The approach is against basal readers (see above) and phonics (see above) in learning to read. Generally the approach supports an holistic and integrated learning of reading, writing, spelling and oracy. The language used must have relevance and meaning to the child. Language development engages co-operative sharing and cultivates empowerment. The use of language for communication is stressed; the function rather than the form of language.

**Withdrawal Classes:** Also known as 'pull-out' classes. Children are taken out of an ordinary class for special instruction.

**Writing Conference:** The teacher and the student discuss the writing the student is to complete, the process of composing. The teacher plans regular discussions with individual students about their writing to promote personal awareness of their style, content, confidence and communication of ideas.

**Zone of Proximal Development:** New areas of learning within a student's reach. Vygotsky saw the zone of proximal development as the distance between a student's level of development as revealed when problem solving without adult help, and the level of potential development as determined by a student problem solving in collaboration with peers or teachers. The zone of proximal development is where new understandings are possible through collaborative interaction and inquiry.

# Bibliography

Ada, A.F. (1995) Fostering the Home–School Connection. In J. Frederickson (ed.) *Reclaiming Our Voices: Bilingual Education, Critical Pedagogy and Praxis*. Ontario, CA: California Association for Bilingual Education.

Adler, M. (1977) *Collective and Individual Bilingualism*. Hamburg: Helmut Buske Verlag.

Aellen, C. and Lambert, W.E. (1969) Ethnic identification and personality adjustments of Canadian adolescents of mixed English–French parentage. *Canadian Journal of Behavioural Science* 1 (2), 69–82.

Alexander, S. and Baker, K. (1992) Some ethical issues in applied social psychology: The case of bilingual education and self-esteem. *Journal of Applied Social Psychology* 22, 1741–1757.

Anderson, C.A. (1966) Literacy and schooling on the development threshold. In C.A. Anderson and M. Bowman (eds) *Education and Economic Development*. London: Frank Cass.

Appel, R. and Muysken, P. (1987) *Language Contact and Bilingualism*. London: Edward Arnold.

Baca, L.M. and Cervantes, H.T. (1998) *The Bilingual Special Education Interface* (3rd edn). Upper Saddle River, NJ: Prentice Hall.

Baetens Beardsmore, H. (1986) *Bilingualism: Basic Principles*. Clevedon: Multilingual Matters.

Baker, C. (1996) *Foundations of Bilingual Education and Bilingualism*. Clevedon: Multilingual Matters.

Baker, C. (2000) *A Parents' and Teachers' Guide to Bilingualism* (2nd end). Clevedon: Multilingual Matters.

Baker, C. and Jones, S.P. (1998) *Encyclopedia of Bilingualism and Bilingual Education*. Clevedon: Multilingual Matters.

Barth, F. (1966) *Models of Social Organization* (Occasional Paper No. 23). London: Royal Anthropological Institute.

Ben-Zeev, S. (1977a) The influence of bilingualism on cognitive strategy and cognitive development. *Child Development* 48, 1009–1018.

Ben-Zeev, S. (1977b) The effect of bilingualism in children from Spanish–English low economic neighbourhoods on cognitive development and cognitive strategy. *Working Papers on Bilingualism* 14, 83–122.

Bialystok, E. (ed.) (1991) *Language Processing in Bilingual Children*. Cambridge: Cambridge University Press.

Bialystok, E. (1987) Influences of bilingualism on metalinguistic development. *Second Language Research* 3 (2), 154–166.

Bialystok, E. (1988) Levels of bilingualism and levels of linguistic awareness. *Developmental Psychology* 24 (4), 560–567.

Bullivant, B.M. (1981) *The Pluralist Dilemma in Education: Six Case Studies*. Sydney: Allen and Unwin.

Butts, R.F. (1980) *The Revival of Civic Learning*. Bloomington, IN: Phi Delta Kappa.

Calero-Breckheimer, A. and Goetz, E.T. (1993) Reading strategies of biliterate children for English and Spanish texts. *Reading Psychology: An International Quarterly* 14 (3), 177–204.

Casanova, U. (1991) Bilingual education: Politics or pedagogy? In O. García (ed.) *Bilingual Education: Focusschrift in Honor of Joshua A. Fishman*. Amsterdam/Philadelphia: John Benjamins.

Cenoz J. and Genesee, F. (1998) Psycholinguistic perspectives on multilingualism and multilingual education. In J. Cenoz and F. Genesee (eds) *Beyond Bilingualism: Multilingualism and Multilingual Education*. Clevedon: Multilingual Matters.

Chambers, J.K. and Trudgill, P. (1980) *Dialectology*. Cambridge: Cambridge University Press.

Cline, T. and Frederickson, N. (eds) (1996) *Curriculum Related Assessment, Cummins and Bilingual Children*. Clevedon: Multilingual Matters.

Cline, T. and Frederickson, N. (1991) *Bilingual Pupils and the National Curriculum: Overcoming Difficulties in Teaching and Learning*. London: University College London.

Cline, T. (1993) Educational assessment of bilingual pupils: Getting the context right. *Education and Child Psychology* 10 (4), 59–68.

Cloud, N. (1994) Special education needs of second language students. In F. Genesee (ed.) *Educating Second Language Children*. Cambridge: Cambridge University Press.

Coelho, E. (1994) Social integration of immigrant and refugee children. In F. Genesee (ed.) *Educating Second Language Children: The Whole Child, the Whole Curriculum, the Whole Community*. Cambridge: Cambridge University Press.

Coelho, E. (1998) *Teaching and Learning in Multicultural Schools*. Clevedon: Multilingual Matters.

Cook, V.J. (1992) Evidence for multicompetence. *Language Learning* 42 (4), 557–591.

Corson, D. (1990) *Language Policy Across the Curriculum*. Clevedon: Multilingual Matters.

Coulmas, F. (ed.) (1997) *The Handbook of Sociolinguistics*. Oxford: Blackwell.

Crawford, J. (1999) *Bilingual Education: History, Politics, Theory and Practice*. Los Angeles: Bilingual Educational Services.

Cummins, J. (1978) Metalinguistic development of children in bilingual education programs: Data from Irish and Canadian Ukranian–English programs. In M. Paradis (ed.) *Aspects of Bilingualism*. Columbia: Hornbeam Press.

Cummins, J. (1981b) The role of primary language development in promoting educational success for language minority students. In California State Department of Education (ed.) *Schooling and Language Minority Students: A Theoretical Framework*. Los Angeles: California State Department of Education.

Cummins, J. (1984) *Bilingualism and Special Education: Issues in Assessment and Pedagogy*. Clevedon: Multilingual Matters.

Cummins, J. (1986) Empowering minority students: A framework for intervention. *Harvard Educational Review* 56 (1), 18–36.

Cummins, J. (1986a) Bilingual education and anti-racist education. *Interracial Books for Children Bulletin* 17 (3&4), 9–12.

Cummins, J. (1987) Bilingualism, language proficiency and metalinguistic development. In P. Homel, M. Palij and D. Aaronson (eds) *Childhood Bilingualism: Aspects of Linguistic Cognitive and Social Development*. New Jersey: Erlbaum.

Cummins, J. (1996) *Negotiating Identities: Education for Empowerment in a Diverse Society*. Ontario, CA: California Association for Bilingual Education.

Cummins, J. (2000) *Language, Power and Pedagogy: Bilingual Children in the Crossfire*. Clevedon: Multilingual Matters.

Davidman, L. and Davidman, P.T. (1994) *Teaching with a Multicultural Perspective*. A Practical Guide. New York: Longman.

De Houwer, A. (1995) Bilingual language acquisition. In P. Fletcher and B. Macwhinney (eds) *The Handbook of Child Language*. Oxford: Blackwell.

Delgado-Gaitan, C. and Trueba, H. (1991) *Crossing Cultural Borders: Education for Immigrant Families in America*. New York: Falmer.

Delgado-Gaitan, C. (1990) *Literacy for Empowerment: The Role of Parents in Children's Education*. New York: Falmer.

Delpit, L.D. (1988) The silenced dialogue: Power and pedagogy in educating other people's children. *Harvard Educational Review* 58 (3), 280–298.

Di Pietro, R. (1977) Code-switching as a verbal strategy among bilinguals. In F. Eckman (ed.) *Current Themes in Linguistics*. Washington, DC: Hemisphere Publishing.

Dicker, S.J. (1996) *Languages in America: A Pluralist View*. Clevedon: Multilingual Matters.

Dutcher, N. (1995) *The Use of First and Second Languages in Education: A Review of International Experience*. Washington, DC: World Bank.

Dyson, A. (1989) *The Multiple Worlds of Child Writers: A Study of Friends Learning to Write*. New York: Teachers College Press.

Edelsky, C. *et al.* (1983) Semilingualism and language deficit. *Applied Linguistics* 4 (1), 1–22.

Edelsky, C. (1996) *With Literacy and Justice for All: Rethinking the Social in Language and Education* (2nd edn). London: Falmer.

Edwards, J.R. (1994) *Multilingualism*. London/New York: Routledge.

Edwards, J.R. (1985) *Language, Society and Identity*. Oxford: Basil Blackwell.

Edwards, J.R. (1994) *Multilingualism*. New York: Routledge.

Edwards, V. and Redfern, A. (1992) *The World in a Classroom: Language in Education in Britain and Canada*. Clevedon: Multilingual Matters.

Edwards, V. (ed.) (1995) *Building Bridges: Multilingual Resources for Children*. Clevedon: Multilingual Matters.

Edwards, V. (1995) Community language learning in the UK: Ten years on. *Child Language Teaching and Therapy* 11 (1), 50–60.

Edwards, V. (1995) *Reading in Multilingual Classrooms*. Reading: University of Reading.

Edwards, V. (1996) *The Other Languages: A Guide to Multilingual Classrooms*. Reading, United Kingdom: Reading and Language Information Centre.

Ekstrand, L.H. (1989) The relation between language, affection and cognition in bilingualism. Paper presented at the First European Congress of Psychology, Amsterdam, 2–7th July, 1989.

Ferguson, C. (1959) Diglossia. *Word* 15, 325–340.

Fishman, J.A. (1972) *The Sociology of Language*. Rowley, MA: Newbury House.

Fishman, J.A. (1980) Bilingualism and biculturalism as individual and as societal phenomena. *Journal of Multilingual and Multicultural Development* 1, 3–15.

Fishman, J.A. (1989) *Language and Ethnicity in Minority Sociolinguistic Perspective*. Clevedon: Multilingual Matters.

Fishman, J.A. (1991) *Reversing Language Shift*. Clevedon: Multilingual Matters.

Fishman, J.A. (ed.) (1999) *Handbook of Language and Ethnic Identity*. New York: Oxford University Press.

Fishman, J.A. (1997) *Language and Ethnicity: The View from Within*. In F. Coulmas (ed.) *The Handbook of Sociolinguistics*. Oxford: Blackwell.

Freire, P. (1970) *Pedagogy of the Oppressed*. New York: Seabury Press/Continuum.

Freire, P. (1973) *Education for Critical Consciousness*. New York: Continuum.

Freire, P. (1985) *The Politics of Education*. South Hadley, MA: Bergin and Garvey.

Galambos, S.J. and Goldin-Meadow, S. (1990) The effects of learning two languages on levels of metalinguistic awareness. *Cognition* 34 (1), 1–56.

Galambos, S.J. and Hakuta, K. (1988) Subject-specific and task-specific characteristics of metalinguistic awareness in bilingual children. *Applied Psycholinguistics* 9 (2), 141–162.

García, O. (1997) Bilingual education. In F. Coulmas (ed.) *The Handbook of Sociolinguistics*. Oxford: Blackwell.

García, O. and Baker, C.(eds) (1995) *Policy and Practice in Bilingual Education: A Reader Extending the Foundations*. Clevedon: Multilingual Matters.

Geach, J. (1996) Community languages. In E. Hawkins (ed.) *Thirty Years of Language Teaching*. London: Centre for Information on Language Teaching and Research (CILT).

Genesee, F., Tucker, G.R. and Lambert, W.E. (1975) Communication skills in bilingual children. *Child Development* 46, 1010–1014.

Gersten, R. and Woodward, J. (1994) The language-minority student and special education: Issues, trends and paradoxes. *Exceptional Children* 60 (4), 310–322.

Ghuman, P.A.S. (1994) *Coping With Two Cultures: British Asian and Indo-Canadian Adolescents*. Clevedon: Multilingual Matters.

Gordon, M.M. (1964) *Assimilation in American Life: The Role of Race, Religion and National Origins*. New York: Oxford University Press.

Graff, H.J. (1979) *The Literacy Myth: Literacy and Social Structure in the 19th Century City*. New York: Academic Press.

Graves, D.H. (1983) *Writing: Teachers and Children at Work*. London: Heinemann.

Gregory, E. (1993) Sweet and sour: Learning to read in a British and Chinese school. *English in Education* 27 (3), 53–59.

Gregory, E. (1994) Cultural assumptions and early years' pedagogy: The effect of the home culture on minority children's interpretation of reading in school. *Language, Culture and Curriculum* 7 (2), 111–124.

Grosjean, F. (1982) *Life with Two Languages: An Introduction to Bilingualism*. Cambridge, MA: Harvard University Press.

Grosjean, F. (1985) The bilingual as a competent but specific speaker-hearer. *Journal of Multilingual and Multicultural Development* 6, 467–477.

Grosjean, F. (1992) Another view of bilingualism. *Cognitive Processing in Bilinguals* 83, 51–62.

Grosjean, F. (1994) Individual bilingualism. In R.E. Asher and J.M. Simpson (eds) *The Encyclopedia of Language and Linguistics* (three volumes). Oxford: Pergamon.

Hakuta, K. (1986) *Mirror of Language: The Debate on Bilingualism*. New York: Basic Books.

Hakuta, K. (1990) Language and cognition in bilingual children, bilingual education. In A.M. Padilla, H.H. Fairchild and C.M. Valadez (eds) *Issues and Strategies in Bilingual Education*. London, New Delhi: Sage Publications.

Hamayan, E.V. and Damico, J.S. (eds) (1991) *Limiting Bias in the Assessment of Bilingual Students*. Austin, TX: Pro-Ed.

Hansegård, N.E. (1975) Tvasprakighet eller halvsprakighet? *Aldus*, Series 253, Stockholm, 3rd edn.

Harding, E. and Riley, P. (1986) *The Bilingual Family: A Handbook for Parents*. Cambridge: Cambridge University Press.

Harris, P.R. and Moran, R.T. (1991) *Managing Cultural Differences: High Performance Strategies for a New World of Business*. Houston, TX: Gulf Publishing Company.

Harry, B. (1992) *Cultural Diversity, Families and the Special Education System: Communication and Empowerment*. New York: Teachers College Press.

Helot, C. (1988) Bringing up children in English, French and Irish: Two case studies. *Language, Culture and Curriculum* 1 (3), 281–287.

Hoffmann, C. (1985) Language acquisition in two trilingual children. *Journal of Multilingual and Multicultural Development* 6 (6), 479–495.

Hoffmann, C. (1991) *An Introduction to Bilingualism*. London: Longman.

Hornberger, N.H. (1989) Continua of biliteracy. *Review of Educational Research* 59 (3), 271–296.

Hornberger, N.H. (1990) Creating successful learning contexts for bilingual literacy. *Teachers College Record* 92 (2), 212–229.

Hornberger, N.H. (1991) Extending enrichment bilingual education: Revisiting typologies and redirecting policy. In O. García (ed.) *Bilingual Education: Focusschrift in Honor of Joshua A. Fishman* (Volume 1). Amsterdam/Philadelphia: John Benjamins.

Hornberger, N.H. (1994) Literacy and language planning. *Language and Education* 8 (1&2), 75–86.

Hudson, R.A. (1996) *Sociolinguistics* (2nd edn). Cambridge: Cambridge University Press.

Ianco-Worrall, A.D. (1972) Bilingualism and cognitive development. *Child Development* 43, 1390–1400.

Jacobson, R. (1990) Allocating two languages as a key feature of a bilingual methodology. In R. Jacobson and C. Faltis (eds) *Language Distribution Issues in Bilingual Schooling*. Clevedon: Multilingual Matters.

Jiménez, R.T., García, G.E. and Pearson, P.D. (1995) Three children, two languages and strategic reading: Case studies in bilingual/monolingual reading. *American Educational Research Journal* 32 (1), 67–97.

Kaur, S. and Mills, R. (1993) Children as interpreters. In R.W. Mills and J. Mills (eds) *Bilingualism in the Primary School: A Handbook for Teachers*. London: Routledge.

Kegl, J. (1975) Some observations on bilingualism: A look at some data from Slovene–English bilinguals. Unpublished Master's Thesis, Brown University.

Kjolseth, R. (1983) Cultural politics of bilingualism. *Sociolinguistics Today* 20 (4), 40–48.

Krashen, S.D. (1999) *Condemned Without a Trial: Bogus Arguments Against Bilingual Education*. Portsmouth, NH: Heinemann.

Lanauze, M. and Snow, C. (1989) The relation between first and second-language writing skills: Evidence from Puerto Rican elementary school children in bilingual programs. *Linguistics and Education* 1 (4), 323–339.

Laurie, S.S. (1890) *Lectures on Language and Linguistic Method in the School*. Cambridge: Cambridge University Press.

Leopold, W.F. (1939–1949) *Speech Development of a Bilingual Child. A Linguist's Record* (4 volumes). Evanston, IL: Northwestern University Press.

Lynch, J. (1986) *Multicultural Education: Approaches and Paradigms*. Nottingham: University of Nottingham School of Education.

Lyon, J. (1996) *Becoming Bilingual: Language Acquisition in a Bilingual Community*. Clevedon: Multilingual Matters.

Lyons, J. (1990) The past and future directions of Federal bilingual education policy. In C.B. Cazdeb and C.E. Snow (eds) *Annals of the American Academy of Political and Social Science* (Vol. 508, pp. 119–134). London: Sage.

Martin-Jones, M. and Romaine, S. (1986) Semilingualism: A half-baked theory of communicative competence. *Applied Linguistics* 7 (1), 26–38.

May, S. (1994) *Making Multicultural Education Work*. Clevedon: Multilingual Matters.

McKay, S.L. (1996) Literacy and literacies. In S.L. McKay and N.H. Hornberger (eds) *Sociolinguistics and Language Teaching*. Cambridge: Cambridge University Press.

McKay, S.L. and Wong, S.C. (eds) (1988) *Language Diversity: Problem or Resource?* New York: Newbury House.

Moll, L.C. (1992) Bilingual classroom studies and community analysis. *Educational Researcher* 21 (2), 20–24.

Multilingual Resources for Children Project (1995) *Building Bridges, Multilingual Resources for Children*. Clevedon: Multilingual Matters.

Myers-Scotton, C. (1972) *Choosing a Lingua Franca in an African Capital*. Edmonton, IL: Linguistic Research.

Myers-Scotton, C. (1991) Making ethnicity salient in codeswitching. In J.R. Dow (ed.) *Language and Ethnicity. Focusschrift in Honor of Joshua Fishman*. Amsterdam/Philadelphia: John Benjamins.

Myers-Scotton, C. (1992a) Comparing codeswitching and borrowing. *Journal of Multilingual and Multicultural Development* 13 (1&2), 19–39.

Myers-Scotton, C. (1992b) *Duelling Languages: Grammatical Structure in Codeswitching*. Oxford: Oxford University Press.

Myers-Scotton, C. (1993) *Social Motivations for Codeswitching: Evidence from Africa*. Oxford, Clarendon Press.

Myers-Scotton, C. (1996) Code-switching. In F. Coulmas (ed.) *The Handbook of Sociolinguistics*. Oxford: Blackwell.

Myers-Scotton, C. and Ury, W. (1977) Bilingual strategies: The social functions of code-switching. *Linguistics* 193, 5–20.

Nieto, S. (1996) *Affirming Diversity: The Sociopolitical Context of Multicultural Education* (2nd edn). New York, London: Longman.

Ogbu, J. (1978) *Minority Education and Caste: The American System in Cross-Cultural Perspective*. New York: Academic Press.

Ogbu, J. (1983) Minority status and schooling in plural societies. *Comparative Education Review* 27 (2), 168–190.

Ogbu, J. (1987) Variability in minority school performance: A problem in search of an explanation. *Anthropology and Education Quarterly* 18, 312–334.

Olneck, M.R. (1993) Terms of inclusion: Has multiculturalism redefined equality in American education? *American Journal of Education* 10 (3), 234–260.

Otheguy, R. (1982) Thinking about bilingual education: A critical appraisal. *Harvard Educational Review* 52 (3), 301–314.

Ovando, C.J. (1990) Essay review: Politics and pedagogy: The case of bilingual education. *Harvard Educational Review* 60 (3), 341–356.

Oxenham, J. (1980) *Literacy: Writing, Reading and Social Organization*. London: Routledge and Kegan Paul.

Paradis, J. and Genesee, F. (1996) Syntactic acquisition in bilingual children: Autonomous or interdependent? *Studies in Second Language Acquisition* 18 (1), 1–25.

Parrillo, V.N. (1994) *Strangers to these Shores* (4th edn). New York: Macmillan.

Parrillo, V.N. (1996) *Diversity in America*. Thousand Oaks, CA: Pine Forge Press.

Paulston, C.B. (1992) *Sociolinguistic Perspectives on Bilingual Education*. Clevedon: Multilingual Matters.

Paulston, C.B. (1994) *Linguistic Minorities in Multilingual Settings*. Amsterdam/Philadelphia: John Benjamins.

Peal, E. and Lambert, W.E. (1962) The relationship of bilingualism to intelligence. *Psychological Monographs* 76 (27), 1–23.

Perez, B. and Torres-Guzmán, M.E. (1996) *Learning in Two Worlds: An Integrated Spanish/English Biliteracy Approach* (2nd edn). New York: Longman.

Perotti, A. (1994) *The Case for Intercultural Education*. Strasbourg: Council for Europe Press.

Quay, S. (1994) Language choice in early bilingual development. Unpublished PhD, University of Cambridge.

Roberts, G.W. (1994) Nurse/patient communication within a bilingual health care setting. *British Journal of Nursing* 3 (2), 60–67.

Romaine, S. (1995) *Bilingualism* (2nd edn). Oxford: Blackwell.

Rueda, R. (1983) Metalinguistic awareness in monolingual and bilingual mildly retarded children. *NABE Journal* 8, 55–68.

Ruiz, R. (1984) Orientations in language planning. *NABE Journal* 8 (2), 15–34.

Saer, D.J. (1923) The effects of bilingualism on intelligence. *British Journal of Psychology* 14, 25–38.

Schermerhorn, R.A. (1970) *Comparative Ethnic Relations*. New York: Random House.

Schiffman, H.F. (1997) Diglossia as a sociolinguistic solution. In F. Coulmas (ed.) *The Handbook of Sociolinguistics*. Oxford: Blackwell.

Skutnabb-Kangas, T. (1977) Language in the process of cultural assimilation and structural incorporation of linguistic minorities. In C.C. Elert *et al.* (eds) *Dialectology and Sociolinguistics*. UMEA: UMEA Studies in the Humanities.

Skutnabb-Kangas, T. (1981) *Bilingualism or Not: The Education of Minorities*. Clevedon: Multilingual Matters.

Skutnabb-Kangas, T. (1991) Swedish strategies to prevent integration and national ethnic minorities. In O. García (ed.) *Bilingual Education: Focusschrift in Honor of Joshua A. Fishman*. Amsterdam/Philadelphia: John Benjamins.

Skutnabb-Kangas, T. and Phillipson, R. (1989) 'Mother tongue': The theoretical and sociopolitical construction of a concept. In U. Ammon (ed.) *Status and Function of Languages and Language Varieties*. New York: W. de Gruyter.

Skutnabb-Kangas, T. and Phillipson, R. (1994) Linguistic human rights, past and present. In T. Skutnabb-Kangas, R. Phillipson and M. Rannut (eds) *Linguistic Human Rights: Overcoming Linguistic Discrimination*. New York: Mouton de Gruyter.

Skutnabb-Kangas, T., Phillipson, R. and Rannut, M. (eds) *Linguistic Human Rights: Overcoming Linguistic Discrimination*. New York: Mouton de Gruyter.

Skutnabb-Kangas, T. and Toukomaa, P. (1976) *Teaching Migrant Children Mother Tongue and Learning the Language of the Host Country in the Context of the Socio-Cultural Situation of the Migrants Family*. Tampere, Finland: Tukimuksia Research Reports.

Street, B.V. (1993) *Literacy in Theory and Practice*. Cambridge: Cambridge University Press.

Street, B.V. (1994) What is meant by local literacies? *Language and Education* 8 (1&2), 9–17.

Street, B.V. (1995) *Social Literacies: Critical Approaches to Literacy in Development, Ethnography and Education*. London: Longman.

Stubbs, M. (1991) Educational language planning in England and Wales: Multicultural rhetoric and assimilationist assumptions. In F. Coulmas (ed.) *A Language Policy for the European Community*. Berlin/New York: Mouton de Gruyter.

Swain, M. and Lapkin, S. (1991) Additive bilingualism and French immersion education: The roles of language proficiency and literacy. In A.G. Reynolds (ed.) *Bilingualism, Multiculturalism and Second Language Learning*. Hillsdale, NJ: Lawrence Erlbaum.

Swigart, L. (19920 Two codes or one? The insiders' view and the description of codeswitching in Dakar. *Journal of Multilingual and Multicultural Development* 13 (1&2), 83–102.

Tabouret-Keller, A. (1997) Language and identity. In F. Coulmas (ed.) *The Handbook of Sociolinguistics*. Oxford: Blackwell.

Takaki, R. (1993) Multiculturalism: Battleground or meeting ground? *Annals of the American Academy of Political and Social Science* 530, 109–121.

Takaki, R. (ed.) (1994) *From Different Shores: Perspectives on Race and Ethnicity in America* (2nd edn). New York: Oxford University Press.

Taylor, D.M. (1991) The social psychology of racial and cultural diversity. In A.G. Reynolds (ed.) *Bilingualism, Multiculturalism and Second Language Learning*. Hillsdale, NJ: Lawrence Erlbaum.

Todd, R. (1991) *Education in a Multicultural Society*. London: Cassell.

Torres, G. (1991) Active teaching and learning in the bilingual classroom: The child as an active subject in learning to write. In O. García (ed.) *Bilingual Education: Focusschrift in Honor of Joshua A. Fishman*. Amsterdam/Philadelphia: John Benjamins.

Tosi, A. (1988) The jewel in the crown of the Modern Prince. The new approach to bilingualism in multicultural education in England. In T. Skutnabb-Kangas and J. Cummins (eds) *Minority Education: From Shame to Struggle*. Clevedon: Multilingual Matters.

Tosi, A. (1991) High-status and low-status bilingualism in Europe. *Journal of Education* 173 (2), 21–37.

Treffers-Daller, J. (1992) French–Dutch codeswitching in Brussels: Social factors explaining its disappearance. *Journal of Multilingual and Multicultural Development* 13 (1&2), 143–156.

Trudgill, P. (1983) *On Dialect: Social and Geographical Perspectives*. Oxford, Blackwell.

Trueba, H.T. (1989) *Raising Silent Voices: Educating the Linguistic Minorities for the 21st Century*. New York: Newbury House.

Trueba, H. T. (1991) The role of culture in bilingual instruction. In O. García (ed.) *Bilingual Education: Focusschrift in Honor of Joshua A. Fishman (Volume 1)*. Amsterdam/Philadelphia: John Benjamins.

Valdés, G. and Figueroa, R.A. (1994) *Bilingualism and Testing: A Special Case of Bias*. Norwood, NJ: Ablex.

Valdés-Fallis, G. (1976) Social interaction and code-switching patterns: A case study of Spanish/English alternation. In G. Keller *et al.* (eds) *Bilingualism in the Bicentennial and Beyond*. New York: Bilingual Press.

Volterra, V. and Taeschner, T. (1978) The acquisition and development of language by bilingual children. *Journal of Child Language* 5, 311–326.

Wei, L., Miller, N. and Dodd, B. (1997) Distinguishing communicative difference from language disorder in bilingual children. *Bilingual Family Newsletter* 14 (1), 3–4. (Clevedon: Multilingual Matters.)

Wells, G. and Chang-Wells, G.L. (1992) *Constructing Knowledge Together: Classrooms as Centers of Inquiry and Literacy*. Portsmouth, NH: Heinemann.

Williams, Cen (1994) Arfarniad o ddulliau dysgu ac addysgu yng nghyd-destun addysg uwchradd ddwyieithog. Unpublished PhD thesis, University of Wales, Bangor.

Williams, Cen (1996) Secondary education: Teaching in the bilingual situation. in C. Williams, G. Lewis and C. Baker (eds) *The Language Policy: Taking Stock*. Llangefni: CAI.

Williams, J.D. and Snipper, G.C. (1990) *Literacy and Bilingualism*. New York: Longman.

Wong Fillmore, L. and Valadez, C. (1986) Teaching bilingual learners. In M.C. Wittrock (ed.) *Handbook of Research on Teaching* (3rd edn). New York: Macmillan.

Young, R.M. (1987) Interpreting the production of science. In D. Gill and L. Levidov (eds) *Anti-Racist Science Teaching*. London: Free Association Books.

# Index

## Author Index

Ada, A.F. 115, 116
Adler, M. 18
Aellen, C. 22, 25
Alexander, S. 19
Anderson, C.A. 107
Appel, R. 28

Baca, L.M. 123, 126, 129, 140
Baetens Beardsmore, H. 20
Baker, C. 8, 15, 41, 47, 50, 52, 69, 92, 94, 121, 122
Baker, K.A. 19
Barth, F. 59
Ben-Zeev, S. 29, 30
Bialystok, E. 30, 71, 72
Bullivant, B.M. 143
Butts, R.F. 144

Calero-Breckheimer, A. 117
Casanova, U. 157
Cenoz, J. 48
Cervantes, H.T. 123, 126, 129, 140
Chambers, J.K. 64
Chang-Wells, G.L. 109, 111, 116
Cline, T. 81, 135, 136, 150
Cloud, N. 140
Coelho, E. 150, 151, 152
Cook, V.J. 9
Corson, D. 157
Coulmas, F. 53
Crawford, J. 159, 162, 163
Cummins, J. 7, 13, 72, 73, 75, 78, 80, 81, 82, 86, 87, 88, 89, 121, 122, 123, 133, 136, 148

Damico, J.S. 136
Davidman, L. 137

Davidman, P.T. 137
De Houwer, A. 30, 40, 42, 47
Delgado-Gaitan, C. 83, 85, 88, 89, 121, 164
Delpit, L.D. 88, 89, 116
Di Pietro, R. 35
Dicker, S.J. 21, 57, 162, 163
Dodd, B. 128
Dutcher, N. 81
Dyson, A. 111

Edelsky, C. 7, 116
Edwards, J.R. 9, 15, 61, 160
Edwards, V. 86, 99, 103, 119
Ekstrand, L.H. 18

Ferguson, C. 61, 62
Figueroa, R.A. 130, 135, 136
Fillmore, L.W. (*see* Wong Fillmore, L.)
Fishman, J.A. 39, 61, 62, 154
Frederickson, N. 81, 150
Freire, P. 115

Galambos, S.J. 72
García, G.E. 117
García, O. 92, 93, 94
Geach, J. 53
Genesee, F. 29, 30, 42, 48
Gersten, R. 137, 138
Ghuman, P.A.S. 163
Goetz, E.T. 117
Goldin-Meadow, S. 72
Gordon, M.M. 160
Graff, H.J. 113, 114
Graves, D.H. 111
Gregory, E. 113
Grosjean, F. 6, 15, 16, 17, 28, 31, 32

Hakuta, K. 69, 72, 157
Hamayan, E.V. 136
Hansegård, N.E. 6
Harding, E. 39, 41
Harris, P.R. 25
Harry, B. 123, 126, 137
Helot, C. 48
Hoffmann, C. 3, 20, 48
Hornberger, N.H. 114, 117, 119, 122
Hudson, R.A. 65

Ianco-Worrall, A.D. 71

Jacobson, R. 100, 103
Jiménez, R.T. 117
Jones, S.P. 8, 15, 52, 92

Kaur, S. 30, 31
Kegl, J. 36
Kjolseth, R. 158
Krashen, S.D. 123

Lambert, W. E. 22, 25, 29, 30, 68, 69
Lanauze, M. 117
Lapkin, S. 108
Laurie, S.S. 67
Leopold, W.F. 70
Li Wei 128
Lynch, J. 141
Lyon, J. 4, 5, 43
Lyons, J.J. 157

Martin-Jones, M. 7
May, S. 143
McKay, S. L. 54, 116, 165
Miller, N. 128
Mills, R. W. 30, 31
Moll, L.C. 84, 85
Moran, R.T. 25
Multilingual Resources for Children Project 85
Muysken, P. 25
Myers-Scotton, C. 33, 34, 35, 36

Nieto, S. 143, 147, 165

Ogbu, J. 55, 56
Olneck, M.R. 145
Otheguy, R. 154, 155, 164
Ovando, C.J. 158
Oxenham, J. 109

Paradis, J. 42
Parrillo, V.N. 57

Paulston, C.B. 160, 162
Peal, E. 68, 69
Pearson, P.D. 117
Perez, B. 116, 119
Perotti, A. 147
Phillipson, R. 4, 5, 155, 156

Quay, S. 42

Rannut, M. 156
Redfern, V. 86
Riley, P. 39, 41
Roberts, G.W. 35
Romaine, S. 3, 6, 7, 28, 39, 41
Rueda, R. 139
Ruiz, R. 153, 155, 156, 159

Saer, D.J. 67
Schermerhorn, R.A. 160
Schiffman, H.F. 62
Skutnabb-Kangas, T. 4, 5, 6, 54, 75, 155, 156, 157, 159, 160
Snipper, G.C. 117
Snow, C.E. 117
Street, B.V. 112, 114, 116
Stubbs, M. 157, 159
Swain, M. 108
Swigart, L. 33

Tabouret-Keller, A. 61
Taeschner, T. 42
Takaki, R. 57, 161
Taylor, D. 160
Todd, R. 147
Torres, G. 117
Torres-Guzmán, M.E. 116, 119
Tosi, A. 8, 161
Toukomaa, P. 75
Treffers-Daller, J. 33
Trudgill, P. 64, 65
Trueba, H.T. 88, 89, 121, 156, 164
Tucker, G.R. 29, 30

Ury, W. 35

Valdés, G. 36, 130, 135, 136
Valadez, C. 103
Volterra, V. 42

Wei, Li (see Li Wei)
Wells, G. 109, 111, 116
Williams, C. 103, 106
Williams, J.D. 117

Wong Fillmore, L. 103
Wong, S.C. 54, 165
Woodward, J. 137, 138

Young, R.M. 146

Zangwill, I. 160

## Subject Index

Acculturation 166
Additive Bilingualism 46, 52, 166
Advantages of Bilingualism 11
Affective Filter Hypothesis 166
Aims of Bilingual Education 90
Anti-Racism 142, 147
Arabic 8
Assessment 130
Assimilation 56, 93, 153, 160, 167
Attitudes to Language 28, 35, 39, 177
Attrition 10, 24
Autonomous Minority Groups 54

Balanced Bilinguals 5, 53, 69, 76, 167
Basic Interpersonal Communication Skills
    (BICS) 78, 167
Bilingual Classrooms 95
Bilingual Education 90
Bilingual Special Education 136
Biliteracy 14, 107, 117, 167

Canada 38, 68, 80, 113
Careers 15
Caste-like Minority Groups 54
Codemixing 32, 168
Codeswitching 31, 34, 43, 49, 104, 168
Cognitive/Academic Language Proficiency
    (CALP) 78, 168
Cognitively Demanding Communication
    79
Cognitively Undemanding Communication
    79
Common Underlying Proficiency 73, 168
Community 51
Community Language Learning 169
Community Languages 52, 85
Concurrent Use of Languages 100
Conflict 60
Consecutive Bilingualism 42, 45
Content Teaching 90, 97, 169
Context Embedded Communication 78, 169
Context Reduced Communication 79, 170
Corpus Language Planning 170
Creative Thinking 14, 69
Criterion-Referenced Tests 134
Critical Literacy 113, 115
Critical Periods 45, 170

Cultural Differences 57
Culture 14, 88, 94, 108, 135, 163, 164, 170

Development of Bilingualism 41
Developmental Interdependence
    Hypothesis 78
Dialects 63
Diglossia 61, 171
Divergent Thinking 69, 172
Dominant Language 5, 46, 49
Dual Language Books 99
Dual Language Schools 93, 97, 172, 187

Economic Advantages 14
Elite Bilinguals 8
Emigration 55
Empowerment 86, 88, 114, 133, 172
English-Only Movement 172
Ethnic Identity 57, 173
Ethnicity 58

Family Relationships 12, 30, 37, 39
Fathers 4
Fractional View of Bilingualism 15
Functions of Language 2, 5, 9, 27, 108
Funds of Knowledge 84

Holistic View of Bilingualism 15
Home and School Relationships 82, 121

Identity 21, 23, 55, 60
Identity Conflict 21
Immersion Bilingual Education 77, 175
Immigrants 20, 21, 54, 55, 150, 152, 161, 175
Integration 162
Intercultural Education 142
Interdependence Hypothesis 86
Intergenerational Transmission 39
Interlanguage 175
Interpretation 30, 133, 176
IQ 66
IQ Tests 67

Language Ability 2, 176
Language Achievement 176
Language Acquisition 176
Language Allocation 95

Language Aptitude 177
Language as a Problem 153
Language as a Resource 153, 158
Language as a Right 153, 155
Language Attrition 10, 24
Language Awareness 177
Language Borrowing 32
Language Boundaries 44, 59, 62, 64
Language Choice 26
Language Competence 1, 4, 169, 177
Language Death 177
Language Delay 126
Language Domains 172
Language Dominance 177
Language Learning 177
Language Loss 178
Language Maintenance 178
Language Minority 53, 178
Language Performance 178
Language Planning 178
Language Proficiency 2, 178
Language Revitalization 178
Language Separation 32, 96
Language Shift 178
Language Skills 2, 179
Language Use 2, 26
Latinos 179
Learning Difficulties 123, 124
LEP (Limited English Proficient) 179
Literacy 107, 108, 117
Loan Words 180
Local Literacies 112

Marriage 22, 48
Metalinguistic Awareness 70, 180
Minority Languages 53, 143, 180
Monolingual View of Bilingualism 15, 20
Mother Tongue 3, 181
Multicultural Education 141, 143
Multiculturalism 94, 112, 141, 163
Multilingualism 8, 47, 92

Networks 51, 182
Norm-Referenced Tests 133

One Person – One Language 40
One-parent Families 40

Parents 83
Passive Bilingualism 47, 182
Personality 17

Personality Principle 62, 182
Pidginization 182
Prejudice Reduction 147
Prestigious Bilingualism 8

Racism 141, 147, 183
Reading 72
Receptive Bilingualism 47, 184
Refugees 56, 57, 150, 152
Register 26, 184

Second Language 184
Self-concept 18
Self-esteem 18
Semilingualism 6, 184
Sensitivity in Communication 28
Separate Underlying Proficiency 72, 184
Sheltered English 184
Simultaneous Bilingualism 41, 185
Social Development 17, 29
Societal Bilingualism 2, 51
Socioeconomic Status 121, 122
Spanish 38, 73, 104
Special Education 130, 136
Special Educational Needs 124
Speech Therapists 128
'Strong' Forms of Bilingual Education 91, 94
Stuttering 17
Submersion Education 93, 185
Subtractive Bilingualism 45, 52, 186

Territorial Principle 62, 186
Thinking 14, 30, 46, 66
Threshold Level 186
Thresholds Theory 75
Transfer 32, 117, 179
Transitional Bilingual Education 93, 186, 187
Translanguaging 104
Translation 100, 132
Trilingual Education 92
Trilingualism 8, 47
Two-Way Bilingual Education (see Dual
    Language Schools)

Under-Achievement 120
United States 20, 58, 64, 80, 97, 124, 130, 136

'Weak' Forms of Bilingual Education 91, 94
Welsh 41
Whole Language Approach 110, 187
Withdrawal Classes 187